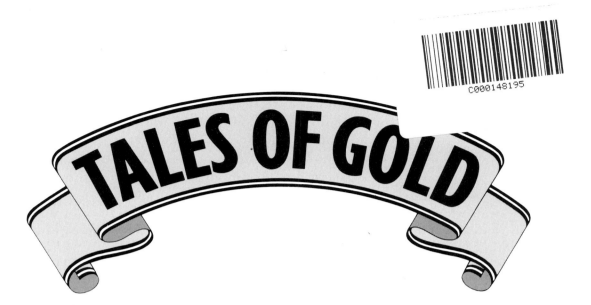

TALES OF GOLD

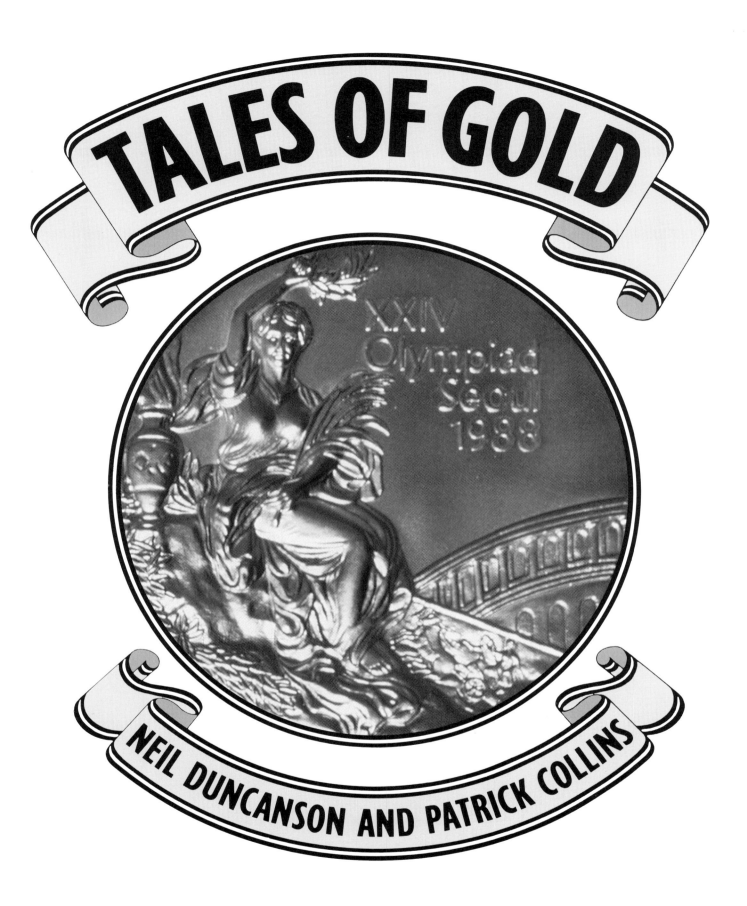

XXIV Olympiad
Seoul
1988

NEIL DUNCANSON AND PATRICK COLLINS

Macdonald
Queen Anne Press

Neil Duncanson is head of sport at Chrysalis Television, and devised and produced the BBC Television series TALES OF GOLD. Following a successful career in newspaper journalism he joined Thames Television, where he produced the award-winning THE FASTEST MEN ON EARTH. After the Seoul Olympics, he moved to LWT before embarking on a freelance career. At Chrysalis he has produced a number of programmes including GAZZA'S SOCCER SCHOOL, RAY OF HOPE and the ITV documentary GAZZA: THE FIGHT BACK. This is his fourth book.

Patrick Collins has been chief sports writer of the *Mail on Sunday* since the newspaper was launched in 1982. He was named British Sports Journalist of the Year in 1989 and 1990 and has written major sports documentaries for ITV and BBC Television. He is married with four children and lives in London.

PICTURE CREDITS

Allsport; Associated Press; British Newspaper Library; British Olympic Association; International Olympic Committee; National Centre for Athletics Literature (Birmingham University); Private Collections of Olympians, collectors and contributors; David Terry

A QUEEN ANNE PRESS BOOK

© Neil Duncanson and Patrick Collins 1992

First published in Great Britain in 1992 by
Queen Anne Press, a division of
Macdonald & Co (Publishers) Ltd
165 Great Dover Street
London SE1 4YA

Design: Peter Champion

A CIP catalogue record for this book is available from the British Library

ISBN 0–356–20784–6

Typeset by Litho Link Ltd, Welshpool, Powys, Wales
Printed and bound in Great Britain by BPCC Hazells Ltd
Member of BPCC Ltd

CONTENTS

INTRODUCTION 6

ACKNOWLEDGEMENTS 8

BRITISH OLYMPIC CHAMPIONS 9

INDEX OF SPORTS 207

INTRODUCTION

It has taken more than four years to complete TALES OF GOLD and detail the lives of the 370 Britons who have won gold medals at the Summer Olympics. Sports historians have argued for much longer about the merits of certain sports and sportsmen and whether their inclusion on the Olympic roll of honour is valid. We have aimed to steer a cautious path through this uncertain territory as in some cases the validity of claims will probably never be proven.

However, we decided early on that the 1906 Interim or 'renegade' Games, held in Athens, were not a true Olympics and the six Britons and two Irishmen who won gold medals there are not included in this work. Indeed, the word Olympiad denotes the four-year period, by ancient Greek chronology, between successive celebrations of the Olympic Games. The Athens Games, held just two years after St Louis, were not supported by the IOC and were in fact a cynical attempt by founder Baron de Coubertin to install them in Greece for ever.

For the record, the British winners were in three sports, athletics, cycling and shooting. In athletics, Henry Hawtrey won the five-mile title and Irishman Con Leahy, often wrongly attributed as a Briton, won the high jump, with fellow countryman Peter O'Connor taking the triple jump. In cycling, Johnnie Matthews and Arthur Rushen won the 2000 metres tandem and Billy Pett the 20-kilometre event. In shooting, Sidney Merlin won gold in the clay pigeon double shot competition and a bronze in the single shot, while Gerald Merlin (no relation) won gold in the single shot and bronze in the double shot.

We have also chosen to omit the Irish competitors who clearly were not competing for Britain but for their own country. Ireland did not participate as a nation in the Games until 1924, but Irish athletes were able to compete, either under their own steam in the early days or using the British flag as a cover. Where they clearly did not take part for Britain or within a British team they have been left out. These athletes are not British Olympians, nor, we felt, would they want to be remembered as such.

A prime example was the tennis player John Boland, who won gold medals in the 1896 singles and doubles. Dublin-born Boland, a lawyer, was a vociferous supporter of Irish affairs and campaigned for the wider use of the Irish language until his death, on St Patrick's Day, in 1958. No British team was sent to the 1904 Games in St Louis, because of the cost and the distance, so decathlon champion Tom Kiely clearly was not a British representative. Born in Ballyneal, County Tipperary, Kiely was offered a free trip by a wealthy backer if he competed for Britain. He refused, paid his own way and took part for Ireland. Limerick-born triple jumper Tim Ahearne won gold at the 1908 London Games and was clearly not representing Britain. When he received his medal he objected to the organisers raising the Union Jack and tried to replace it with the green of Ireland.

Other omissions are made on an historical or competitive basis. For example, some historians credit gold medals to the entire British three-mile team at the 1908 Games, though only the first three scored and received prizes. Consequently, Harold Wilson and Norman Hallows were not awarded gold medals. Australian sprinter Stan Rowley only took part in the British 5000 metres team effort in 1900 when French officials in Paris ordered each team to carry five runners even though only four would score. The team tried to find a volunteer and picked on Rowley, a bronze medallist in the 60, 100 and 200 metres at the Games. He trotted around the first lap and then dropped out. He did not score or receive a medal in the event.

The yachting competition in Paris threw up more anomalies, with scant evidence of a 20 ton and above race. Yet some research suggests there was indeed such a race and that British financier Cecil Quentin won it on his 96-ton boat *Cicely*. However, no crew names are listed and a major question mark remains over whether Quentin was taking part in the competition and, if he was, whether he actually won anything. Similarly, in the 3–10 ton event at Le Havre some historians credit Howard Taylor on his boat *Bona Fide* as a gold medal winner. But he won only one of a series of three races and general opinion favours the Michelet brothers, of France, as the genuine gold medal winners.

One of the most intriguing anomalies concerns the crew of the boat *Scotia*, owned by Lorne Currie and John Gretton. There seems to be a reasonably united view that these two men were on board, but historian Ian Buchanan recently discovered the name of Algernon Maudslay who, it was claimed, was the helmsman aboard the 1900 yacht *Scotia*. Official Olympic records have no knowledge of such a man and we could find no report of him in contemporary material. However, the Paris Games are notorious for their inaccurate records and it is possible he could have been involved.

Many inaccuracies and errors exist in Olympic history, particularly in the early days, and this work will probably not be the last word on British gold medal winners. We would be pleased to hear from anyone who can add to the material included or correct any discrepancies.

ACKNOWLEDGEMENTS

The authors would like to thank the scores of people whose help has made this project possible.

Special thanks go to the Chrysalis Television production team, particularly Ken McGill, Steve Gowans, Sarah Jones, Clare Driver, Sue Youngs and Emma Da Cruz for their tireless efforts. Also to John Bromhead at the National Centre for Athletics Literature, Birmingham University, for his archives, books and tape recordings; the British Olympic Association staff and library; the British Newspaper Library, Colindale, and its helpful staff; the British Museum Library; the Sports Council library; to sports historian Dave Terry and to all the champions, as well as their families and friends.

We received a mountain of material from the many advertisements placed in magazines, newspapers and journals up and down the country and we would like to thank everyone who responded, as well as those publications which carried features and letters. The staff of countless local history libraries also provided us with a fund of material and we would like to thank all of them.

Also thanks to Julie Duncanson and Julie Collins for their patience during the creation of the project.

Neil Duncanson
and Patrick Collins

HAROLD ABRAHAMS

ATHLETICS

1924 Paris
Gold   100 Metres
Silver   4 × 100 Metres Relay

Abrahams' Olympic achievements were beginning to fade from memory when he was immortalised in the Oscar-winning movie *Chariots of Fire*. Though largely fictionalised, the film traced Abrahams' quest for athletic success in an outstanding British team which included Eric Liddell and Douglas Lowe.

Born into the family of a wealthy Lithuanian Jewish financier in December 1899, Abrahams was the youngest of six children. His two older brothers, Adolphe and Sidney, fired his interest in athletics by taking him regularly to watch meetings at Stamford Bridge. At Repton and Caius College, Cambridge, Abrahams' athletic ability began to blossom — though it was Lord Burghley and not Abrahams who completed the Trinity Great Court run as depicted in *Chariots of Fire*. While still a freshman he was selected for the British team in 1920, but went out in the second round of the 100 metres. He teamed up with professional coach Sam Mussabini and began a strict training programme which was completely alien to athletes of the day. But it worked.

Abrahams emerged in 1924 as a radically different athlete from the young man of four years earlier. He posted a wind-assisted time of 9.6 seconds for 100 yards which would have equalled the world record and improved his national long jump record to 7.38m — a mark that was to stand for 32 years. His professional approach to the Olympics extended to taking Mussabini with him to Paris and finding him lodgings close to the stadium. British official-

dom remained unimpressed, but Mussabini's influence paid off, with Abrahams emerging comfortably from the heats. After a difficult semi, Abrahams ran the race of his life to beat tough American opposition in 10.6. In his own words he had 'achieved the ambition of a lifetime'. Harold finished last in the 200 metres final, but helped the relay squad to silver. There were no award ceremonies in Paris and his medals arrived about a month later with insufficient stamps — Abrahams had to pay the excess postage.

He aimed to compete in the long jump four years later in Amsterdam but was prevented by a freak accident when jumping at Stamford Bridge in 1925, when he tore almost every muscle in his right leg. He remained a passionate supporter of British athletics as a journalist, broadcaster, administrator and historian. He was the *Sunday Times* athletics correspondent between 1925 and 1967, a BBC radio commentator for over 40 years and for 50 years held a variety of positions in the AAA. He was much criticised for his dual role as journalist and administrator — poacher and gamekeeper — but remains one of the most significant figures in British athletics this century, on and off the track.

A barrister by profession, he married the opera singer Sybil Evers in 1935 and they adopted two children. Strangely, he received no official recognition for his services to athletics. His CBE was awarded for his work as secretary of the National Parks Commission. When he died, in January 1978, hundreds attended his memorial service and plans were being drawn up for the film based on his life.

Harold Abrahams dives for the tape to become Olympic 100 metres champion in Paris in 1924.

The gold medal-winning 4 x 400 metres relay team of 1920:
(left to right) Guy Butler, Jack Ainsworth-Davis, Robert Lindsay and Cecil Griffiths.

JACK AINSWORTH-DAVIS

ATHLETICS

1920 Antwerp
Gold   4 × 400 Metres Relay

A solid though unspectacular quarter-miler, Ainsworth-Davis ran the third leg in the gold medal-winning relay team. He also finished a very creditable fifth in the individual 400 metres – with just a few days' notice. He had been selected only for the relay, but when team-mate Cecil Griffiths went sick he was drafted into his place.

The son of a zoology professor, Ainsworth-Davis was born in Aberystwyth, Wales, in 1895. He went to Westminster School and managed just a term at Christ's College, Cambridge, before the outbreak of the First World War. He became a captain in the Rifle Brigade before transferring to the Royal Flying Corps where he survived the conflict as a pilot.

After the war he returned to Christ's, where he developed as an athlete despite being eclipsed by the talents of Trinity's Guy Butler. He won his colours in rugby, soccer and tennis, as well as athletics. At the 1920 Olympics he joined his Cambridge rival Butler, along with Griffiths and Robert Lindsay, in the relay squad that beat off the challenge of South Africa, who were led by the individual 400-metre champion Bevil Rudd. In the same year he ran for the British Empire in the match against the Americans.

In 1921, as his medical career progressed his track career suffered and, after finishing fourth in the AAA Championships 440 yards, he virtually retired from competitive athletics. Ainsworth-Davis began his medical studies at St Bartholomew's Hospital and rose through the ranks to become one of the most respected surgeons in the country. A keen musician (especially the violin) and ballroom dancer, he was a member of the 'Original Christi Minstrels' at college and during his spell at Barts he led a dance band, which helped him pay his way through medical school.

During the Second World War he took a commission as wing commander in the RAFVR and ran the surgical division at RAF Cosford. He became secretary of the Royal Society of Medicine council and wrote several books on urology, the field in which he specialised. He also founded the Association of Urological Surgeons. He carried on his practice well into retirement, as emeritus consulting urological surgeon to the Lord Mayor Treloar's Hospital in Alton, and died in Devon, in 1976, aged 80.

DEREK ALLHUSEN

EQUESTRIAN

1968 Mexico City
Gold   Three-Day Event Team
Silver   Three-Day Event

Major Derek Allhusen holds a unique Olympic record – he is the only Briton to take part in both Winter and Summer Games. He made his Olympic debut at the 1948 Winter Games in St Moritz, finishing sixth in the pentathlon – which comprised downhill and cross-country skiing, shooting, fencing and riding. It was while training for this event that he discovered his talent for riding.

He was able to concentrate on his sporting endeavours thanks to the army. During the Second World War he served in the Queen's Royal Lancers and was a troop tank commander. He was twice wounded in active service, first at Dunkirk and then in Italy, though not seriously enough to hinder his sporting career. After the war he trained hard at Aldershot for the Winter Games and was introduced to horse trials, a relatively new discipline at the time. His interest grew and by the mid-1950s he was breeding and training his own horses.

In 1957 he competed for Britain for the first time in the event and won the European gold in Copenhagen, but the high point of his career came 11 years later in Mexico. Given the task of going first in the team competition, which called for a steady, clear round, rather than a race to beat the clock, Allhusen performed a minor miracle to record the second best score of the competition on his mount Lochinvar, earning himself the individual silver. Team-mates Richard Meade and Ben Jones also performed well and the British team easily held off the challenge of the much-fancied Americans and the Australians.

His competitive career ended a year after Mexico when he broke his ankle in a fall, but he continued to work in the sport, breeding and training horses on his farm in Norfolk. He bred and trained his famous horse Laurion, who was the mother of Lauriston, a horse he lent to Richard Meade for the Munich Olympics – where he won two gold medals.

Born in 1914 and educated at Eton and Trinity College, Cambridge, Allhusen is still passionate about his sport and hopes his grandson, a leading pentathlete at Cambridge, will follow the family's Olympic tradition.

EDWARD AMOORE

SHOOTING

1908 London
Gold   Small-Bore Rifle Team
Bronze   Small-Bore Rifle – Disappearing Target

An excellent all-round sportsman, Amoore learned his rifle craft while serving with the Hon Artillery Company. Lance Corporal Amoore started competitive shooting in 1906 and joined the Southfields Rifle Club. He began winning competitions almost immediately, but the following year he won several majors, including the Daily Mirror Championship and the 'Two Twenty' at Bisley. His performances through 1907 earned him selection at four events for the London Olympics.

He became known as 'Peepo' because of his proficiency with peep sights, and his unusual left-handed stance made him easy to pick out on the range. In London he was the lowest-scoring member of the gold medal-winning small-bore team that beat Sweden and France for the title, but in the small-bore 25-yard disappearing target event he was among eight marksmen – seven of them British – who scored a maximum 45 points. He was relegated to the bronze medal spot only on the count back. He competed in two other events, finishing fifth in the individual small bore and an unusual last in the moving target, with a score of just three from a possible 45 points.

Amoore was a keen artist, but was better known in sporting circles as an excellent cyclist; he was captain of the Bath Road Cycling Club and a winner of many trophies and medals. He was also a fine race walker, swimmer, boxer and roller skater.

WILLIE APPLEGARTH

ATHLETICS

1912 Stockholm
Gold   4 × 100 Metres Relay
Bronze   200 Metres

The greatest British sprinter of the early part of the century, Applegarth was the man who inspired the young Harold Abrahams. He held three world records during a glittering track career and then turned professional and toured the lucrative Australian circuit.

Born in Guisborough, Yorkshire, in 1890, Applegarth first sprang to attention when he came home third in the 1910 AAA 100 yards. The young post office clerk, running for the great Polytechnic Harriers club, then made stunning progress and in 1912 – Olympic year – won the championship 220 yards and was third in the 100. This performance earned him selection for the Games in Stockholm, where he was eliminated from the 100 metres in the semis, held off Germany's great Richard Rau to take a bronze in the 200 metres, then anchored the British relay team to victory in a final marred by disqualifications. The Americans had already been disqualified in the semis, and when Germany were disqualified in the final for passing out of the changeover zone, the only other finishers, behind Britain, were the host nation. The British time of 42.4 seconds was a new Olympic record. Applegarth then went on a European tour and embarked on a wholesale demolition of records. He set a new world best of 19.8 for the 200 yards, equalled the world 100-metre record of 10.6, set a new British mark of 21.8 for the 220 yards and twice equalled the British 100 yards record of 9.8 – all in the space of a few months.

The following year he took both the 100 and 220 yards titles at the AAA Championships, a feat he repeated in 1914 in what was to be his last amateur season. He finished impressively, lowering the world 220-yard record to 21.2 – a time that stood for 14 years. It was in these years, at Stamford Bridge, that Harold Abrahams was captivated by Applegarth's performances and vowed to become a sprinter himself.

Applegarth then turned professional, beating some of the world's great fast men. After the war he emigrated to the USA, where he became track and soccer coach at Mercersburg Academy in Pennsylvania, where he also played in the fledgling US soccer league and ran exhibition sprints. In 1925 he joined the General Electric Company as a welder, where he remained until his retirement in 1955. He died three years later in Schenectady, New York.

JOHN ASPIN

YACHTING

1908 London
Gold   12 Metres Class

Aspin was a member of the ten-man crew aboard the *Hera* and of the Royal Clyde Yacht Club. Born in Glasgow in 1877, he was a wealthy varnish manufacturer and belonged to most of the leading yacht

Willie Applegarth, winner of two medals at the 1912 Stockholm Games – gold in the 4 x 100 metres relay and bronze in the 200 metres.

The victorious coxless four of 1932: (left to right) Felix Badcock, Jumbo Edwards, Jack Beresford and Rowland George.

clubs. In 1908 he was recruited by Thomas Glen-Coats, also from the RCYC, to take part in the Olympics. There were only two entries: *Hera*, from the RCYC, and *Mouchette*, which was crewed exclusively from Merseyside. It was decided to stage the event on the Clyde rather than sail all the way down to Cowes. It thus became the only Olympic event to be staged in Scotland. In a three-race series, the local craft won the first two to take the gold medal.

Aspin died in Partick, Glasgow, in 1960, aged 82.

J.J. ASTOR

RACKETS

1908 London
Gold Doubles
Bronze Singles

The son of a wealthy American businessman, Astor was born in New York yet became one of the cornerstones of the British establishment. He became a British citizen when he was just three years old and enjoyed the advantages of American money and British social position. Educated at Eton and New College, Oxford, where he excelled at cricket, Astor left early in 1911 to take a commission in the Life Guards. He first served as ADC to the Viceroy of India, Lord Hardinge, but when the First World War began he rejoined his regiment and saw action in France. Tragically, a few weeks before Armistice he lost his right leg.

He had excelled as a rackets player at school and when the 1908 Olympics were staged in London he joined the small number of entrants for the competition. He took a bronze in the singles after Henry Leaf beat him in the semi-finals, but in the doubles he joined forces with Vane Pennell and they got through to the final, where they beat fellow Britons Edward Bury and Cecil Browning in five sets, 6–15, 15–7, 16–15, 15–6, 15–7.

After the war he entered Parliament, as an MP for Dover, a seat he held until 1945. In the same year that he became an MP he also became proprietor of *The Times*. The loss of his right leg did not appear to hinder his sporting prowess – he won the Parliamentary squash rackets championship in 1926 and 1927. In 1937 he became the first non-British-born President of the MCC and in 1956 was created Baron Astor of Hever. Six years later he moved to the South of France to escape the heavy British death duties. He died in Cannes in 1971, aged 85.

CHARLES ATKIN

HOCKEY

1920 Antwerp
Gold Hockey Team

A keen player at Marlborough College, Atkin won a hockey blue when he went up to Caius College and represented Cambridge at inter-varsity matches. Born in 1889 in Sheffield, he became a medical student on leaving Cambridge and studied at London's St Bartholomew's Hospital.

Just before the war he played hockey for England and then served as an officer in the RAMC before returning to Sheffield to join the family's general practice. Atkin played right-back in the English side which won the Olympic title in Antwerp. They won all three of their games, against Denmark, Belgium and France, scoring 17 goals and conceding just two.

Britain did not field a hockey team until 1948, so it was left to the strongest home nation to compete. The only other time hockey had been played at the Olympics – in 1908 – the home nations also played independently. After the 1920 Games, Atkin made his eighth and final international appearance for England. He died in Sheffield in 1958.

STANLEY BACON

WRESTLING

1908 London
Gold Middleweight Freestyle

The finest product of an amazing south London wrestling family, Bacon was the eldest of five brothers who dominated the sport in Britain for more than a decade. He competed in three Olympic Games and had there been a freestyle event in Stockholm in 1912, Bacon would surely have added to his gold in London.

Born in Camberwell in 1885, he soon followed the family's sporting traditions, excelling as a diver, boxer and rugby player, as well as a wrestler. The five Bacon brothers won a staggering 30 national titles during their careers, and Stanley accounted for no fewer than 15 of them. A stocky 5ft 3½in, he also won titles on the Continent, including both the German and Swiss Opens in 1904, and the lightweight Cumberland title in 1906.

At the 1908 Games he beat three British wrestlers to reach the middleweight freestyle final, where he faced fellow Londoner George de Relwyskow, the reigning national champion. It was a tense and even battle and Bacon eventually came out on top, winning the first two bouts of the best-of-three series – both on points – to take the gold. Bacon also took part in the Greco-Roman event in London but it was really not a style suited to him and he went out in the first round. With no freestyle events in Stockholm he was forced to have another tilt at Greco-Roman in 1912 but, again, he was eliminated early on. Incredibly, he made a third Olympics. He went to Antwerp in 1920, aged 35, but was beaten on his first outing.

A lifelong civil servant, he represented the service at a variety of sports, including boxing – he was middleweight champion – and played for the first XV at rugby. He made a final appearance at the Olympics, in Amsterdam in 1928, as a wrestling judge. He died in Streatham in 1952.

FELIX BADCOCK

ROWING

1928 Amsterdam
Silver   Eights

1932 Los Angeles
Gold   Coxless Fours

One of the few British Olympic rowing champions not to have rowed at school, Badcock grew up on the River Thames. His family had been in the boat building and dock business for more than a century and the river was like a second home to the young man.

Born in West Ham, east London, in 1903, he went to Merchant Taylor's School, began rowing with the famous Thames Rowing Club and made his Olympic debut with them in the eights at the 1928 Games. He was joined in the team by top rowers such as Jack Beresford and Gully Nickalls, but they just missed out on the gold by two seconds to the United States. Four years later he joined Rowland George, Jumbo Edwards and the legendary Beresford in the coxless fours in Los Angeles. The team rowed brilliantly, with Badcock at stroke, to hold off the highly fancied German four and eventually won by two lengths.

The Olympics were important to Badcock for another reason – it was there that he met his future wife Joyce Cooper, Britain's top female swimmer of the day who won four medals at the 1928 and 1932 Games and a gold at the 1930 Empire Games. Their two sons followed in father's footsteps, one rowing for Oxford in the Boat Race, the other for

England in the Commonwealth Games.

Badcock spent his life running the family's riverside business and died in 1976, in Petersfield, Hampshire.

HORACE BAILEY

ASSOCIATION FOOTBALL

1908 London
Gold   Soccer Team

An outstanding, though diminutive, goalkeeper, Bailey enjoyed a vintage year in 1908. He helped his club side Leicester Fosse to promotion to the First Division, won his first England caps at both amateur and full international level, and topped the year with a gold medal in the London Olympics.

Born in Derby in 1881, he followed both family and city traditions by working on the railways. He joined his home town team, Derby County, in 1899, but could not hold a regular place in the side. He moved to Ripley Athletic and Leicester Imperial before joining Fosse in 1907. He leaped to notice in the promotion side and won his first amateur cap against Wales, followed shortly by his full debut, also against Wales. He won five full caps in 1908, four coming in England's tour of Europe in June. Bailey's last England appearance was against Bohemia on that tour, although he continued to play at amateur level until 1913, making a total of eight appearances. In 1910 he rejoined Derby, then went to Birmingham, where he eventually decided to retire from the game. England won all three of their Olympic matches, conceding just a single goal – an own goal.

Bailey continued to work on the Midland Railway and died in retirement in Biggleswade, in 1960.

LOUIS BAILLON

HOCKEY

1908 London
Gold   Hockey Team

Hockey was played for the first time at the London Olympics and the home nations decided to field individual teams. The competition was won by England, who triumphed in all three of their games, against Ireland, Scotland and Wales, scoring 24 points and conceding just three.

The son of a Falkland Islands sheep farmer, Baillon was born in 1881 and grew up in Northampton. He soon attracted attention as a natural sportsman, especially at hockey, soccer and tennis. He played hockey nine times for England, at left-back, and was selected for the Olympic side that took the gold. On retiring from competitive sport — he also played soccer for Wandsworth — he went into business and became a director of Phipps Brewery. He died in 1965.

PAUL BARBER

HOCKEY

1984 Los Angeles
Bronze   Hockey Team

1988 Seoul
Gold   Hockey Team

Rated as one of the best defenders in the game and believed to be the hardest striker of a ball in world hockey, Barber announced his retirement from the international scene when he collected his gold in Seoul. He was just one cap short of his century for England and would certainly have been favoured for selection in Barcelona.

Barber, born in Peterborough in 1955, was educated at the local King's School where he took up the game. He played for England in the 1978 European Cup, where they finished third, and won a silver in the 1986 World Cup and 1987 European Championships. He played 67 times for Britain, usually at left-back, and made his Olympic debut in Los Angeles, when the British side was included as a last-minute replacement for the Soviet Union who boycotted the 1984 Games. The team provided a much needed boost to the sport in Britain by winning a bronze, the nation's first hockey medal for more than 60 years. When they returned to Olympic competition, in Seoul, Barber was vice captain and scored in their first five games as a striker. He then played a key role in the 3–1 defeat of West Germany in the final to secure a famous victory and the gold.

Although he then retired from international hockey, Barber, who works as a quantity surveyor, still plays for Slough, one of Britain's top teams.

EDWARD BARRETT

TUG OF WAR

1908 London
Gold   Tug of War Team
Bronze   Wrestling – Heavyweight Freestyle

The tug of war competition at the London Games sparked a bizarre Olympic controversy. The Americans were easily beaten in the first round by Liverpool Police and then protested that the British side had illegal cleats on their heavy boots. They made an official protest, but it was not upheld and the Americans had to back down. However, the Liverpool team was eventually beaten in an all-British final by the City of London police team. In tug of war, the first team to pull the other six feet was declared the winner, but if neither could manage the distance inside five minutes the team that had pulled the furthest was declared the winner.

City policeman Edward Barrett, born in Ballyduff, County Kerry, was a powerfully built athlete who had already won a gold medal for hurling as part of the London Irish team that beat Cork in the All-Ireland final in 1901. At the 1908 Games he competed in no fewer than six events and, after winning his gold in the tug of war, moved on to his best event — wrestling. Barrett had won the British heavyweight title shortly before the Games, when he beat the giant Irishman Con O'Kelly. The two men met in the third round of the Olympic competition, but this time the 221-pound O'Kelly managed to pin Barrett in 2 minutes 14 seconds and went on to take the gold, leaving Barrett to take the bronze. Barrett also took part in the discus and javelin competitions and finished a very creditable fifth in the shot, with a put of 42ft 3½in. He also competed in the Greco-Roman wrestling event, but was eliminated in the early rounds. He went on to claim a second British heavyweight freestyle title in 1911.

In 1914 he resigned from the City Police and returned to Ireland.

The Great Britain football XI which took the Olympic soccer title in 1908.

The City of London police tug of war team who became Olympic champions in 1908.

FREDERICK BARRETT

POLO

1920 Antwerp
Gold   Polo Team

1924 Paris
Bronze   Polo team

An exceptional steeplechase jockey, Barrett became a top British polo player after learning to play in India with his regiment, the 15th Hussars. Born in County Cork, Barrett played the game only for fun until a serious fall during a steeplechase curtailed his competitive career. He then took up polo with renewed gusto and considerable success.

In 1914 he captained the British side to victory in the hotly contested Westchester Cup against the United States and his performances earned him selection for the Olympic team in Antwerp. The team, which included Tim Melville, John Wodehouse and Vivian Lockett, beat Spain 13–11 in the final to clinch the gold medal. He was on the losing side in the 1921 Westchester Cup and returned to the Olympic fold in Paris, where Britain took bronze behind the USA and Argentina, the eventual winners.

When he first returned from India, Barrett married and took over an estate in Wiltshire. On retiring from the army he used part of the estate as a base for training steeplechasers. He was again successful and his notable achievement was to train Annandale to victory in the 1931 Scottish Grand National. He died in Wiltshire in 1949.

ROPER BARRETT

LAWN TENNIS

1908 London
Gold   Indoor Men's Doubles

1912 Stockholm
Silver   Indoor Mixed Doubles

Despite two appearances in Wimbledon singles finals, Roper Barrett is regarded as a far more accomplished doubles player. He played six times in Wimbledon doubles finals, winning three and losing three, with two different partners.

Born in Upton Park, east London, in 1873, Barrett learned to play at school and joined the local Forest Gate Club. He first made his mark in tournaments on the Continent, winning the Belgian Open four times, the Austrian Open and other smaller events. His favourite British event was clearly the Suffolk Championships, which he won 17 times. In Olympic year 1908, Barrett reached the Wimbledon finals of the singles and doubles, losing both. The singles title went to Arthur Gore, who also happened to be his doubles partner. Barrett and Gore had better fortune at the Olympics when they won the indoor doubles final, beating fellow Britons George Simond and George Caridia in four sets.

The following year the pair won the Wimbledon doubles title for the first time, then lost again in 1910. In 1911 Barrett lost his last singles final to New Zealand's Tony Wilding and failed to make the doubles final. He then swapped partners and joined with Charles Dixon, who like Barrett was a solicitor and a talented doubles player. They won the 1912 Wimbledon doubles title, but with the Olympics around the corner, Barrett decided to team up again with Gore to defend their title in Stockholm. But they were beaten in a bronze medal play-off by Dixon and Arthur Beamish. Barrett and his partner Helen Aitchison took home a silver medal as beaten finalists in the mixed doubles. Their opponents were Dixon and singles winner Edith Hannam.

Barrett and Dixon regrouped, won the 1913 Wimbledon doubles, then lost the title in 1914 before war broke out. Barrett also played the first-ever Davis Cup match for Britain, in Boston in 1900, and captained the side to success in the 1930s. He served as Chairman of the LTA in 1924, was prominent in civic affairs in the City and died in Horsham, Sussex, in 1943.

J.E. BARRIDGE

ASSOCIATION FOOTBALL

1900 Paris
Gold   Soccer Team

Barridge played centre-half for the Upton Park side which won the first Olympic soccer tournament. The English defence had their work cut out: the Parisian team they faced in late September 1900 had already beaten a Belgian side 7–4 in the tournament's only other match. The French representatives met with a far stronger defence this time. While Upton Park's attack scored four, Barridge and the other backs defended stoutly, keeping a clean sheet and helping Great Britain's representatives to the gold.

CHARLES BARTLETT

CYCLING

1908 London
Gold   100km Track Race

Widely considered to be the most important cycling event of the Games, the 100km track race attracted a massive entry and the Prince of Wales agreed to present the medals and a special cup to the winner. The clear favourite was the three-time world champion over the distance, Britain's Leon Meredith, and after two heats had whittled down the numbers to a more manageable 17 finalists, all the top names were still there.

Bartlett, despite winning the British 50-mile title in Olympic year, was just 23 and considered something of an outsider. Born in London in 1885, he took up cycling as a teenager and began to make an impression on the scene when he joined the Polytechnic Cycling Club.

The 1908 Olympic final was hampered by appalling weather and part of the track was already under water when the race began. Meredith, hindered by a puncture and a three-man fall, was gradually pushed backwards down the field as the race wore on. Although Bartlett suffered a puncture some 20 miles from home and dropped almost a lap behind, he effected a swift repair, remounted and was soon back in contention. At the bell, Bartlett was in front and held off a stiff challenge from fellow Briton Charles Denny to win by a length in two hours, 41 minutes and 48 seconds. After playing second fiddle to the likes of Meredith, Billy Pett and other British riders for so long, Bartlett had won the most important event of the year.

He went on to win the British 50-mile title, at Herne Hill, in the following year and when he finally retired from cycling he established a successful packing business. His interest in the sport remained and he was for many years President of the Pickwick Bicycle Club. He died in Enfield, Middlesex, in 1968, aged 83.

STEVE BATCHELOR

HOCKEY

1984 Los Angeles
Bronze   Hockey Team

1988 Seoul
Gold   Hockey Team

Batchelor came into the 1988 Olympic hockey tournament as one of Britain's goalscoring hopes, but failed to hit the net even though the team won the gold.

Born in Dorking, Surrey, in 1961, Batchelor made his England debut as a 19-year-old just after leaving Millfield School. He was part of the British side that took bronze at the Los Angeles Olympics, and silver in the 1986 World Cup and the 1987 European Cup. In Seoul, hopes for a medal were high, but Australia were favourites for the gold. Batchelor played in all seven games, either starting or coming on as a substitute. After a patchy group performance Britain faced Australia in the semifinals and beat them 3–2, the winner coming just over a minute from the end. In the final they overcame the tough West German side 3–1 to win the gold medal.

Batchelor currently plays for East Grinstead and may step back into the international scene if selected for Barcelona. He is a partner in a company specialising in hockey, tennis, cricket and golf coaching, especially for children, for whom sports holidays and coaching camps are organised.

CHARLES BEACHCROFT

CRICKET

1900 Paris
Gold   Cricket Team

One of the more intriguing stories surrounding the early Games concerns Britain's Olympic cricket champions in Paris. Cricket was on the original list of sports approved by Baron de Coubertin just before the first Games in Athens, but there was so little interest that a cricket competition did not take place. In Paris many of the athletics competitions were held under the banner of the Paris Exposition. Indeed, many athletes did not realise they had been competing in an Olympic Games until years later.

Charles Bartlett comes in first to take the 100km track race title at the 1908 London Games.

Cambridge's Trinity College crew that won gold in the coxless fours in 1928: (left to right) John Lander, Michael Warriner, Richard Beesly and Edward Bevan.

The 1900 cricket competition was held between Devon County Wanderers, representing Britain, and an eleven from the French Athletic Club, known as All Paris but consisting mainly of expatriates.

Virtually unnoticed by the press, the Devon side arrived in Paris on Saturday, 18 August 1900, having left Exeter the day before to travel, by boat and train, for a round fare of £2 6s 3d. The two-day game was held at the velodrome in Vincennes, south-east of Paris, with the Devon side winning comfortably by 158 runs. The official scores were: Britain 117 and 145 for 5 declared, France 78 and 26. Few details about the game or the players remain, but sports historians prompted a re-enactment of the match at the original venue, in period costume, in 1987. On this occasion the match was a draw.

Little is known about Beachcroft, who was the opening batsman for Britain and a prominent local cricketer in Devon circles, having played for the Exeter first XI in 1900 and a local side called Starcross. In the Olympic match he scored 23 and 54, being run out in the second innings.

RICHARD BEESLY

ROWING

1928 Amsterdam
Gold   Coxless Fours

A member of Cambridge's hugely successful Trinity College crews that won gold in the coxless fours at successive Games, Beesly was elected President of the University Boat Club after their Olympic triumph. Born in Worcestershire in 1907, he was educated at Oundle before going up to Trinity. He rowed at number two in the winning Boat Race crews of 1927, 1928 and 1929, the spot he occupied at the Amsterdam Games, where he joined fellow Trinity oarsmen John Lander, Michael Warriner and Edward Vaughan Bevan.

The Americans and Germans were installed as favourites and it looked as if Britain were on their way out in the semi-final when the Germans pulled half a length clear with 50 metres to go. Then suddenly one of their crew slumped forward on his oars and while the rest of the crew stopped rowing the British boat powered past to win. Fortunately, he had only fainted, but the Germans did not make the starting line-up so only three boats, Britain, the USA and Italy, contested the final. Again the British crew were behind for most of the race, but with 100 metres to go they put on a finishing spurt and caught the Americans with about 20 metres left, going on to win by half a length. As Trinity had represented and won the fours in 1924, the crew

had successfully defended the title for Britain, the university and the college.

Beesly retired from competitive rowing after the Games and went into business, later running his own light engineering firm and farming in Shropshire. He died in tragic circumstances when he was killed by a bull which attacked him on his farm in Ashford Hall, near Ludlow, in 1965.

MILES BELVILLE

YACHTING

1936 Berlin
Gold   6 Metres Class

A Herefordshire farmer, Belville's introduction into the world of first-class sailing was an unusual one. He was called up to crew Tommy Sopwith's famous boat *Endeavour* in the 1934 America's Cup after the original crew had been sacked for going on strike for higher wages. Sopwith, the aircraft pioneer, brought in 13 amateurs from the Royal Corinthian Yacht Club, where Belville was a member. The new-look crew put up a good show, winning the first two races of the series, but eventually went down to Mike Vanderbilt's American boat *Rainbow* by 4–2. Galvanised by this experience, Belville joined the five-man crew of *Lalage* for the Berlin Olympics and they held off the Norwegians and Swedes to take the gold at Kiel.

Born in Leicester in 1909, Belville was educated at Malvern and Jesus College, Cambridge, where he excelled as an oarsman. During the Second World War he served as a major in the Royal Marine Commandos and won the Military Cross in 1942 for his action in attacking a Vichy French base in Madagascar. The following year he was also awarded the MBE for his services to the war effort. After the war he returned to his Herefordshire farm and served as Sheriff of Hereford between 1966 and 1969. He died in Bromyard in 1980.

Miles Belville on the winner's rostrum following his victory in the 1936 6 metres class yachting competition.

Charles Bennett, Olympic gold medallist in both the 1500 metres and 5000 metres team race in 1900, leading the field in the 1898 AAA four miles.

CHARLES BENNETT

ATHLETICS

1900 Paris
Gold   1500 Metres
Gold   5000 Metres Team Race
Silver   4000 Metres Steeplechase

Bennett began a great tradition of British success in Olympic middle-distance events by winning the 1500 metres in Paris, but he was fortunate in that two of the world's top metric milers had decided not to run because the race was held on a Sunday. However, nobody could dispute Bennett's right to the gold after he smashed the world record by more than four seconds in a dramatic sprint for the line with Henri Deloge of France.

Bennett was born near Wimborne, Dorset, in 1870, and worked on his father's farm, where he trained by running across the fields and chasing the horses. He started running as a schoolboy and graduated through the ranks of Finchley Harriers. His first major success came in 1897, when he won the AAA four-mile title. He followed this two years later by winning the British cross-country championship, as well as the AAA four miles and ten miles.

In Olympic year he managed to hold his cross-country title and rather surprisingly took the AAA mile, in a disappointing field and an even more disappointing time of 4:28.2. But in Paris, America's John Cregan and Alex Grant pulled out on religious grounds, leaving Bennett to canter around the 500-metre grass track, in the Bois-de-Boulogne, in a world best of 4:06.2, a mark that lasted more than four years. In doing so, Bennett became Britain's first-ever winner of a track and field Olympic title.

A week later he added to his gold tally when he helped Britain to defeat France in the 5000 metres team race, having already taken silver in the 4000 metres steeplechase. Bennett, who had a reputation as something of a ladies' man, celebrated his Olympic success with a visit to the Folies-Bergère.

During his career he was a fanatical trainer and relied on a favourite diet of boiled rice with a pinch of salt and a cocktail comprising three raw eggs with sauce. After the Paris Games a special challenge race was arranged between Bennett and 800-metre champion Alf Tysoe in Manchester. But Tysoe was too quick and won a keenly fought contest over three quarters of a mile.

Bennett then retired from competitive athletics, part of a marital arrangement made with Sarah Lewis, a 19-year-old seamstress, with whom he had fallen in love. She was not keen for him to travel around the country from meeting to meeting. He was due to inherit the family farm, but when his father married his housekeeper shortly before his death he forgot to make a will and Bennett received only a smallholding. He was forced to sell most of his medals and trophies to start his own farming concern and continued this until his death in a Bournemouth hospital in 1949.

JOHN BENNETT

HOCKEY

1920 Antwerp
Gold   Hockey Team

A genuine all-round sportsman, Bennett represented his college at hockey, cricket, football and rugby. Born in Chorlton, Lancashire, in 1885, he went to Harrow and then Magdalen College, Oxford, where he won a hockey blue. He studied law at Oxford and was called to the Bar in 1911, the same year in which he made his international hockey debut for England.

He played club hockey for Hampstead and Surrey and during the First World War he served with the Royal Warwickshire Regiment and was wounded in action. Despite this setback he recovered to play 34 internationals for England at left-back, the position in which he played for the English side at the Antwerp Games which comfortably took the title by disposing of Denmark, Belgium and France. Bennett also played cricket for minor league Berkshire. He died in the seaside town of Budleigh Salterton, Devon, in 1973, aged 87.

ISAAC BENTHAM

SWIMMING

1912 Stockholm
Gold   Water Polo Team

Wigan-born Bentham made his only Olympic appearance as a forward in the successful British water polo team in Stockholm. The 25-year-old swimmer helped Britain to a 100 per cent record in their three matches; they scored 21 goals and conceded just eight. They beat Austria 8–0 in the Olympic final.

JACK BERESFORD

ROWING

1920 Antwerp
Silver   Single Sculls

1924 Paris
Gold   Single Sculls

1928 Amsterdam
Silver   Eights

1932 Los Angeles
Gold   Coxless Fours

1936 Berlin
Gold   Double Sculls

In the words of one of his contemporaries: 'Jack Beresford was rather too good for the average man.' The remark was intended as a compliment, an admission that Beresford had set standards of dedication and determination which were far beyond the scope or understanding of ordinary mortals. 'We admired him,' said that same contemporary, 'but we also regarded him as being a bit unreal.'

The merest glance at Beresford's Olympic achievements simply reinforces that air of unreality. He competed at the Games of Antwerp, Paris, Amsterdam, Los Angeles and Berlin. He won a medal at each Olympics, three gold and two silver. He was actually in training for a sixth Olympic appearance when world war aborted the Games of 1940. Jack Beresford was, quite simply, the finest Olympic oarsman in history.

He was helped by the fact that his father had himself won an Olympic silver medal in the coxless fours in 1912 and was an eminent rowing coach, but Jack's talent was primarily the product of a fierce will and an utterly competitive nature. Born by the Thames at Chiswick on the first day of 1899 into a family which set great store by sporting excellence, he combined his early rowing with a keen enthusiasm for rugby football, and at Bedford School he captained the first XV and also stroked the eight. But his rugby ambitions were ended a few weeks before the close of the First World War, when he was shot in the leg while serving with the Liverpool Scottish Regiment.

He was sent to Cornwall to recuperate and he worked to regain his strength by rowing a dinghy around the coast, a hazardous task in the heaviest of seas. By 1920, he had established a formidable reputation as one of the most promising talents in British rowing, and he was selected for the single sculls at the Antwerp Olympics. After a memorable duel with the American Jack Kelly, the father of the girl who was to become Princess Grace, Beresford was beaten by one second. But the silver medal represented the overture to an extraordinary Olympic career.

The first gold medal arrived four years later, also in the single sculls, and after another fierce battle against American opposition. Beresford was beaten in the heats by William Garrett-Gilmore, but he reached the final after a repechage and avenged the defeat by the comfortable margin of almost five seconds.

The scope of his talent seemed almost unlimited and he marked his third Olympics, at Amsterdam in 1928, by winning a silver medal in the eights, just two seconds behind the victorious American crew. By now, his discipline and determination had acquired the status of legend. He simply set himself targets, prepared meticulously and achieved his goals. Came the Games of Los Angeles in 1932, and he secured his second gold medal, this time in the coxless fours.

Inevitably, he was dominating the domestic scene as he assembled a dazzling sequence of success, with seven victories in the Wingfield Sculls, four in the Diamond Sculls and two each in the Stewards, the Grand and the Silver Goblets. Yet it was his Olympic triumphs which seized the public imagination, and his fifth Olympiad was to prove the most memorable and dramatic of all.

Beresford was selected for Berlin at the age of 37. He was to compete, with his protégé Dick Southwood, in the double sculls. As a tribute to his long and distinguished Olympic service, Jack carried the British flag at the opening ceremony, but it was generally believed that he was long past his best; that he could not reasonably expect further reward from his fifth Olympics.

A few weeks earlier, at Henley Regatta, Beresford and Southwood had been training for their Olympic event under the eye of the British professional coach, Eric Phelps. He had been employed to coach the German Olympic scullers and, after watching the British pair, he informed them that they had no chance of success at the Games. To prove his point, he challenged them to race; Phelps in the single, Beresford and Southwood in the double. He beat them easily, and they turned to him for advice. He told them that they had to acquire a lighter boat – one was built for them within three weeks – and that they needed to follow the training programmes he had devised for the Germans. He also confided that the Germans would make their break 200 metres from the line. If the British pair could reach the final and somehow hang on to the pace, they were in with a small chance.

They worked desperately to meet Phelps' demands, yet all their efforts were threatened by a crisis on the eve of the Games. The new boat disappeared, lost in transit. Moreover, the Germans refused to lend them another boat in which to

Jack Beresford, whose Olympic career lasted 16 years and brought him three gold and two silver rowing medals.

The 1912 water polo team which beat Austria 8–0 in the Olympic final in Stockholm.

practise. Finally, the boat was discovered in a railway siding near Hamburg, and they entered the competition determined to avenge their discomforts.

They lost to the Germans, Joachim Pirsch and Willy Kaidel, in the heats and reached the final through a repechage. But, after that opening heat, it seemed to them that the Germans had been guilty of a false start. As they prepared for the final, Southwood noticed that the Belgian umpire was using a huge megaphone, and when he raised it to his mouth, it was impossible for him to see any of the crews. So, in the final seconds before the race, Southwood said: 'Jack, I'm going to go as soon as the Germans move.' And, ignoring the umpire, they moved off with their rivals to save themselves precious seconds.

The race evolved just as Eric Phelps had forecast, with the British pair hanging on until the closing stages, then making the burst which proved decisive. In the final 100 metres, they moved away with every stroke and eventually came home six seconds clear.

With the onset of the war Beresford finally conceded that his active rowing career was over. For a time, he tried his hand at coaching, but he was not a natural teacher. He continued to train and retained much of his old fitness and he was closely associated with Henley Regatta, at which he acted both as a steward and an umpire. He was honoured by the IOC with the Olympic Diploma of Merit in 1949 and in 1964 he received the CBE for his services to rowing. An autocratic man, he seems to have mellowed with the years, although his daughter Libby recalls that he was: 'A tremendous stickler for the National Anthem. That, and the Queen's speech at Christmas.'

His family believe that a tragic accident on the Thames at Pangbourne, when he was 70 years old, provoked the illness which was to overshadow his final years. He attempted to rescue a young boy who had fallen into the river, but, after an heroic struggle, his efforts failed and the boy drowned. The emotional trauma of that day took its toll. He lost the sight of an eye some time later and his general health deteriorated. He died, at his home by the Thames, in December 1977. Jack Beresford, the finest Olympic oarsman in history. The very best of his breed.

JOHN BERESFORD

POLO

1900 Paris
Gold   Polo Team

The only British Olympic champion born prior to 1850, Beresford was 53 years old when he played in the polo semi-final of the Paris Games in 1900.

Born in Ireland in 1847, Captain Beresford learned to play in his regiment, the 7th Hussars, but was regarded as only an average talent at the Hurlingham Club, where he played. His appearance in the Games was as a replacement for team-mate Foxhall Keene in the game against France. It was a largely informal tournament and although records show that Britain — in the shape of the Foxhunters team — defeated the Anglo-USA Wanderers team 3–1, there was a great degree of 'mix and match' in the team nationalities.

A British Westchester Cup player, Beresford died in Ireland in 1925.

ARTHUR BERRY

ASSOCIATION FOOTBALL

1908 London
Gold   Soccer Team

1912 Stockholm
Gold   Soccer Team

One of only two men to win two Olympic gold medals for soccer, Berry was an 'up and at 'em' winger of the old style. His footballing talents came to the fore when he went to Wadham College, Oxford, where he won his blue. He played 32 amateur internationals during a glittering career and just once for the full England side, against Ireland, in 1909.

Born in Liverpool in 1888, Berry studied law at Oxford and was selected for the Olympics while still at the university. The British side won their three games and clinched the gold with a 2–0 victory over Denmark.

Berry's success at amateur level (he played for several teams, including Liverpool, where his father was a director, and Everton) earned him selection for the 1912 Games. He played in two of the three games, and featured prominently in the final against Denmark, which the British side won 4–2.

A year later, after appearing in the FA Amateur

Cup final for Oxford City, which they lost 1–0 in a replay with South Bank in Bishop Auckland, he retired from soccer. His decision was prompted by his call to the Bar, and after war service in France he returned to Liverpool to join the family's legal practice. He died in the city in 1953.

EDWARD BEVAN

ROWING

1928 Amsterdam
Gold   Coxless Fours

One of the few early British Olympic oarsmen never to have rowed in a Boat Race, Bevan was nevertheless a member of a fine rowing dynasty at Trinity College, Cambridge. Born in Chesterton, Cambridgeshire, in 1907, the third son of Professor Bevan, he went with his three brothers to Bedford School and then to Trinity, where he excelled at rugby and boxing.

Though he never won a blue, Bevan rowed successfully at Henley, in the Trinity crews that took the Ladies Plate in 1927 and the Visitors Cup in 1928. His four at Henley was selected to represent Britain at the Amsterdam Olympics and, surprisingly, they came back with the gold after the Germans pulled out of the semi-final and they caught the American crew, almost on the line, to win the title. Bevan, at stroke, joined Richard Beesly, John Lander and Michael Warriner in the four.

On leaving Cambridge Bevan went to St Mary's Hospital, where he qualified as a doctor, and became the United Hospitals heavyweight boxing champion. He became a much respected GP in Cambridge and maintained a keen interest in rowing, acting as treasurer to the University Boat Club and the county's rowing association. During the Second World War he served as a major in the RAMC and after the war continued his practice with British shot putter Rex Salisbury Woods.

As a Cambridge conservator he was granted a special licence to have a motor attached to his bicycle and this made him a celebrated figure in the city. A Henley Steward, Bevan was also appointed a deputy lieutenant of Cambridgeshire in 1969 and was chairman of the city's Samaritans. He died in February 1988.

KULBIR BHAURA

HOCKEY

1984 Los Angeles
Bronze   Hockey Team

1988 Seoul
Gold   Hockey Team

India have taken the Olympic hockey title on no fewer than eight occasions, so it was fitting that when Britain took their first Olympic gold an Indian-born player should be in the side. Born in Jullundur in 1955, Bhaura was a member of England's silver medal-winning sides at the 1986 World Cup and 1987 European Championships. He was also part of the bronze medal-winning team at the Los Angeles Games in 1984, where Britain were the surprise package of the tournament, only having arrived in America at the last minute to replace the absent Soviet Union team.

The Hounslow centre-forward was then selected for the Seoul Olympics and played a significant role in securing the gold. The team lost only one group game – against West Germany – a defeat they avenged in the final, beating the Germans 3–1. The only game in which Bhaura did not play was a group match against his native India, which Britain won 3–0.

Formerly a computer systems analyst, Bhaura now works as the marketing manager of Britain's only specialist hockey goods company.

NORMAN BINGLEY

YACHTING

1908 London
Gold   7 Metres Class

Bingley was a crew member of the *Heroine* boat which had no opposition in the 7 metres class competition at the London Games. A member of the Royal Victoria Yacht Club in Cowes, which hosted the Olympic Regatta, he was brought on board by *Heroine*'s owner Charles Rivett-Carnac. The 13-nautical-mile course started and finished at Ryde Pier Head and there was due to be one other boat competing in the class. But when it withdrew at the last moment *Heroine* made its two sailings alone to claim what was arguably the easiest gold medal in British Olympic history.

Britain's football team of 1912, who beat Denmark 4–2 in the final to retain the Olympic title.

Harry Blackstaffe, winner of the single sculls rowing competition in 1908.

ARTHUR BIRKETT

CRICKET

1900 Paris
Gold   Cricket Team

The Exeter-born batsman, who like many of the British Olympic side attended Blundell's School and played for their first XI, was just 24 when he captained the side to victory at Vincennes and went on to play for the Castle Cary club. Birkett batted at number two, making just a single in the first innings and not batting in the second. He died at Hammersmith Hospital in April 1941, aged 65.

HARRY BLACKSTAFFE

ROWING

1908 London
Gold   Single Sculls

One of the most remarkable gold medal winners in Olympic history, Blackstaffe had passed his 40th birthday when he lined up for the final of the sculls at Henley. His career featured countless rowing victories – 28 alone in open sculling competitions – confirming him as one of the sport's premier oarsmen.

Born in Islington, north London, in 1868, Blackstaffe took to rowing early in life, joining first the Maurice Rowing Club in Hammersmith, and then the famous Vesta Rowing Club. In 1892 he stroked the successful junior eight in the Metropolitan competition, then won the Vesta Invitation Sculls in the following year, followed by the Junior Sculls – despite having been ordered by his doctor to stay in bed.

Over 14 years Blackstaffe, a butcher by trade, built up an incredible record of rowing success, including nine London Cups, five Wingfield Sculls and a Diamond Sculls. He considered retirement in 1907 but was so attracted to the Olympics that he decided to try for the British team. In the run-up to the Olympic Regatta he put himself through a strict physical regimen, bringing his weight down from 12st 6lb to 10st 10lb. He recorded his daily routine in *The Field*: 'Rose at 3.45am, drank half a tumbler of water, ate an orange, caught 4.37 train and ate a few dry biscuits. Arrived London 5.15, ate some dry toast, had a cup of tea. Sound breakfast at 9.15 – beef steak or fish, with coffee, toast, marmalade, oranges. Ordinary lunch at one. Slept from 2.30 to 5. After tea and biscuits went to Putney and sculled eight or nine miles. Then ran two miles in warm clothes, finished off with a glass of beer. Light supper, mile walk, glass of barley water and bed at 10.' The routine clearly worked wonders: he was chosen as second string to Oxford's 21-year-old Alexander McCulloch for the Olympics. He fought his way to the final where he met his British team-mate McCulloch – almost half Blackstaffe's age and rated the world's best sculler. The race was among the best of the regatta with the older man edging the gold by a length and a quarter.

It was to be his last race. He duly retired and was made a Freeman of the City of London. In his competitive career he won 231 prizes and was still sculling into his sixties as well as working as a Vice President of the Amateur Rowing Association.

CHRIS BOARDMAN

YACHTING

1936 Berlin
Gold   6 Metres Class

Like many of the early Olympic yachtsmen, family money enabled Boardman to indulge in his sport. Born in Norwich in 1903, the eldest son of architect Edward Boardman, he attended Norwich School, the Royal Naval College in Dartmouth and Trinity College, Cambridge. On leaving university he took up a senior position at the family firm of Colman's Mustard. Promotion to the Board of Directors allowed him sufficient time for sailing and, as a former captain of Cambridge, he became a member of a variety of yachting clubs.

Two years before the Berlin Games, Boardman was involved in Tommy Sopwith's unsuccessful challenge for the America's Cup, on board the *Endeavour*. In 1936, in Kiel, he was helmsman of the *Lalage*, joining owner Charles Leaf and a crew comprising Miles Belville, Russell Harmer and Leonard Martin. They took the gold medal by just a single point from a Norwegian crew.

After war service as commander of a corvette on the Atlantic convoys, he returned to the family business and the Boardman home, How Hill, near Ludham, which is now a nature park, boasting a well-known garden in which he took a great interest. His younger brother Humphrey was an Olympic athlete; he rowed in the double sculls in 1928 and won a double gold at the 1930 Empire Games. Boardman died in a residential home for the elderly, at Aylsham, Norfolk, in 1987.

DAVID BOND

YACHTING

1948 London
Gold   Swallow Class

The Olympic Regatta at Torbay was a huge success, drawing large crowds for the six days' racing. Competition was even and lasted until the final day in most cases, with 25 countries taking part and nine sharing the medals. British interest was kept alive right up to the last moment in the Swallow class, the first and last time the event was included in the Olympic programme. Swallow class boats were similar to Star class boats, but they had a smaller sail area. Britain's entry *Firefly*, with Stewart Morris at helm and David Bond crewing, was well placed throughout the competition. However, when the last race began the pair knew they had to finish fourth to win the gold from the Portuguese Bello brothers. They managed it by just ten seconds.

Born in Falmouth, Cornwall, in 1922, Bond went to Harrow and served as an aircraft engineer with the RAF during the war. Later, he worked for the British Aircraft Corporation and built yachts in Cornwall. He is now retired and lives in Truro.

ALFRED BOWERMAN

CRICKET

1900 Paris
Gold   Cricket Team

A keen all-rounder, Bowerman batted at number six in the British Olympic side and was the match's top scorer. He made just seven runs in the first innings, took a wicket in the French first innings and then scored an impressive 59 to set Britain on the path to victory.

Born in Bridgwater, Somerset, in 1873, Bowerman was one of only two players from the Olympic side to play cricket at county level, albeit two appearances for Somerset five years apart – and one of those as an amateur. He played for the Castle Cary club, emigrated to Australia and died in Brisbane in 1959.

BOB BRAITHWAITE

SHOOTING

1968 Mexico City
Gold   Clay Pigeon

Braithwaite won Britain's first Olympic shooting gold medal for more than 40 years when he took the clay pigeon title in Mexico. He performed brilliantly in the two-day competition in which 59 top marksmen from all over the world took part.

Born in Scarborough, Yorkshire, in 1925, Braithwaite was a veterinary surgeon in the north-west when he took up the sport. He competed in the Tokyo Games, where he finished seventh. But from 1965 until 1968 he was virtually unbeatable, winning every British Grand Prix, and ended a glittering international career with a gold in Mexico.

At the end of the first day Braithwaite was lying in second place, having missed just two of his 100 clays, the fifth and 13th. But on day two he hit every shot to score a perfect 100 and an aggregate score of 198, two better than American silver medal winner Tom Garrigus. He equalled the world record of Italy's great two-time world champion and reigning Olympic champion Ennio Mattarelli. Braithwaite has now retired from his veterinary practice and from competitive shooting.

CHRIS BRASHER

ATHLETICS

1956 Melbourne
Gold   3000 Metres Steeplechase

When a man wins an Olympic gold medal at the age of 28, he runs the risk of leading the rest of his life in the shadow of that achievement. If that danger ever occurred to Christopher William Brasher, then certainly he never offered the faintest indication.

For Brasher, the Olympic steeplechase title which he won in Melbourne in 1956 was simply a stage in a crowded and extraordinary life. Subsequently, he was to become Sports Editor and later athletics correspondent of the *Observer*, Head of General Features, BBC Television, an immensely successful businessman and, above all, the creator of the London Marathon, one of the finest ideas that British sport has ever known.

Until his Olympic success, Brasher seemed destined to be remembered as one of the men who had helped pace Roger Bannister to the first four-minute

The 1948 Swallow class competition was the only time the event has been included in the Olympic programme. Britain's David Bond and Stewart Morris eventually won in *Firefly*.

Chris Brasher on his way to gold in the 1956 3000 metres steeplechase.

mile in 1954. In his own event, although he had reached the final of the Helsinki Olympic steeplechase in 1952, he had been forced to live in the shadow of his gifted compatriot, John Disley.

He clinched his place in the 1956 Olympic team with a personal best of 8 minutes 47.2 seconds, finishing second behind Disley in an international match against Czechoslovakia. Yet even when he reached his second Olympic final, he remained the least regarded of the British competitors, form preferring the chances of both Disley and Eric Shirley.

In the event, the outsider landed the prize, driving for home with 300 metres remaining and finishing in a new British and Olympic record of 8:41.2, more than two seconds ahead of his nearest challenger, the Hungarian Sandor Rozsnyoi. Yet before the celebrations could begin, it was announced that Rozsnyoi was the new Olympic champion. Brasher had been disqualified after the judges had decided that he had impeded the third finisher, Norway's Ernst Larsen, while crossing a barrier.

The British lodged a protest and, remarkably, they were supported by the three men who had most to gain from Brasher's disqualification: Rozsnyoi, Larsen and Germany's Heinz Laufer, who finished in fourth place. After three long hours, the decision was reversed and the Olympic steeplechase title was in British hands for the first time in 36 years. Brasher had been vindicated. Now he could get on with the rest of his life.

RON BREBNER

ASSOCIATION FOOTBALL

1912 Stockholm
Gold   Soccer Team

The bravery of goalkeeper Ron Brebner earned him a fine reputation in British football in the early part of the century but also contributed to his untimely death. He enjoyed a nomadic career around some of the famous clubs in the Football League and played 23 times for England's amateur side.

Born in Darlington, County Durham, in 1881, Brebner was a dentist by profession and made his League debut with Chelsea in 1906. As an amateur he moved around the country playing for sides such as Huddersfield Town, Sunderland, QPR and his home town team Darlington. His form in the Chelsea goal earned him selection for Britain's Olympic side and he conceded five goals in the three matches. However, the impressive British attacking force scored 13 times to ensure the title

remained in the country. The team confirmed their quality with a 4–2 win over Denmark in the final.

Two years after winning his gold medal Brebner was dead, the result of a freak accident while playing in goal for Leicester Fosse. He suffered a head injury diving at the feet of an opposing forward and never recovered. He died ten months later in London, at the age of 33.

GODFREY BROWN

ATHLETICS

1936 Berlin
Gold   4 × 400 Metres Relay
Silver   400 Metres

The three old gentlemen sat in a Cheshire garden, sipping their tea and telling their stories. Over the past half-century, their lives have taken very different directions, yet they spoke with the easy familiarity of old friends.

Godfrey Rampling, born in May 1909, was the oldest of the trio; a large, bluff man of unmistakably military bearing. He was once a lieutenant colonel in the Royal Artillery, later the secretary of a Home Counties golf club. One of his contemporaries described him as: 'A good chap to have on your side', and few would dispute that assessment.

Godfrey (A.G.K.) Brown was born in February 1915. A quieter, more reflective man, he was a graduate of Peterhouse College, Cambridge. He pursued an academic career and for 28 years was Headmaster of Worcester Royal Grammar School.

Bill Roberts was host for the day; a thoroughly amiable Lancastrian, swift to chuckle and eager to entertain his guests. A patently contented man, he spent his working life in his family's furniture business.

The trio was once a quartet, and from time to time a small silence would still their conversation as they remembered their fallen friend. Freddie Wolff was a power in the City, the head of his grandfather's firm of commodity brokers and formerly chairman of the London Metal Exchange. He died in January 1988, at the age of 77, on the very day that all surviving British Olympic medallists were honoured at a Buckingham Palace reception.

Rampling, Brown and Roberts had travelled to the Berlin Olympics of 1936 with high expectations of individual honours. They carried with them this commendation from the correspondent of *The Times*: 'The British hand is strongest in the . . . 400 metres, which is a stride or two shorter than the quarter-mile. There, without a trace of over-confidence, great things may be expected.'

Great things, indeed. Rampling was a seasoned international; Empire champion in 1934 and a silver medallist in the 4×400 metres relay at the Los Angeles Games of 1932. Roberts was Europe's foremost quarter-miler in 1935 and AAA champion in that same year. While Brown was perhaps most talented of all; the shining star of university athletics and a man who combined a sprinter's speed with the strength of a half-miler.

At the time of the Berlin Olympics, Adolf Hitler had been Chancellor of Germany for three and a half years. Opposition parties had been banned, the Nuremberg decrees had denied Jews the right to citizenship, concentration camps had become an obscene reality and all the apparatus of a totalitarian state was in place, although the more noxious manifestations were concealed for the duration of the Games. Both Roberts and Brown had seen some evidence of the anti-Jewish feeling on a visit to Munich in 1935, and on their arrival at the Berlin Olympic Village the British team had been greeted by thousands of Germans with arms raised in the Nazi salute. Rampling recalls little of a political nature: 'My life consisted of shuttling from the village to the track and back to the village,' he says. 'I might have been in Timbuktoo instead of Berlin.' He did, however, form an unfavourable impression of the Führer, having watched him at the Olympic Stadium: 'Hitler? Well, he just stood there like a silly little man. With a rather stupid moustache.'

Although the British one-lap runners were rich in talent, their preparation was sadly inadequate. Only Brown, by courtesy of Cambridge, had done a winter's training. For Roberts, 'Training was a foreign word'. While Rampling remembers: 'I was stationed in Shoeburyness at the time. I used to run once round the cricket field, twice a week. And that was it. One just did what one thought one needed, and then turned up at the Olympics. The Americans had coaches for everything. They thought we were crazy.'

Certainly, the lack of preparation sabotaged their hopes of individual achievement. Rampling, easing up too early, was eliminated in the semi-final and while his colleagues qualified for the final they each ran naively and experienced bitter disappointment. Brown misjudged his effort and, although he set a European record of 46.7 seconds, he had to settle for silver behind the American Archie Williams, while Roberts, who recorded a personal best performance of 46.8, finished in fourth place behind another American James LuValle.

The chores of training were still scrupulously avoided. Says Rampling: 'I remember saying one day: "Look here, chaps, we really ought to practise some baton-changing." But we soon got bored and packed it in.' Yet the collective attitude of the British relay team had changed radically. As Brown recalls: 'We discovered we were in the same class as the Americans. We didn't know that before. I thought: "We can beat these blighters. There's no doubt about it."'

After the first leg, it seemed that their confidence was ill-founded. Freddie Wolff was the weakest of the quartet and, moreover, he was short of full fitness. The other main contenders had placed their strongest men on the opening leg, and while Wolff ran a courageous lap, he faded swiftly over the last 30 metres and handed Rampling a deficit of some ten metres. Yet Britain was still in touch, and Rampling was in the mood for something extraordinary. 'I wanted to show, perhaps, that I wasn't too bad an athlete,' he says. 'I don't remember a thing about the race. When you're running well, you're in a cocoon of concentration. It's almost as if the other runners don't matter.' Both the Americans and Canadians were overhauled within a magnificent leg and Bill Roberts was presented with a two-metre advantage.

Godfrey Brown had been so captivated by Rampling's effort that he forgot to remove his tracksuit in preparation for the final leg. But he ripped it off as Roberts flew around the track, and he saw enough of that penultimate lap to decide that: 'Bill's running was the best exhibition of quarter-mile sprinting that I've ever seen. It was absolutely superb; so relaxed yet so powerful. Perfection!' In fact, Roberts surrendered the lead to America for a few strides, but he piled on the pace off the final bend and eventually presented Brown with a four-metre lead. 'I knew I had the beating of the American,' says Brown, 'and I thought to myself: "Well, unless you make an absolute fool of yourself, there's a gold medal at the end of this race." It was a wonderful way to run 400 metres.' He cruised around that final lap, widening the margin almost with every stride. In the end, he brought the British team home with two full seconds to spare in 3 minutes 9 seconds. It was an overwhelming victory.

Brown could not resist a small gesture of triumph, a lapse for which he now apologises: 'It wasn't done in those days, not done at all.' Then the team gathered for several manly shakes of the hand and pats on the back. 'We said: "Congratulations, old man", that sort of thing,' says Rampling. 'Yes,' says Roberts, '"Well done. Thanks very much for your help."'

The gold medals, they say, made only a marginal difference to their future lives. Roberts insists that nobody really wanted to look at his medal. 'The chap in the local chippie wanted to see it and I took it down there one day,' he says. 'But some years later, the house was broken into and the medal was stolen.' Rampling feels the same: 'The important thing was winning,' he says. 'Whether we'd got a medal, a teapot or a glass vase is immaterial. The fact was that we'd won. That was the great thing. We'd won.'

They were never again to experience such heights.

The final of the 1936 4 x 400 metres relay: Godfrey Rampling, with a clear lead, hands the baton to Bill Roberts on the third leg.

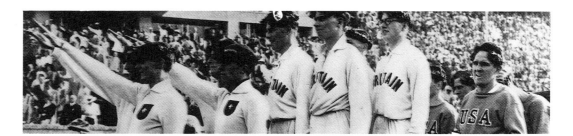

The 1936 relay team on the victory rostrum: (left to right) Rampling, Roberts, Freddie Wolff (partly hidden) and Godfrey Brown.

The Leander crew which represented Britain in the eights competition at the 1908 London Games.

Wolff and Rampling retired with ambitions fulfilled, Brown made a brief competitive appearance after the war, but then followed his friend into retirement. Bill Roberts was most tenacious of all, finding the energy and form to captain the British team in the first post-war Olympics in 1948 at the age of 36. He was eliminated in the second round of the individual 400 metres and his team narrowly missed a place in the relay final before he too turned his back on the track.

And now there are three; old men, sitting in a Cheshire garden, drinking tea and telling stories. Many years ago, they performed great deeds in a vast stadium. Many years ago, those deeds were witnessed by a huge German crowd, which included an eerily familiar little man. With a rather stupid moustache.

JOHN BUCHANAN

YACHTING

1908 London
Gold   12 Metres Class

The 12 metres competition at the London Games was a unique event, contested as it was by just two boats – in Scotland. It was the first and last time an Olympic competition has been staged north of the border.

The 1908 sailing regatta was held at Cowes but the only two entries for the 12 metres class were from Glasgow and Liverpool. Therefore, it was agreed that they would not make the long journey to the Isle of Wight, but that the Liverpool boat would sail to the Clyde. The 26-mile course along the river was won over two races by the Scottish boat *Hera*. They beat the Merseyside boat *Mouchette* by one minute 37 seconds in the first race and one minute and two seconds in the last to take the gold.

Buchanan, like all *Hera*'s crew, was a member of the Royal Clyde Yacht Club and was brought on board by the owner Thomas Glen-Coats. He was born in Rhu in 1884, and was a farmer. He carried on sailing – notching up a victory in the 1936 Tabert Cup sailing his own boat – until his death in 1943.

CLAUDE BUCKENHAM

ASSOCIATION FOOTBALL

1900 Paris
Gold   Soccer Team

Buckenham was one of the leading figures in Essex sport during the early part of the century, and represented the county at both cricket and football. Born in Wandsworth, south-west London, in 1876, the gangling full-back and fast bowler attended Alleyn's School before beginning his football career with Leyton. In 1899 he made his debut for the county cricket side.

In 1900 he played for Upton Park FC in the inaugural Olympic soccer tournament. Reports of the time indicate that Buckenham played a prominent role in Upton Park's victory over a Parisian eleven, helping to secure the gold for Great Britain. However, Buckenham was better known as a dangerous pace bowler, both with Essex and the MCC, and he played a significant part in the latter's South African tour of 1909–10.

In 1914 Buckenham moved north of the border and became a resident cricket professional. After serving with the Royal Garrison Artillery in the First World War, he returned to civilian life and a cricketing career, coaching the students of Repton School. Buckenham died, at the age of 61, in Dundee, Scotland.

GEORGE BUCKLEY

CRICKET

1900 Paris
Gold   Cricket Team

A little-known amateur cricketer from the Devon leagues, Buckley played low in the batting order for the Olympic side. He was bowled for two in the first innings and his batting services were not required again in the match. He took a fine catch to dismiss France's number three who was looking a threat on a score of 15.

HENRY BUCKNALL

ROWING

1908 London
Gold   Eights

A top-class oarsman at Eton, Bucknall was soon installed as stroke at Oxford when he went up to Merton College. Born in Portugal in 1885, he stroked the winning Oxford crew in the 1905 Boat Race and the losing crew of 1906. In 1907, during his tenure as President of the Oxford University Boat Club, he switched to number two in the eight when the crew was reshuffled to try and gain an advantage – but still they lost.

He went back to stroke in the Leander crew which represented Britain and entered the eights competition at the London Games. Despite a brave effort by the Belgians in the final, Leander were too strong and won by two lengths in 7 minutes 52 seconds.

On leaving Oxford, Bucknall joined a ship building firm in Newcastle and he died in Scotland in 1962.

RICHARD BUDGETT

ROWING

1984 Los Angeles
Gold   Coxed Fours

Britain's four was a highly rated unit in Europe and was widely tipped to win a gold medal in Los Angeles. But the team – Budgett, Steven Redgrave, Andrew Holmes, Martin Cross and cox Adrian Ellison – certainly felt the pressure of global TV coverage and the weight of British hopes as they lined up on California's Lake Casitas. With the Eastern Bloc boycotting the Games, the competition was, in truth, not as tough as it could have been, but the British four rowed superbly in the final to hold off the Americans and the much-fancied New Zealanders, winning in 6 minutes 18.64 seconds. Budgett had already won a rowing medal, bronze in the 1981 world championships coxed pairs, but this was his first major international success.

Born in Glasgow in 1959, Budgett went to Radley and then Selwyn College, Cambridge, before qualifying as a doctor. Now retired from competitive rowing, he currently works at the British Olympic Medical Centre, at Northwick Park Hospital in Middlesex.

CHARLIE BUGBEE

SWIMMING

1912 Stockholm
Gold   Water Polo Team

1920 Antwerp
Gold   Water Polo Team

One of Britain's top water polo players before and after the First World War, Bugbee won two golds with the British teams of 1912 and 1920 – then returned for a farewell Olympic appearance in 1924. By then West Ham-born Bugbee, a City of London policeman, was nearly 37 years old and he retired from competitive water polo shortly after the Paris Games.

In the 1912 Games he played in Britain's three successful matches, including the final where they beat Austria 8–0. In Antwerp, the British side were led from the pool under police protection after they defeated the host nation Belgium 3–2 in a fiercely competitive final.

Bugbee died in Middlesex in 1959.

JANE BULLEN

EQUESTRIAN

1968 Mexico City
Gold   Three-Day Event Team

In Mexico Jane Bullen became the first British woman to take part in an Olympic three-day event and was given special leave from her nursing studies at Middlesex Hospital to compete in the Games. She finished a creditable 18th in the individual competition, despite the twin hazards of heat and altitude and a cross-country course that was partially obliterated by swollen rivers and torrential rain. But with her three team colleagues Allhusen, Meade and Jones registering second, fourth and fifth places, there was no need to record her score. Nevertheless, she was able to join her scoring colleagues on the rostrum to receive a gold medal after winning the team event.

Born in Bridport, Dorset, in 1948, she was taught privately before going to Westwing School, in Bristol, and then embarking on her nursing career. She later became a state registered nurse.

A few months before the Mexico Games, Bullen won the Badminton Horse Trials on her tiny horse Our Nobby. Ten years later, as Mrs Holderness-

The British water polo team of 1920 score a goal in their 3–2 win over host nation Belgium in the Olympic final.

With a totally new crew, the Leander Club staged a successful defence of the eights title in Stockholm in 1912.

Roddam, she clinched the title again. In between, she won the Burghley Trials in 1976. She also worked as an administrator in the sport and served as chairman of the selectors for the British three-day event team.

JAMES BUNTEN

YACHTING

1908 London
Gold   12 Metres Class

Bunten was a member of the ten-man crew aboard the *Hera* which won the 12 metres class event on the River Clyde. The Olympic Regatta was held at Cowes, but only two boats entered the 12 metres class – one from Glasgow, the other from Merseyside – so it was decided to allow the competition to take place in Glasgow.

Bunten, a mechanical engineer from Glasgow (born 1875), was a member of the Royal Clyde Yacht Club and had been taken on by owner Thomas Glen-Coats. *Hera* won both its races against the Liverpool-based *Mouchette* on the 26-mile Clyde course to take the gold. Bunten died in Glasgow in 1935.

FRANCIS BURCHELL

CRICKET

1900 Paris
Gold   Cricket Team

Burchell's contribution to the British Olympic effort was minimal. He was nought not out in the first innings as the tenth man and was not called to bat again.

Born in Bristol in 1873, he died in Worthing, Sussex, in 1947, aged 73.

EDGAR BURGESS

ROWING

1912 Stockholm
Gold   Eights

The Leander Club had won the eights at the 1908 London Games and sent a completely new crew to defend the title in Stockholm. Burgess, born in London in 1891, was the only man in the eight who had not won a blue at the time of the Games. He remedied this situation the following year, stroking Oxford to victory in the 1913 Boat Race.

He was educated at Eton and Magdalen College and, although a total of 11 crews took part in the eights competition, Leander's toughest opponents proved to be another one from Britain. New College, Oxford, were just four seconds behind their illustrious team-mates in the final, with the Germans in third place.

Burgess studied law at Oxford and became a member of the Inner Temple on leaving university before accepting a post in the Sudan Political Service. He enjoyed the North African lifestyle and on retirement chose to spend the rest of his days there. He died in Tangier in 1952.

LORD DAVID BURGHLEY

ATHLETICS

1928 Amsterdam
Gold   400 Metres Hurdles

1932 Los Angeles
Silver   4 × 400 Metres Relay

A few years ago, an old gentleman approached Lady Victoria Leatham with an anecdote about her late father. She still smiles at the story. 'This chap was a green keeper, and he was working at the playing grounds in Stamford one day when a young man asked him to help set up some hurdles. Well, he put aside his lawn mower and arranged the hurdles, and the young man hurdled away happily for a couple of hours. When he was finished, the old man asked him where he was off to. "Actually," said the young man, "I'm leaving on Tuesday for Amsterdam. It's the Olympics, you know." And, of course, he came home with a gold medal.'

Of course he did, for Lord David Burghley, sixth

Marquess of Exeter, was never one to ruin a good story. Burghley served the Olympic movement for most of his life but he never allowed it to become his obsession. 'I always got the impression from him,' says his daughter, 'that it was a wonderful club to which he had belonged.'

In truth, Burghley was eminently suited to club life. Born in 1905 at the family's ancestral home of Burghley House in Stamford, Lincolnshire, and educated at Eton, Le Rosey in Switzerland and Magdalene College, Cambridge, he inherited a lifestyle which the modern Olympian could not begin to comprehend.

Hunting was his consuming passion. Even as a schoolboy he had his own pack of harriers which he used to hunt with the help of conscripted villagers. But he discovered a rare athletic talent while at Cambridge, where for three consecutive years he won both high and low hurdles at the Inter-Varsity Sports and where he also completed the famous run around the Great Court of Trinity College before the clock had completed the midday chimes, a feat which the film *Chariots of Fire* misleadingly attributed to his contemporary Harold Abrahams.

By this time he had already competed as a 19-year-old in his first Olympics, at Paris in 1924, where he was eliminated in the first round of the 110 metres hurdles. But his improvement was rapid, helped by his idiosyncratic training trick of balancing a matchbox on the hurdle and attempting to dislodge it with his leading heel. Again, *Chariots of Fire* indulged in romantic fantasy by replacing matchboxes with glasses of champagne. Lady Leatham offers a withering rebuttal: 'He was never one to waste champagne at the best of times,' she says. 'I can't imagine he would have risked the glasses, either.'

By 1927, he was established as one of the world's leading performers over the one-lap hurdles and at the AAA Championships of that year he set a world record of 54.2 seconds for the 440 yards hurdles. It lasted only a matter of hours, for in Nebraska on the same day America's John Gibson ran 52.6, but it installed Burghley as one of the leading contenders for the 1928 Games in Amsterdam.

The experience gained in Paris served him well in his second Olympics. He cruised through his heat in a sluggish 57 seconds and arrived in peak form for the final. His chief rivals were the Americans Morgan Taylor, the defending champion, and Frank Cuhel. They each ran the creditable time of 53.6, but Burghley hurdled magnificently and came home for the gold medal in 53.4 seconds, the first non-American to win the event. He would not comment on his own performance after the race; indeed his only reaction was to praise his rivals: 'Americans', he said, 'are frightfully good losers.'

His track career continued until 1933, and was lavishly littered with honours. He won eight AAA hurdles titles, three Empire Games gold medals and, in the 1932 Los Angeles Games, he ran a 46.7-second leg in Britain's silver medal-winning 4 × 400 metres relay team. In those same Games, Burghley finished fifth in the high hurdles and, defending his 400 metres hurdles title, he ran his fastest time of 52.2 seconds but finished fourth behind the winner, Ireland's Robert Tisdall.

As his athletic career declined, he adapted to his new life as a man of affairs. At the general election of 1931, he won for the Conservatives the Labour-held seat of Peterborough with a majority of 12,434. He continued to hold the seat until resigning in 1943 to become Governor of Bermuda.

He became President of the AAA in 1936 and held the position for 40 years. He was President of the International Amateur Athletic Federation from 1946 to 1976 and, in 1933, he became a member of the International Olympic Committee, a position which he held until his death 45 years later and which saw him fight several political battles, notably with those opposed to the British team's presence at the Moscow Games of 1980.

The years of active sport had left him with severe arthritis, yet he did not allow it to curtail his hunting activities. From 1935 to 1939, he hunted his own private pack of foxhounds and he continued to hunt throughout his life. 'He was extremely courageous towards the end,' recalls his sister, Lady Romayne Brassey, 'because it really almost needed a crane to put him on to his horse, his arthritis was so bad.' That crippling disease required him to undergo three hip replacement operations in his later years, yet he treated them all with aristocratic disdain.

His daughter, Lady Leatham, recalls it with a shudder: 'The first replacement was done in the very early years of that operation, and he had his own bone replaced with a very heavy metal joint. Well, he messed that up by insisting on going hunting. When they took the metal one out, it was such a wonderful shape that my mother took it to London in a carrier bag and walked into the jewellers and said: "This is my husband's hip. I'd like you to crest it and put his coat of arms on it and underneath I'd like you to put: To A Loyal Supporter, with the dates on which it was inside him." They used it as a mascot on our Rolls Royce after that.'

For all his cavalier eccentricities, Burghley was pre-eminently a great Olympian, and he rendered his finest service to the Olympic movement when he organised the 1948 London Games within the space of two years – an achievement which secured the future of the modern Games.

As befits a man of his era, he held an absolute belief in the creed of amateurism. 'He minded terribly that people shouldn't take part in sport for profit or gain,' says Lady Leatham.

It is his daughter who offers the epitaph which reflects his feelings about the Olympic movement;

Selected for both the 110 and 400 metres
hurdles in 1928, Lord Burghley won gold
over the longer distance.

Amateur Athletic Association

Telegraphic Address:
"Athlete, London."

Telephone:
Gerrard 7212

10, John Street
Adelphi,
London, W.C.2

July 10th, 1928

IXth OLYMPIAD

AMSTERDAM
July-August, 1928

Dear Lord Burghley,

It is with great pleasure that we
write to inform you that you have been
selected to represent Great Britain
at the Olympic Games in the

110 and 400 metres Hurdles.

We are asked to convey to you the
heartiest congratulations and best
wishes of the Association.

Yours sincerely,

Harry S. Barclay
Hon. Sec.

Harold M. Abrahams
Team Captain

J.F. Wadmore.
Team Manager

three sentences which he would have appreciated above all others:

'What he really loved was the fact that everybody was joining in just for the pleasure of racing each other. It didn't matter what nation you came from, what colour you were. Nothing mattered, just the fact of taking part.'

TOM BURN

ASSOCIATION FOOTBALL

1912 Stockholm
Gold   Soccer Team

Tom Burn was one of two members of Britain's triumphant 1912 gold medal-winning soccer side to die during the First World War. An uncompromising right-back, Burn was born in Berwick-on-Tweed, Northumberland, in 1888, and played 12 times for the England amateur side. A fixture at the back for his club side London Caledonians, he played in all three games during the Stockholm Olympics, in which Britain enjoyed a 100 per cent record, winning the final 4–2 against Denmark.

Burn's career was curtailed by the war and he died in action in France, in 1916. Two years later his team-mate, left-half Joe Dines, was also killed.

CHARLES BURNELL

ROWING

1908 London
Gold   Eights

A keen soccer player at Eton, Burnell also attracted attention as an excellent schoolboy oarsman. During his time at Eton he won the junior sculls and rowed in the Eton eight at Henley. He went up to Magdalen College, Oxford, in 1895 and rowed in four successful University Boat Races. As a member of the Leander eight he won the Grand for four consecutive years around the turn of the century, as well as securing three victories in the Stewards.

Burnell served as a captain in the London Rifle Brigade and was awarded the DSO during the First World War. After the war he rejoined the family's City stockbroking firm Wise & Burnell. He was chairman of Wokingham Rural Council for more than 30 years and was awarded the OBE in 1954 for his services to Berkshire. His son Richard also won Olympic gold, in the double sculls in 1948, while his grandson Peter rowed in the Boat Race. Burnell died in Oxfordshire, aged 93, in 1969.

RICHARD BURNELL

ROWING

1948 London
Gold   Double Sculls

When Richard Burnell won the double sculls in London he and his father Charles became the only father and son in Olympic history to win gold medals in rowing.

Born in Henley in 1917, Richard followed closely in the footsteps of his father, winner of a gold in the eights in 1908, and attended Eton and Magdalen College. He was in the victorious Oxford crew in the 1939 Boat Race and after the war went straight back to rowing, taking the 1946 Wingfield Sculls at Henley.

At the 1948 Olympic Regatta, also held at Henley, he joined forces with Bertie Bushnell. The combination showed how two scullers of different size and style can forge a successful partnership; Burnell, the powerful oarsman who tended to scull a little short, with Bushnell, a smaller man who tended to over-reach. The net result was a perfect sculling team. However, they started less than perfectly at the Games, losing to France in the first round. But, after winning the repechage and the semi-final, they lined up confidently alongside favourites Denmark and Uruguay in the final. They won by four seconds to take the gold medal – one of only three events won by the host nation in the Games, two of them in rowing.

Burnell continued rowing after London and won a bronze in the eights at the 1950 Commonwealth Games and then the Double Sculls Challenge Cup at Henley in 1951, with P. Bradley. He kept rowing in the family by marrying the daughter of 1912 gold medal-winning oarsman Arthur Garton. Completing a third generation of Boat Race oarsmen, their son rowed in the 1962 event.

Burnell is well known in today's rowing circles as a journalist and leading historian of the sport.

BERTIE BUSHNELL

ROWING

1948 London
Gold   Double Sculls

Bushnell and partner Richard Burnell only came together as a pair in Olympic year, after Bushnell had been surprisingly overlooked as a single sculler by the selectors. Bushnell felt a little aggrieved, especially as he had won the Wingfield Sculls at Henley in 1947.

Born in Woking, Surrey, in 1909, Bushnell went to Henley Grammar School and grew up around boats. His family ran a boatyard on the Thames at Wargrave and also had a yard at Henley. But as a youngster Bushnell was apprenticed as an engineer to Thornycroft's, a company owned by the winner of a 1908 gold medal for motor boating, Tom Thornycroft. The Olympic ideal was clearly sown in young Bushnell and, despite his disappointment at not sculling at the London Games, he prepared diligently for the double sculls with Burnell. They made a good pair: Burnell, a big, strong oarsman who tended to scull short, and Bushnell, a slighter figure who would often over-reach. But together they performed well.

In London the Olympic Regatta was held on their home course, Henley, and although they started badly, losing to France in the first round, they bounced back to make the final, where they held off the Danes and Uruguayans to take the gold. Bushnell, then nearly 40, retired from competitive rowing and went back to the family boat building business. He now lives in retirement on the Algarve, in Portugal.

GUY BUTLER

ATHLETICS

1920 Antwerp
Gold   4 × 400 Metres Relay
Silver   400 Metres

1924 Paris
Bronze   400 Metres
Bronze   4 × 400 Metres Relay

One of the greatest athletes produced in Britain during the first half of the century, Butler never quite peaked in Olympic years despite winning four medals. He was a supremely gifted athlete over the quarter-mile and was unfortunate to compete in the same era as the great South African Bevil Rudd and the Scotsman Eric Liddell.

He was born in Harrow, Middlesex, in 1899 into a great sporting family. His father had been a top athlete and cricketer at Cambridge and young Guy soon followed in his footsteps. As a Harrovian he won three events at the 1917 Public Schools Sports before joining the Royal Military College, Sandhurst, and then Trinity College, Cambridge. In his first attempt he took the AAA 440 yards title in 1919, but then fell foul of Rudd and Liddell in future British championship battles.

Selected for the individual event and the relay at Antwerp, Butler was thwarted once again by Rudd and had to settle for a silver in the 400 metres, but then anchored the relay team to victory in 3:22.2 – two seconds ahead of Rudd's team. He twice finished runner-up in the AAA 440 yards in the years leading up to the Paris Olympics, where he was chosen for the same two events. Things looked promising when he smashed the European 400 metres record in 48 seconds flat in the semi-finals, only to see Liddell storm to a new Olympic and European mark of 47.6 to take gold, leaving him to trail America's Horatio Fitch for the bronze. He then added a second bronze to his medal tally in the relay, behind Sweden and winners America.

In 1926 he equalled the world 300-metre mark of 30.6, took the AAA 220 yards title and began serious training for the 1928 Olympics in Amsterdam. But when he was eliminated in the heats of the 200 metres he decided to end his marvellous track career. He began to coach in the 1930s and worked as a journalist, writing on athletics for the *Morning Post*. He died in St Neots, Cambridgeshire, in 1981.

CHARLES CAMPBELL

YACHTING

1908 London
Gold   8 Metres Class

Campbell was a member of the five-man crew aboard *Cobweb*, the boat that won the 8 metres class at Cowes. Like the owner Blair Cochrane and the rest of the crew, he lived on the Isle of Wight and was a member of the Royal Victoria Yacht Club, which played host to the Olympic Regatta.

Campbell was born in Torquay, Devon, in 1881, the son of a New Zealand sheep farmer, and went to Eton where he began sailing. At the 1908 regatta

Richard Burnell (right) and Bertie Bushnell,
double sculls champions in 1948.

The five-man crew of *Cobweb*, winners of the 8 metres class yachting event at Cowes in 1908.

Cobweb won two of the three 16-mile races, beating the Swedes and a second British boat for the gold. During the First World War he served in the Life Guards, the Royal Tank Corps and on the personal staff of General Sir Alex Godley. His elder brother was killed in the hostilities and when his father died in 1919 he inherited the family baronetcy. Sir Charles Campbell Bt. died on the Isle of Wight in 1948.

COLIN CAMPBELL

HOCKEY

1920 Antwerp
Gold   Hockey Team

Campbell was one of four squad members who did not play in the two matches at the Antwerp Games, but it is understood they were still awarded gold medals. He joined McGrath, McBryan and Cassels on the sidelines as England cruised through their matches to win the Olympic title. The side beat Denmark 5–1, then Belgium 2–1, to reach the final with France.

It is possible that the four reserves would have played in the final game – France had already been beaten by Belgium and Denmark and were almost certain to be defeated by England. But the French team scratched from the competition claiming an epidemic of flu at the school in which they were staying. England were awarded a walkover and the four non-players went home with gold medals without setting foot on a playing field.

GEORGE CANNING

TUG OF WAR

1920 Antwerp
Gold   Tug of War Team

Tug of war made its last Olympic appearance at the 1920 Games in Antwerp and was then consigned to the growing list of discontinued sports. Strangely, the last contest was probably the most representative, with five teams taking part from five different countries.

Britain was represented by the City of London police team, gold medallists in 1908, and they easily defeated the USA, Belgium and Holland to win the competition. Canning, a City constable, retired from the force in 1935.

ARTHUR CARNELL

SHOOTING

1908 London
Gold   Small-Bore Rifle

Carnell benefited from one of the most dreadful episodes of bureaucratic bungling in Olympic history. Britain decided to field a total of 12 marksmen in the small-bore event at the London Games, but one of their nominee's entry forms went astray. While officials tried to rectify the situation, Philip Plater was drafted in as the 12th entrant. When the competition started the officials had managed to get the original man in and nobody noticed that Britain had 13 men shooting.

In the event Plater won the competition with a world record 391 points, with Carnell second with 387. But when the British team management realised what had happened they were forced under Olympic rules to accept the original entry – and not Plater – as their 12th man. Plater was subsequently disqualified, his record expunged, and his name appears in only a few publications of the day, several of them still naming him as Olympic champion.

Captain Carnell, born in London in 1862, was a member of the Mansfield Rifle Club. He shot well during the 50- and 100-yard events, in rain-sodden Bisley, and accepted the gold. He maintained his association both with the sport and his Highgate club throughout his life and died in London in 1940.

HAROLD CASSELS

HOCKEY

1920 Antwerp
Gold   Hockey Team

One of only two British gold medal winners to emerge from a prisoner-of-war camp to take an Olympic title, Cassels was shot down in a dogfight over France during the First World War. Born in China in 1898, where his father was a missionary, he was sent home to school at St Lawrence College, Ramsgate, where he excelled in all sports, especially hockey. When he left school in 1917 he joined the

Royal Flying Corps and soon after was mentioned in despatches before being captured by the Germans. On his release he went to Queens' College, Cambridge, where he won a hockey blue and joined the squad for the 1920 Olympics, the only time he achieved international selection. Able to play anywhere across the half-back line, Cassels was a useful squad player and, although he did not play for England in Antwerp, he still received his medal as England romped to a clean sweep in the tournament, beating Denmark, Belgium and France to take the gold.

On leaving Cambridge he returned to China and taught at the Cathedral School in Shanghai. He then travelled to Australia and the Middle East before settling back in England, where he became a house master at Millfield School. He died in Taunton, Somerset, in 1975.

ALFRED CHALK

ASSOCIATION FOOTBALL

1900 Paris
Gold   Soccer Team

An Essex man through and through, Chalk was born in West Ham in 1874. The right-half was a leading figure in east London football at the start of the century. At various times he turned out for Ilford, Barking Woodville, Essex County and, most notably, Upton Park.

Upton Park's tour of 1900 began with three games in five days, at Dorchester, Yeovil and Weymouth. Then it was across the Channel for a game against a Parisian XI at the World Exhibition. The match was also the first Olympic soccer final. Chalk was the side's outstanding half-back as they beat the French team 4–0, securing the gold medal. The Essex team continued their tour with another game in France and two in the Channel Islands. Finally, Chalk and his fellow Olympic champions returned home, completing their travels with a match in the less exotic surroundings of Basingstoke.

FREDERICK CHAPMAN

ASSOCIATION FOOTBALL

1908 London
Gold   Soccer Team

A fine central defender, Frederick Chapman was unfortunate enough to be responsible for the only blemish on Great Britain's defensive record during their 1908 Olympic triumph. In the match against Sweden he put through his own goal, the only goal Britain conceded in the tournament.

Born in Nottingham in 1883, Chapman was educated at the city's High School. He began his football career locally, with Notts Magdala FC, but left the club when they broke away from the Football Association to join the newly-founded Amateur Football Association. During a career in which he won 16 amateur caps, Chapman played for Oxford City, Nottingham Forest and South Nottingham. He was also a leading light of the English Wanderers, a touring football club formed exclusively from amateur internationals. Other members included the great Vivian Woodward (captain) and Lord Kinnaird (President).

In the First World War Chapman served as a gunner with the Royal Artillery and then as a major in Mesopotamia. After the war he gave up football, focusing instead on his business interests — Lord and Chapman Ltd, a ladies' fashion manufacturers based in Nottingham. He died in his native Nottinghamshire at the age of 68, in 1951.

FRED CHRISTIAN

CRICKET

1900 Paris
Gold   Cricket Team

Christian played a major role in Britain's defeat of France in the Olympic 'final'. He took seven wickets in the French first innings, including four French batsmen for ducks. He scored six with the bat and then took a catch in the French second innings.

The City of London police team, gold medallists in 1908, regained their tug of war title at the 1920 Games in Antwerp.

Lewis Clive (left) partnered Jumbo Edwards to Olympic gold in the 1932 coxless pairs competition in Los Angeles.

Britain won the three miles team race in 1908 through the efforts of Arthur Robertson, Joe Deakin and Bill Coales. Harold Wilson (left) did not score in the event and therefore did not receive a medal.

The famous Manchester Osborne Swimming Club represented Britain in the 1900 water polo competition. Tom Coe is seated on the left.

ROBERT CLIFT

HOCKEY

1988 Seoul
Gold   Hockey Team

Current captain of the British side, Clift's experience will be important as Britain seek to defend their Olympic title in Barcelona.

Born in Newport, South Wales, in 1962, Clift went to Nottingham University and made his England debut in 1982. He was a member of the silver medal-winning sides at the 1986 World Cup and 1987 European Cup before Seoul. An incisive midfielder, Clift was playing at Southgate at the time of the 1988 Games, alongside the star strikers Sean Kerly and Steve Batchelor. That familiarity clearly paid off as Britain lost only one group match – to West Germany – to reach the semi-finals, where they defeated favourites Australia 3–2. In the final they gained revenge for their group defeat by beating the Germans 3–1 to take the gold.

Clift, who has since moved to the East Grinstead club, works in the commercial department of Midland Bank.

LEWIS CLIVE

ROWING

1932 Los Angeles
Gold   Coxless Pairs

Born in London in 1910, Clive excelled as an oarsman from an early age. His father, Lt. Colonel P.A. Clive of the Grenadier Guards, died in action in France in 1918. Young Clive went to Eton and then Christ Church College, Oxford, where he rowed in the 1931 and 1932 Boat Races, but he turned down the chance of joining Leander, the world's oldest rowing club. He was selected to join Jumbo Edwards, one of the finest British oarsmen of the decade, in the coxless pairs at the 1932 Olympics in Los Angeles. Clive was regarded as an impetuous talent by the rowing team, but Edwards' experience saw them comfortably home in the competition, more than two seconds ahead of New Zealand.

Clive's left-wing beliefs had made him something of a rarity in pre-war Oxbridge rowing circles. A staunch Labour Party supporter, he became a councillor for Kensington Council in the 1930s, writing dozens of books and pamphlets, many for the Fabian Society. His ultimate aim was to win a Labour seat in the Commons, but he never achieved his ambition: he decided his presence was required in the fight against fascism in the Spanish Civil War. It was there that he was shot and killed, in Gandesa in 1938, at the age of just 27.

BILL COALES

ATHLETICS

1908 London
Gold   Three Miles Team Race

At just 22, Coales went into the London Games with a growing reputation as one of the up and coming stars of the British cross-country scene. Born in Aldwincle, Northamptonshire, in 1886, he had won his first major race as a teenager when he took the local three-mile handicap, beating the 1900 Olympic champion Sidney Robinson in the process. He continued to excel at handicap races and cross-country; he took the Midland title in 1908 and finished a close second to the great Arthur Robertson in the National Championships.

Slightly built, at just 5ft 6in and weighing barely eight stone, he finished fifth in the AAA ten miles, on the track, just before the London Games, where he was selected for the three-mile team race. Only three men in the team scored, and Britain completed a clean sweep, taking the first three places, with Coales the third man home just edging out the American John Eisele. Britain's two odd men out, Norman Hallows and Harold Wilson, finished some way down the field and out of the medals. A few hours after accepting his gold medal, Coales lined up for the individual five-mile race; but, clearly tired from the morning's exertions, he dropped out with a mile to go.

BLAIR COCHRANE

YACHTING

1908 London
Gold   8 Metres Class

The owner of the *Cobweb* boat that won the 8 metres competition at Cowes, Cochrane was also a key organiser of the Olympic Regatta. The events were hosted by the Royal Victoria Yacht Club and Cochrane was club committee chairman. The crew were a family unit, with both Cochrane and John

Rhodes married to daughters of Sir Richard Sutton. Sutton's son Henry was also on board. *Cobweb* won the first two races of the competition and held off the Swedish boat *Vinga* and a second British boat *Sorais* for the gold.

After the Games Cochrane became Rear Commodore of the RVYC until the outbreak of the First World War, where he was a captain in the Royal Horse Artillery and was awarded the OBE for his services in 1919. The Isle of Wight was his home for many years and he served as Deputy Sheriff of Hampshire. He died in Bembridge in 1928.

SEBASTIAN COE

ATHLETICS

1980 Moscow
Gold   1500 Metres
Silver   800 Metres

1984 Los Angeles
Gold   1500 Metres
Silver   800 Metres

When Sebastian Coe was omitted from the British team for the 1988 Seoul Olympics, the President of the International Olympic Committee made an unprecedented offer. Señor Juan Samaranch suggested that the British runner be given a 'wild card' to the Games in order that he might defend his 1500 metres title.

The offer caused almost as much controversy as the omission. Some urged Coe to grasp his last chance of Olympic competition while others protested at this special treatment for an individual athlete. Coe winced at the uproar, made it known that he could not accept a place on those terms and the suggestion was withdrawn. It was, said Coe, 'A bit of a poisoned chalice'. Yet the incident demonstrated the extraordinary regard in which Sebastian Newbold Coe was held by the most powerful man in the Olympic movement. Of all the tributes Coe had received in the course of a dazzling career, that gesture from Samaranch was perhaps the most remarkable.

The career yielded three world indoor records and nine world records outdoors, three of them set within 42 summer days in 1979. Those records alone entitle him to a measure of athletic immortality, yet his Olympic achievements are surely destined to linger even more warmly in public memory.

Peter Coe, Seb's father and coach, had discerned the potential at an early stage and had attempted to warn his son about what lay in store. 'I remember coming off a rain-soaked training track in Sheffield when I was about 14,' says Seb. 'And my father said to me, very calmly: "Look, I don't want this to come as a major surprise to you, but you will be going to the Olympic Games in 1980. I've seen a lot of athletes wilt under that kind of pressure, and I want you to get used to it now." Well, that was terrific. But I was only 14!'

In fact, running was never a hardship to the young Coe. 'I got enormous physical enjoyment from running,' he says. 'Without that, careers don't tend to last too long. And I didn't miss out on things through running. I was European indoor champion at 19. I was getting a breadth of experience that no 19-year-old was getting in the normal course of events. I was flying the world and competing and doing something I enjoyed. And I was coming back to a normal, happy family.'

He first became aware of the man who was to prove his fiercest and most respected rival when he visited his first English Schools Championships. 'I'd finished something like 13th in the 3000 metres,' he says, 'and there was Steve Ovett, coming off the bottom bend in the 400 metres and waving to his mates in the stands. Even then, I knew this was a massive talent.'

The rivalry was as keen as it was inevitable, and as the pair won their titles and broke their world records, the entire world of sport began to anticipate with relish the conflict of the Moscow Olympics. The Americans may have boycotted the event, but no matter; there was still Ovett versus Coe. 'The interest was incredible,' recalls Coe. 'For foreign journalists, the British Team HQ was their first port of call in the morning. "How had they slept? What did they have for breakfast?" Thankfully, the rivalry never spilled over into a slanging match in the press. It's something I'm particularly proud of. I spoke to Steve about this recently and he feels the same. We never made disparaging comments about each other in the newspapers. If we had, the whole thing would have just gone completely out of control.'

More than a decade after Moscow, Coe concedes that he shared the popular view of how the two crucial races were likely to finish: 'I felt I would have to run pretty badly if I was to blow the 800 metres, but I knew the 1500 would be very different because that was really Steve's strength.' In fact, he ran untypically poorly at 800 metres, and the disappointment is still with him: 'I should have won an Olympic title at the distance I felt I dominated for the best part of a decade,' he says. 'Looking back, if I'd made the Olympic team in 1976 and learned to live under that pressure, I'd have been a lot stronger for it in Moscow. But the race I ran had inexperience and pressure and nerves written all over it.' The silver medal he won in a slow-run race behind Ovett was scant consolation.

After the 800, he got the frustration out of his system with what he describes as 'An horrendously

Seb Coe celebrates his victory in the 1980 1500 metres, a title he went on to retain four years later in Los Angeles.

hard training session', of a kind which most athletes would not contemplate in the middle of a major championships. His motivation was also sharpened by a newspaper which carried a picture of Coe on a long training run under the headline: 'Coe's Trail of Shame.' The 1500 offered the chance of redemption and, despite the fact that his chance had been widely dismissed, he was determined to take it. 'Funny,' he says, 'I can't remember a single stride of the 800 metres, but I could take you through every footstep of the 1500.' He ran a tactically perfect race, covering every break, refusing to show his hand too early, accommodating the frenzied third lap which the East German Jurgen Straub inflicted upon the field and kicking irresistibly off the pace to float home in style and comfort. 'There was relief,' he says, 'real relief. It wasn't the joy of having won an Olympic title, it was the relief of having finished a pretty intense and occasionally nasty series of experiences. I also realised that if I didn't alter my mental approach, and if I continued to let the pressures affect me, then my career probably wouldn't last that long.'

Such was his talent that he decided, quite deliberately, to run for the sheer hell of it and to break records along the way. His riotous success was reflected in the statistics as the world records fell almost to order. Yet he still retained the belief that the Olympic Games offered the most fulfilling challenge, and he set himself the task of retaining his title, a feat which no athlete had accomplished in modern times. He suffered with a blood disorder which virtually erased his 1983 season, yet he was mentally far tougher than he had been in Moscow. He was still only 27 years old, yet some pundits were starting to write him off. He used that rejection to fuel his sense of grievance. He became even more single-minded. He was ready to create a little history.

The Los Angeles programme demanded that he run seven races in nine days: 'That was the thing which pleased me most,' he says. 'I ran them and lived to tell the tale!' Ovett was not a factor, a virus having robbed him of his speed and strength, and Coe himself was no longer quite the athlete he had been at 800 metres. Yet he discovered sufficient pace to run 1:43.64 and take the silver medal behind the gifted Brazilian, Joaquim Cruz. In the 1500 metres, he delivered one of those perfect races once again; drifting with the pace, flicking through the gears off the final bend and surging away from the field to finish almost a second ahead of his countryman Steve Cram in a new Olympic record of 3:32.53. For a few moments he directed a rare show of anger at those journalists who had doubted his credentials, but the mood quickly passed as the reality of his achievement dawned.

Sadly, the competition which provided him with his greatest triumphs was also the source of his deepest disappointment. After a poor run in the Olympic Trials, he was not selected to run for Britain in the Seoul Games of 1988. He resented the fact that he was not given more time to find his real form and that his record at major championships was not taken into account ... except by Señor Samaranch. Privately, he is convinced that he would have won a third title at 1500 metres. Publicly, he says: 'I had the opportunity of making history. And it wasn't the greatest of Olympic finals . . .'

In fact, the controversy of Seoul simply hastened his departure from active athletics. He made an attempt to win a Commonwealth title in New Zealand in 1990, but injury betrayed him and he retired after the games. Shortly after, he was adopted as Conservative candidate for the marginal constituency of Falmouth and Camborne, and won the seat at the General Election of April 1992.

He now looks back with pride and affection upon one of the most astonishing careers in modern sport. He even feels genuine affection for his fiercest Olympic rival. 'I think Steve Ovett's the greatest runner I ever competed against, probably the most complete athlete I knew,' he says. 'We came through a very difficult period in both our lives and we came out the other side as pretty reasonably balanced people. These days, I don't see as much of him as I would like to. But, yes, I count him as a friend.'

TOM COE

SWIMMING

1900 Paris
Gold   Water Polo Team

A huge contingent from the famed Manchester Osborne Swimming Club made the trip to Paris for the 1900 Games. With no other water polo team in France it was decided the club would represent Britain in the competition. Twenty-year-old Coe played in both matches, beating France and then Belgium's Swimming et Water Polo Club 7–2 in the final to take the gold.

ROBERT COLEMAN

YACHTING

1920 Antwerp
Gold   7 Metres Class

Coleman was a member of the four-man crew aboard the *Ancora* which won the 7 metres event in Ostend. The 32-year-old was a member of the Royal Burnham Yacht Club, where he met Cyril Wright and was invited to take part in the Olympic Regatta. The *Ancora* had a tough battle with the Norwegians, who won the first race, but the British crew fought back to win the last two and clinch the gold.

Coleman died in Brentwood, Essex, in 1960.

HAROLD COOKE

HOCKEY

1920 Antwerp
Gold   Hockey Team

A diminutive right-half, Birmingham-born Cooke was spotted playing for Warwickshire by the British selectors. He played four times for England, including his two appearances during the Olympics in Antwerp. England had little problem during the tournament, crushing Denmark, Belgium and France by huge margins to take the gold. In the same year he left Birmingham University and began a career in the steel industry.

CHARLOTTE COOPER

LAWN TENNIS

1900 Paris
Gold   Women's Singles
Gold   Mixed Doubles

Chattie Cooper holds the distinction of being the first woman ever to win an Olympic gold medal. There were no women at the first Games in Athens in 1896, and only a handful appeared in Paris, but tennis was an event in which a sizeable number of mainly French and British women took part.

However, Cooper was hardly an unknown quantity, even in France. She had been in the Wimbledon ladies' singles final six times before the Paris Games, winning on three occasions. In Paris she met local heroine Helene Prevost in the final and comfortably beat her in straight sets 6–1, 6–4. She then took another gold in the mixed doubles with partner Reg Doherty, the elder of the famed tennis brothers, again beating Prevost, who was partnered by Ireland's Harold Mahony. The score: 6–2, 6–4.

Born in Ealing, Middlesex, in 1870, Cooper first took the Wimbledon title in 1895, after which she cycled back to her brother's house in Surbiton, where she was staying during the championships. Her brother was pruning roses in the front garden. 'What have you been doing Chattie?' he enquired. 'I've just won the championship,' she replied. Her brother said nothing and carried on pruning the roses.

In 1901 Cooper married Alfred Sterry, who went on to become President of the Lawn Tennis Association. She won two more Wimbledon singles titles, in 1901 and 1908. She also won seven Wimbledon mixed doubles titles and two ladies' doubles, as well as a host of other championships, including eight Irish titles, the Scottish singles and a variety of covered court events. Her daughter Gwen was a top player between the wars and her son Rex was a vice chairman of the All England Club.

The world's first woman Olympic champion died in Scotland in 1966, aged 96.

MALCOLM COOPER

SHOOTING

1984 Los Angeles
Gold   Small-Bore Rifle – Three Positions

1988 Seoul
Gold   Small-Bore Rifle – Three Positions

One of the greatest marksmen in the history of the sport, Cooper has devoted his life to shooting. Born in Camberley, Surrey, in 1947, he first picked up a rifle as a teenager in New Zealand, where he lived for three years during his father's foreign posting as a lieutenant in the Royal Navy. He began competitive shooting in Auckland and continued to progress in the sport. When he eventually returned home to England, he competed first at club level, then county, then national and finally international.

Cooper made his Olympic debut in Munich in

1972, where he finished 18th; he then duplicated this performance in Montreal. With the British shooting team following the Government's advice to boycott the Moscow Games in 1980 he was unable to show his improvement, but in Los Angeles he took the gold by ten points from Switzerland's Daniel Nipkow, equalling the world record into the bargain. Bronze medallist in that competition was Britain's Allister Allan and it was he who would push Cooper to the limit in Seoul.

Before the Korean Games Cooper had established himself as the world's premier small-bore exponent, winning countless titles and consistently breaking world records. At the 1985 European Championships he won all five events and the following year he set five world records at the World Championships. He has established an incredible 17 world records during his outstanding career. In Seoul, he was suggesting retirement but he pipped Allan in the final – after the Scotsman had led him earlier in the competition – to win in a new Olympic record and become the first man successfully to defend an Olympic rifle title.

His wife Sarah, part of a unique British shooting duo, also took part in Seoul and finished 36th in the women's small-bore competition. Together they run a shooting supplies business on Hayling Island.

WALTER CORBETT

ASSOCIATION FOOTBALL

1908 London
Gold   Soccer Team

A quick, intelligent full-back, Corbett was born in 1880 in Wellington, Shropshire. Although he made appearances for both Aston Villa and QPR, Corbett spent most of his club career with Birmingham. However, a year after playing an important role in Great Britain's Olympic triumph, he returned to his birthplace to play for Wellington Town.

Corbett played 18 times for England's amateur side between 1907 and 1911 and, like the Olympic side's goalkeeper, Horace Bailey, won full honours on the England tour of Central Europe in 1908.

HARRY CORNER

CRICKET

1900 Paris
Gold   Cricket Team

Another member of the Olympic side to emerge from the Blundell's School old boys network, Corner was selected for the trip to Paris at the last minute after it was mutually agreed to allow 12 players a side. Born in Taunton, Somerset, in 1874, Corner played for Devon's Castle Cary club and in both Britain's Olympic innings, going lbw for four in the first and standing at five not out when Britain declared in the second. He also took a wicket in France's second innings of just 26 runs.

A director of a Welsh wool merchants, Corner died in Radyr, Glamorgan, in 1938, aged 63.

GEORGE CORNET

SWIMMING

1908 London
Gold   Water Polo Team

1912 Stockholm
Gold   Water Polo Team

Scottish railwayman Cornet was the oldest member of the victorious British water polo side at the London Games. He then went on to play in his second Olympic final in Stockholm and claim a second gold medal.

Born in Inverness in 1877, he swam for his local club and represented Scotland 17 times, the last occasion being in 1912. The competitive defender was an intimidating sight for opposition players; he stood 6ft 3in and weighed 15st 7lb.

At the London Games Britain outclassed Belgium 9–2, and in Sweden the margin, this time over Austria, was a one-sided 8–0. Cornet died in Scotland in 1952.

Malcolm Cooper, on target for gold in the small-bore rifle (three positions) shooting event at the 1988 Seoul Olympics.

At the 1908 London Games Britain's water polo team beat Belgium 9–2 to take the Olympic title.

CHARLES CRICHTON

YACHTING

1908 London
Gold   6 Metres Class

Crichton was a member of the three-man crew aboard the *Dormy* boat which won the 6 metres class at Cowes. He and Gilbert Laws were crew to owner Tom McMeekin in the event and helped win the first two of the three 13-mile races, placing third in the final race to clinch the gold.

Crichton was born in Colchester, Essex, in 1872, and was educated at Radley. He joined the Royal Cruising and Royal Southern Yacht Clubs and even sailed while on military service in India. He won the DSO for his actions with the 10th Hussars during the First World War and was promoted to lieutenant colonel. He married in 1912 and died in Wales in 1958, aged 86.

ERIC CROCKFORD

HOCKEY

1920 Antwerp
Gold   Hockey Team

A first-class hockey and cricket player, Crockford was one of two Warwickshire players to make the English Olympic team. He joined Harold Cooke in the side that easily defeated Denmark, Belgium, and France to win the gold.

Born in Wylde Green, Warwickshire, in 1888, Crockford went to school in Eastbourne before returning to his home county to establish a solicitor's practice.

Playing at centre-half, he won the first of his 17 England caps in Olympic year while playing for Sutton Coldfield. He also excelled as a cricketer, appearing many times for his county in the early 1920s. He died in Sutton Coldfield in 1958.

MARTIN CROSS

ROWING

1980 Moscow
Bronze   Coxless Fours

1984 Los Angeles
Gold   Coxed Fours

The most experienced member of the Los Angeles crew, Cross made his mark on international rowing as a member of the Thames Tradesmen Rowing Club. He had become a significant oarsman in the late 1970s when he landed bronze medals in Britain's coxless fours at the 1978 and 1979 World Championships. In the following year, at the Moscow Olympics, he claimed another bronze in the coxless fours behind the Soviets and winners East Germany.

In Los Angeles, Britain were firm favourites for the coxed fours gold, especially with the absence of the boycotting East Europeans. But the Americans and the New Zealanders were also strong contenders. Cross described his feelings as he waited to get into the boat before the final: 'There is a sense of destiny that what you are about to take part in is somehow different from any other race that you have been in. Here is the chance to grab sporting immortality. I was more nervous than I have ever been in my life – and I was supposed to be the experienced one!' Their tactics seemed to go awry as the Americans led them with 500 metres to the finish. But then the British crew began to sprint for the line, gradually overhauling the US crew and crossing the line less than two seconds ahead.

Cross, born in London in 1957, went on to win a silver in the pairs at the 1985 World Championships and a gold in the coxed fours at the 1986 Commonwealth Games. His greatest personal achievement was to win the pairs at the Lucerne Regatta in 1986 – by two seconds after being five seconds adrift with 500 metres to go! In 1988 he returned to Olympic competition and rowed once again in the coxed fours, this time finishing fourth.

Cross works as a history teacher at Hampton School and is also secretary of the local Labour Party.

REX CRUMMACK

HOCKEY

1920 Antwerp
Gold   Hockey Team

A wealthy cotton broker, Crummack became an influential administrator in hockey and golf. Born in Salford, Lancashire, in 1887, he travelled south to London on leaving school to learn the cotton trading business in the City. Crummack was a fine all-round sportsman and played hockey, soccer and golf at county level before his career was interrupted by the war. He served as a captain in the Prince of Wales Volunteers and was mentioned in despatches.

As a hockey player, he won five England caps and was selected for the Olympics at inside-forward. England cruised through the competition, beating Denmark, Belgium and France by substantial margins to take gold. He won his last England cap in 1926 and became an England selector.

Meanwhile, he had built up a thriving cotton trading business and was able to spend more time on his favourite pastime – golf. He was three times Lancashire's amateur champion, based at the Royal Lytham St Anne's Golf Club, and played all over the country in amateur competitions, so much so that in 1953 he was appointed to the General Committee of golf's ruling Royal & Ancient. He died in Stockport, Cheshire, in 1966.

COLLIER CUDMORE

ROWING

1908 London
Gold   Coxless Fours

The 1908 coxless fours was a duel between two of the great rowing forces of the day – and they were both British. Only four crews entered the competition: Canada, Holland and the two British boats – Leander and Magdalen College, Oxford. Cudmore, born in Australia in 1885, came to England to study law at Oxford and was immediately recognised as a talented oarsman. He rowed at bow in the Magdalen crew that won both the Stewards and Visitors at Henley, as well as for Oxford in the Boat Race.

The Olympic competition began with Magdalen easily beating Canada's Argonaut Rowing Club in the first heat, while Leander did likewise with the Dutch. The final was eagerly awaited on the home course at Henley but Magdalen emerged comfortable winners, in eight minutes and 34 seconds, as Leander struggled to find a decent course.

Cudmore rowed in the Oxford boat in 1909, was called to the Bar in the following year and then returned to Australia to establish a legal practice. The outbreak of the First World War brought him back to Europe and he served with the Royal Field Artillery in France, where he was twice wounded. He returned to Australia at the end of the war and built up a thriving legal business, using it latterly as a base to launch a political career which saw him become leader of the influential Liberal and Country Party. In 1958 he was knighted for his services to politics in Australia. He died in Adelaide in 1971, aged 85.

FRED CUMING

CRICKET

1900 Paris
Gold   Cricket Team

Top scorer with 38 runs in Britain's first innings in the Olympic final against France, Cuming was another Blundell's School old boy. Born in Tiverton, Devon, in 1875, he also scored 18 for Britain in the second innings and took a catch. He had a good summer in 1900: he scored 86 for the Bradninch club against the Blundell's second XI and played for Exeter. He died in London in 1942.

LORNE CURRIE

YACHTING

1900 Paris
Gold   Open Class
Gold   0.5–1 Ton Class

Currie was the owner of the *Scotia* at the 1900 Olympic Regatta which was held at Meulan on the River Seine. There has been some doubt as to whether he actually participated in the two events or was simply listed on official records because he was the owner. Although press reports of the day are few and far between, it is unlikely that he would have allowed his boat to be sailed in such a competition without him. It seems certain that three men were on board and in the Open class competition the British boat beat Germany by two minutes to take the gold, while in the 0.5–1 ton class the *Scotia* out-sailed the local French crew. Currie died in France in 1926, aged 55.

DENIS DALY

POLO

1900 Paris
Gold   Polo Team

A privileged background in Ireland enabled Daly to spend plenty of time on his polo ponies, and he became one of the country's top players. Born in County Galway in 1862, the son of Lord Dunsandle, Daly joined the army from school and served in the 18th Hussars where he perfected his polo talents. He retired from the Hussars in 1893 but continued to play polo, which ensured his selection for the Olympic tournament in Paris.

Daly played in all the games including the final, in which Britain, represented by the Foxhunters team, beat the Wanderers, an Anglo-US team, 3–1. He rejoined the army in 1914 and served as a major in the Army Remount Department. He died in Oxfordshire in 1942, aged 80.

VIC D'ARCY

ATHLETICS

1912 Stockholm
Gold   4 × 100 Metres Relay

One of the best British sprinters of the pre-First World War era and a member of two Olympic relay teams, D'Arcy leaped to prominence the year before the Stockholm Games, when he beat the country's number one fast man Willie Applegarth.

Born in Rotherhithe, south London, in 1887, he ran for the famous Polytechnic Harriers and boasted a fine record at national championships. After the celebrated defeat of Applegarth in the Kinnaird Trophy meeting, he went on to take second in the 1911 AAA 100 yards and then equalled the British record of 9.8 seconds in the event at a meeting in Vienna. He never managed an AAA title, but finished four times in the first three and ran in four successful medley relay teams.

It was in the relay that he saw success at the Stockholm Games, after crashing out of the individual sprints in the early rounds. The American favourites were disqualified in the semi-finals and Britain – David Jacobs, Henry Macintosh, D'Arcy and Applegarth – just edged the Germans on the line, in a new Olympic record of 42.4. The Germans were then disqualified, leaving the Swedes to take silver behind Britain.

D'Arcy returned to the Olympics after the war, when at 33 he ran the third leg in the 4 × 100 metres relay final in Antwerp, in a team that included the young Harold Abrahams. But they were just pipped for a bronze medal by Sweden. After running in the traditional post-Games Empire match at the White City, he retired from competitive athletics. He later emigrated to South Africa, where he died in 1961.

CHRIS DAVIES

YACHTING

1972 Munich
Gold   Flying Dutchman Class

Chris Davies learned to sail with his father close to their Cornish home and was competing from the age of ten. He successfully worked his way through the system and crewed for reigning Olympic champion Rodney Pattisson at the Munich Olympics. Their victory ended his first-class competitive career, although he still takes part in minor events around the country. In fact, he and Pattisson won an event at the Poole Harbour Yacht Club in the autumn of 1991.

Born in 1946, Davies met Pattisson less than a year before the Munich Olympics, but their partnership was an instant winner. Their boat K263 *Superdoso* was the star of the show as far as Davies is concerned, but when they stepped ashore at Kiel after clinching the gold their triumph was soured by the news of the terrorist atrocity in Munich.

Davies worked for many years with the boat building firm Vosper-Thornycroft, but in 1991 he took on the post of lecturer in marine engineering at the Southampton Institute of Higher Education. He currently lives in Fareham, Hampshire, and has two children, a boy and a girl, both of whom are keen sailors.

The victorious 4 x 100 metres relay squad of 1912: (left to right) Willie Applegarth, Vic D'Arcy, David Jacobs and Henry Macintosh.

George de Relwyskow (standing, second left) won two medals in the 1908 freestyle wrestling competition: gold in the lightweight division and silver at middleweight. Also pictured are Con O'Kelly (standing, centre) and Stanley Bacon (second right), gold medallists at heavyweight and middleweight respectively.

Lynn Davies, Olympic long
jump champion in 1964.
Receiving the congratulations of
the great Jesse Owens crowned
his moment of glory.

LYNN DAVIES

ATHLETICS

1964 Tokyo
Gold   Long Jump

They met on a summer afternoon, at the schools championships in Cardiff. The coach was bursting with ideas and searching for athletes who could put them into practice. The miner's son from Nant-y-moel was promising, but he was uncertain about a future in track and field. Lynn Davies remembers it well. 'Ron Pickering had just been appointed national coach for Wales. He came up to me and I'll never forget this big man with his tremendous enthusiasm. He said: "I've seen you long jump and you've got great ability. If you're prepared to concentrate on athletics, I'd say you could be one of the best athletes this country's ever had."'

Davies was unready for that kind of compliment. Athletics had never been a sport which was taken seriously at his grammar school in the Ogmore Valley, where the real games were rugby and soccer and the heroes were Cliff Morgan and Stanley Matthews. Only once had he long jumped, and he had covered 21 feet, which explained his presence in Cardiff for the championships.

But he thought about Pickering's remarks, and he continued to think about them when he returned to Cardiff to study physical education at the local college. When he arrived, he discovered that Pickering had just moved to the same city. 'Luck and circumstance,' says Lynn. 'I'd been used to drinking eight pints with the rugby team on a Tuesday night and turning out without training. Suddenly I started working with Ron and I discovered the meaning of discipline. Suddenly I was an athlete.' Pickering was working with enviable raw material. Davies was blessed with natural speed but, more importantly, he possessed the appetite for work which would lift him to the highest level.

The coach believed that explosive events required the kind of specialised weight-training which would improve the athlete's power—weight ratio and develop his essential spring. Six months of intensive work brought a dramatic improvement in distances and times. Yet, in the early 1960s, the Olympics were no more than a distant dream.

'An athlete measures his career by a series of milestones,' says Lynn. 'You climb one ladder, and you realise you're only the best in the Welsh Schools Championships. Then you have to win the Welsh Championships, then try to get into the top six in Great Britain, then it's the Commonwealth Games, then the European Championships. But Ron could motivate you, he could sow the seeds. You'd heard him say: "You could be Britain's greatest

long jumper. The Olympics are a possibility." And you always had that sneaking feeling in the back of your mind that he might be right.'

Davies passed his milestones. In 1962 he made his international debut at the European Championships. Later that year, he finished fourth in the Commonwealth Games with a British record of 7.72m. The Tokyo Games of 1964 were acquiring a sharper perspective.

He opened his Olympic season with a Commonwealth record of 8.01m in May, and added a further centimetre in July. But he was also required to cope with a crisis. Now a qualified teacher, Lynn had to shape his training around his working day, and his performance with the weights had started to suffer. Pickering saw the decline, saw the effect it was having upon his protégé and joined Lynn in the weights room. In the course of one gruelling session, the coach succeeded in out-lifting the athlete, pricking his competitive pride and restoring his motivation.

Yet alongside the confidence there was a sobering realism. Both Ralph Boston of America and Igor Ter-Ovanesian of the Soviet Union had jumped a foot better than Davies and, in truth, the expectations of coach and athlete extended no further than the bronze medal.

Lynn's Olympics started in disappointing fashion. Selected at 100 metres, he failed to survive his heat in 10.7 seconds. When he barely qualified for the long jump final with his last jump, expectations were not high. But on the morning of the final, he looked out of his window in the athletes' village and his spirits rose. 'The Welsh gods must have been looking down on Tokyo that day, because it was pouring with rain,' he recalls. 'Not only that, but we found we had a five-metre headwind blowing into us. I'd jumped in those conditions many times in South Wales and I was well used to them. I'm convinced that had it been a warm, sunny day in Tokyo, I wouldn't have won the gold.'

As the afternoon wore on, he became convinced that he could jump eight metres in those conditions. Then, as he prepared for the fifth round, he remembered something Pickering had told him: 'Look at the flag at the top of the stadium. If it drops, it's a fair indication that the wind could be about to drop inside the stadium.' He saw the flag drop, and swiftly accelerated into his run-up. As soon as he landed in the pit, he knew it was a big jump. The officials took two minutes to measure it, and when they came up with 8.07m, Davies was leading the Olympic final. Both Boston and Ter-Ovanesian responded with soaring leaps, but each was a handful of centimetres short. The pride of Nant-y-moel was the new Olympic champion.

He celebrated with Pickering that evening and they met again at breakfast the following morning, when their meal was interrupted by an elderly gentleman who came across to offer congratulations.

'Hello, Mr Davies,' he said. 'I saw you compete yesterday. It was a great performance.' Lynn's Olympics were complete. He had won the approval of Jesse Owens.

And then it was home, to face the nation's applause. There was a reception at Buckingham Palace and another at Paddington Station, which was decorated by a huge banner: Welcome Home Lynn. Four thousand awaited him in Cardiff and a motorcade carried him home the 30 miles to Nant-y-moel. 'Amazing!' he says. 'They'd given the children a day off from school and they'd all turned out to see me and my medal. There was bunting outside the houses, all the way down the valley. Outside my little house in Nant-y-moel there were 3000 people, all celebrating. The whole thing meant a lot to a small mining community like that. It was a wonderful day.'

But Pickering looked to the future, pointing out that no athlete had ever won Olympic, European and Commonwealth gold medals. That became Lynn's task and such was his talent that the goal was delivered within two weeks in 1966, when he won the Commonwealth title in Jamaica, and the European Championship in Budapest.

In the Olympic year of 1968, he became the first Briton to jump 27 feet (8.23m), and he was strongly favoured to retain his Olympic title at the Games of Mexico. But that was the year of Bob Beamon, who almost leaped out of the pit with his first jump of the competition, adding almost two feet to the old figures and setting, at 8.90m, a world record which was to stand for 23 years.

After his achievement, Beamon walked over to Davies and said: 'Do you think I should jump again?' 'No,' said Lynn, 'go and sit in the stand now, Bob. You can afford to watch the rest of this competition.' Davies was destroyed by that jump and finished a distant ninth, but in the following year in Stuttgart he actually defeated Beamon for one of his most satisfying victories.

Davies retained his Commonwealth title at the Edinburgh Games of 1970, but that was to prove his last major victory. He captained the British team at his third Olympics, the Munich Games of 1972, but he was handicapped by injury and failed to make the long jump final. Soon after, he retired, having extended the British record by almost two feet in the course of his career.

He spent six years as technical director of Canadian athletics and later returned to British sport as a team manager for the Games of 1980 and 1984. He worked with the Sports Council for Wales and dabbled successfully in BBC Television's *Superstars*. Eventually, he accepted a sports broadcasting post with BBC Wales, where he has become one of the most popular presenters.

A man utterly unaffected by his fame, he looks back and gives thanks for his sporting life. 'I believe sport is one of the greatest things we can offer our young people,' he says. 'There's nothing we can hand on to the next generation which has so much value.' He thinks for a moment, then he breaks into a sad little smile. 'Ron Pickering was very fond of saying that,' says Lynn.

GEORGE de RELWYSKOW

WRESTLING

1908 London
Gold   Lightweight Freestyle
Silver   Middleweight Freestyle

Londoner George de Relwyskow held the record of being the youngest Olympic wrestling champion for almost 70 years. He was just a month past his 21st birthday when he claimed the gold in the freestyle lightweight division at the London Games.

Born in Kensington in 1887, de Relwyskow was generally regarded as, pound-for-pound, the most talented wrestler in Britain going into the Olympics. He was reigning British champion in both lightweight and middleweight divisions, having already won both titles in 1907. By the time of the 1908 Games he had won 35 open titles and even managed runner-up prizes in two heavyweight tournaments.

In the Olympic middleweight division he was pipped by the great Stanley Bacon, who won 15 national titles during his career, with the two bouts of the best-of-three series going on points decisions after neither wrestler managed a winning move within the 15-minute time limit. But de Relwyskow made amends in the lighter division, beating the novice Briton Bill Wood to take the gold. The cleverer de Relwyskow won the first two bouts on points from the stronger Wood.

He went on to coach wrestling and took the 1924 British team to the Paris Olympics. As a fitness coach and masseur, he became a familiar figure on the Yorkshire wrestling scene. A builder and decorator by trade, he died in Leeds in 1942.

JOE DEAKIN

ATHLETICS

1908 London
Gold   Three Miles Team Race

Veteran track star Joe Deakin led Britain to a clean sweep in a tactically run team race at the London Games. He sprinted the last 200 yards to pull away from the field and win by a clear 30, dragging along with him his two British team-mates to ensure another athletics gold. Deakin was nearly 30 when the 1908 Olympics began and he used all the experience garnered from hundreds of races around the world to lead the three-mile team to victory.

Born in Shelton, near Stoke-on-Trent, in 1879, he first sprang to prominence by winning the 1901 Irish Steeplechase Championship in Belfast. Serving with the Rifle Brigade he saw action in the Boer War, but still continued to run, setting South African records in the 880 yards and the mile. Back in Ireland he took the mile and four-mile titles and after joining Herne Hill Harriers became one of the country's finest cross-country athletes. His cross-country victory in the 1908 Southern Championships, when it seemed there was no way back for him, ensured selection for the Olympics and he came into the team race having finished sixth in the 1500 metres on the previous day.

Like three-mile team-mate Bill Coales, a few hours after receiving the gold medal Deakin entered the five-mile individual race, held on the same afternoon. Consequently he dropped out of the event after less than four miles. Deakin continued to compete after the war, in which he was temporarily blinded, moving up to the marathon and trying his hand at road races as well as his beloved cross-country. He was still running well into his eighties and died in south London three years after his last race, in 1972, aged 93.

BILLY DEAN

SWIMMING

1920 Antwerp
Gold   Water Polo Team

One of the top water polo forwards of his day, Dean learned his trade under the wing of George Wilkinson — the greatest goalscorer in the sport. Dean was born in Manchester in 1887 and took to swimming at a very early age, winning the Royal Humane Society's medallion at the tender age of ten. He played polo for his local Manchester Swan and Salford Club and made his England debut while still a teenager. When he moved a few miles down the road to Hyde he swapped clubs to the formidable Hyde Seal, arguably Britain's number one swimming team, where he joined forces with Wilkinson. With the two men playing up front the club was virtually unbeatable at home and abroad, winning the national title three times and the European three times. In regional competition they were even more dominant, winning the northern counties water polo title for 21 successive years.

Dean played 18 games for England, as captain in six of them, and earned selection for the Antwerp Games towards the end of his career, long after Wilkinson had retired. The British side beat the host nation Belgium 3–2 in a stormy final, and the team had to be led from the pool by armed guards to protect them from the angry crowd.

A keen all-round sportsman, Dean was on the books of Manchester United as a goalkeeper and started his own electrical engineering company, which he ran until his death in his native Lancashire in 1949.

ROB DERBYSHIRE

SWIMMING

1900 Paris
Gold   Water Polo Team

1908 London
Gold   4 × 200 Metres Freestyle Relay

One of the country's top swimmers around the turn of the century, Derbyshire was the first Briton to break the one-minute barrier for 100 yards. He collected no fewer than ten national titles and took part in three Olympic Games spanning 12 years.

Born in Manchester in 1878, John Henry Derbyshire was always known as Rob — an abbreviation of a childhood pet name. He had an immediate introduction to the water, as his father was superintendent of Manchester Baths. His aquatic talents were soon evident and he won his first prize at the age of six. As a young man he joined the Manchester Osborne Swimming Club which represented Britain at the Paris Games and defeated Belgium 7–2 in the final. A few years after internal wrangling had split Osborne, he left to found the Old Trafford Club and continued to compete for them until he eventually moved to London.

Derbyshire went to the 1906 'renegade' Games in Athens, where he won a bronze in the 4 × 250

Rob Derbyshire, the talented swimmer who won two Olympic golds at the turn of the century – in the water polo competition of 1900 and in the 1908 4 x 200 metres freestyle relay.

The 1912 indoor mixed doubles tennis final: (left to right) Edith Hannam and Charles Dixon beat Helen Aitchison and Roper Barrett in four sets.

metres relay, and two years later was in the gold medal-winning British relay team that beat Hungary in a thrilling final. His ten national titles included six victories in the 100 yards, from 1898 to 1904, but he made little impression on the 100-metre event in London, or when he made his last Olympic appearance four years later in Stockholm.

After working as a baths manager in Manchester for some years he moved to London, where he competed for a short while for the Amateur SC and ran Lime Grove Baths. His wife Alice was also well known in swimming circles; she founded Hammersmith Ladies and remained active in the sport many years after the death of her husband, in Derbyshire in 1938.

JOE DINES

ASSOCIATION FOOTBALL

1912 Stockholm
Gold   Soccer Team

Joe Dines was one of two members of Britain's gold medal-winning soccer team in Stockholm to be killed during the First World War. Born in King's Lynn in 1886, Dines was an incisive and strong tackling left-half and one of the play-makers of the amateur side. A teacher by profession, he worked in Essex and was captain of the local Ilford side. He played 24 times for the England amateur side and his displays on the left side of the midfield earned him almost automatic selection for the Olympics. Britain confirmed their superiority in Sweden, maintaining a 100 per cent record from their three matches and beating Denmark 4–2 in the final to take the gold.

The war ended Dines' career, though he did play a game for Liverpool when he was commissioned into the city regiment. He was killed less than a fortnight after being sent to the front in 1918. He and five other officers, along with 125 men, died in an ill-conceived advance on enemy positions at Ribecourt. He was just 32.

CHARLES DIXON

LAWN TENNIS

1908 London
Bronze   Men's Doubles

1912 Stockholm
Gold   Indoor Mixed Doubles
Silver   Indoor Men's Singles
Bronze   Indoor Men's Doubles

Unfortunately, Dixon's multi-medal-winning successes at the Olympics were not truly reflected in major international competitions. He won just two Wimbledon titles, both doubles, despite playing well in countless tournaments.

Born in Grantham, Lincolnshire, in 1873, he studied law at Clare College, Cambridge, and became a solicitor. Even though he played four Davis Cup matches during his spell at Clare he failed to win a blue at lawn tennis. Despite placing in the 1901 singles at Wimbledon, his first major tennis success was the 1908 Olympic Games, where he took a bronze medal in the doubles with Charles Cazalet. He again fared well in the 1911 Wimbledon singles, but it was in Stockholm that the 39-year-old player saw his finest hour, winning gold, silver and bronze.

The gold came in the indoor mixed doubles. Dixon, with his partner Edith Hannam, beat Roper Barrett and Helen Aitchison in four sets. He then took silver in the indoor singles, losing to Frenchman André Gobert, after beating reigning Wimbledon champion Tony Wilding in the semis. And finally, he won a bronze in the indoor doubles, beating Arthur Gore and Arthur Beamish in a play-off. A few weeks after this triumph, Dixon won his first Wimbledon title, the doubles, alongside Roper Barrett, a feat they repeated a year later. They lost the 1914 final before war shut down the tournament.

A keen golfer, he died in south London in 1939.

RICHARD DIXON

YACHTING

1908 London
Gold   7 Metres Class

Although he was born in Australia, Dixon came to Britain as a child and was a member of the crew aboard the *Heroine* boat which won the 7 metres class completely unopposed.

Dixon was educated at Harrow and the RMA Woolwich before being commissioned into the Royal Engineers in 1885. His yachting career began a few years later and continued for more than half a century and more than 1000 victories. He joined the Southampton Yacht Club and was a founder member of the Yacht Racing Association, serving on its ruling council for nearly 40 years.

At the 1908 Games Dixon joined *Heroine* owner Charles Rivett-Carnac, Norman Bingley and Carnac's wife Frances for the 7 metres class. They were due to race against just one boat, but when that withdrew at the last minute they were awarded the gold medal on a sail over.

Dixon died in Cornwall in 1949, a week before his 84th birthday.

WILLIAM DOD

ARCHERY

1908 London
Gold   York Round

William Dod could easily have been a creation of Edwardian literature rather than one of Britain's Olympic champions. He had a fine pedigree as an international class archer – one of his ancestors was Sir Antony Dod, who commanded the bowmen at the Battle of Agincourt.

Born in Cheshire in 1867, Dod did not actually enter an archery competition until he was 39. He and his sporting sister Lottie, who is rated by many as the greatest ever female athlete, simply played the sport for enjoyment. But it was clear when he began to take archery more seriously that he had a genuine talent. At the London Games, Dod and his fellow archers were forced to endure appalling conditions and the competition was repeatedly held up because of torrential rain. Eventually Dod managed to pull away from the rest of the field, scoring heavily over the three distances – 60, 80 and 100 yards – to win by some 47 points from fellow Briton Reginald Brooks-King. It was Dod's 41st birthday.

In true Wodehouse fashion, Dod was a man of leisure, relying on apparently endless family funds and never having to work a day in his life. His father, a wealthy City financier, enabled Dod to travel the world and indulge his passion for archery, golf and shooting.

After the Olympics Dod twice won the British championships, in 1909 and 1911, before retiring from competition. He took up golf, in which he had been a scratch player and South of Ireland champion in 1901, and in 1912 he reached the fourth round of the British Amateur Championships.

Dod enlisted in the army in 1914 and at 47 served as a private in the trenches in France. He transferred to the navy and found himself back in France as an administrative officer for the Royal Navy Air Service before he was invalided out in 1916. He lived for much of his life in Devon, latterly with his sister Lottie, who won Wimbledon at 15, was British golf champion, an Olympic silver medal-winning archer and an international hockey player. They helped run the Royal North Devon Golf Club, but in 1950 she moved back to London and he followed two years later. Neither married and William died in 1954, aged 87.

RICHARD DODDS

HOCKEY

1984 Los Angeles
Bronze   Hockey Team

1988 Seoul
Gold   Hockey Team

One of the most influential members of Britain's gold medal-winning team, Dodds retired from the international game soon after the Seoul success. Born in York in 1959, Dodds learned to play at Kingston Grammar School before moving up to St Catharine's College, Cambridge, where he won a hockey blue. He then went to St Thomas's Hospital, south London, where he trained as a surgeon and played hockey for the hospital side. Dodds won bronze in the British side of 1984, then silver in the 1986 World Cup and 1987 European Championships before captaining the side for Seoul. Britain were tipped to do well, but the team exceeded all expectations by beating favourites Australia in the semi-finals and then West Germany 3–1 in the final.

Dodds, a midfield player for the Southgate club, was narrowly beaten in the 1988 Player of the Year poll. He played 79 times for England and 65 for Britain and was awarded the OBE for his services to the game. He continues to have an influence as the sport's representative on the national Olympic committee and has qualified as a surgeon.

William Dod won the Olympic archery title on his 41st birthday at the 1908 London Games.

Reggie (left) and Laurie Doherty, the tennis-playing brothers who dominated the sport at the turn of the century.

LAURIE DOHERTY

LAWN TENNIS

1900 Paris
Gold   Men's Singles
Gold   Men's Doubles

The legendary tennis-playing Doherty brothers, Laurie and elder brother Reggie, could have been drawn from the pages of Victorian schoolboy fiction. They arrived on the tennis scene at a time when the game was flagging, Wimbledon was on its knees and the sport generally needed a genuine lift.

The Dohertys became sporting heroes around the turn of the century and dragged the game of tennis up with them. Laurie was born in Wimbledon in 1875 and was educated at Westminster School and Trinity Hall, Cambridge. His interest in tennis was sparked by Reggie and also by their elder brother Rev William Doherty, who captained Oxford at tennis and then decided not to pursue the game seriously. As a singles player Laurie had a better record than his brother, winning five Wimbledon titles in a row, from 1902 to 1906, the US title in 1903 – the only foreign player to win it in 44 years – and 12 victories out of 12 in the Davis Cup. As a doubles pair, the Dohertys won eight Wimbledons, two US titles and were unbeaten in the Davis Cup. Laurie was an excellent sprinter at school and his speed around the court, superb tactical brain and flawless strokes made him a very difficult opponent.

The 1900 Olympics were not regarded by the Dohertys as a major tournament, but both went to Paris, where they were drawn to play each other in the semi-finals of the men's singles. Reggie decided he could not play his brother in such a 'minor event' and stood down, allowing Laurie to go into the final and beat defending champion, Irishman Harold Mahony, in straight sets. In the doubles the brothers defeated an American-French pairing, and Laurie came home with two gold medals.

After Laurie won his last singles title in 1906 his delicate health forced him to retire. He suffered severe dyspepsia and he decided to quit at the top and concentrate on golf, playing in amateur championships and taking life easy. However, he joined the Royal Navy Reserve in 1914 and served on an anti-aircraft unit, which seemed to hasten the final breakdown of his fragile health. He died in 1919 at a sanatorium in Broadstairs, Kent, aged 43.

REGGIE DOHERTY

LAWN TENNIS

1900 Paris
Gold   Men's Doubles
Gold   Mixed Doubles
Bronze   Men's Singles

1908 London
Gold   Men's Doubles

The elder of two great tennis-playing brothers and the dominant force in the game at the turn of the century, Reggie Doherty first came to Wimbledon as a Cambridge undergraduate. A natural sportsman, 'Big Do', as he was affectionately known to tennis followers, was born in Wimbledon in 1872, and excelled at cricket and football at Westminster School before going up to Trinity Hall. Reggie played in the 1895 Wimbledon singles and reached the final of the covered court championships in the same year – even though there were only two entries. He was already being hailed as a star of the future and a correspondent of *The Field* commented: 'He has capital ground strokes, volleys hard, serves a capital length and keeps a cool head.'

The Doherty reign began in 1897 when Reggie won the first of his four consecutive singles titles. Such was the revival of interest in tennis brought about by the Dohertys' sportsmanship, style and off-court modesty, that the All England Club was able to use the money generated from the next two years' championships to help build a new pavilion. The 1900 Olympics were staged a few weeks after Reggie took his last singles title. After stepping aside in the singles semi to allow Laurie a clear path to the final, he took gold in the doubles with his brother and in the mixed with Charlotte Cooper. He was warned by doctors that his fragile health would not stand too much competition, but he decided to enter Wimbledon in 1901. After leading by a set and 5–2, his strength deserted him and he lost to Arthur Gore.

He carried on playing doubles until 1906, when Laurie retired, and, despite his mother's protestations, played in the 1908 Olympics, winning a gold, with George Hillyard, in the doubles. He then went to South Africa in 1909 and won two titles at their championships. Reggie died the following year after returning to London from a break at a Swiss nursing home.

WILLIAM DONNE

CRICKET

1900 Paris
Gold   Cricket Team

Donne founded the Devon County Wanderers side which represented Britain at the Paris Games. A leading light in Somerset civic life, Donne was born in Wincanton in 1876 and was educated at King's School, Bruton, before joining the family's rope manufacturing business. He was a captain in the Somerset Light Infantry during the First World War and enjoyed numerous appointments in his home county, including JP, alderman and governor of his old school. Donne was best known for his administrative work in rugby and his obituary in *The Times* noted: 'For many years he had devoted much of his spare time to the rugby game and in an official capacity did a lot to assist the struggling clubs by grants from the county union. He also lent many a small match the encouragement of his cheery presence.'

He served the Somerset RU for 38 years, including spells as honorary secretary and president. He was elected President of the RFU in 1924–25 and his noted diplomatic skills were called into use to defuse a potentially explosive international sporting incident, when an All Black forward became the first player to be sent off in an international match. He died in 1934 at his home in Castle Cary, aged 57.

JOHNNY DOUGLAS

BOXING

1908 London
Gold   Middleweight

One of the most extraordinary champions of the early Olympic era, Douglas is probably better known as the captain of England's cricket team than as a boxer. He was born in Clapton, Middlesex, in 1882, the son of a wealthy timber merchant and amateur boxing champion, and was a naturally talented sportsman from an early age. Following the example of his father – as he did throughout his life – Douglas quickly turned to boxing and while at Felsted was the Public Schools middleweight champion in 1899 and 1901, with a reputation as a strong hitter with an impenetrable defence.

A few weeks after leaving school in 1901, he made his first-class cricket debut for Essex against champions Yorkshire, scoring nought in both innings. But it was the start of an amazing cricket career for Essex and England in which he played in 651 first-class matches, scoring 24,531 runs, including 26 centuries, and taking 1893 wickets. Superbly fit, Douglas also excelled at soccer and played before and after the First World War for the famous Corinthians side, usually as a defender, and also for England's amateur XI.

Douglas had claimed the ABA middleweight title in 1905, but his greatest boxing achievement came at the London Olympics. The final, against the tough Australian 'Snowy' Baker, was a classic, and after three rounds of what the *Times* correspondent described as 'one of the most brilliant exhibitions of skilful boxing allied to tremendous hitting ever seen', the judges could not separate them. The 1908 rules allowed for an extra minute to be boxed at the end of the final round and the judges then awarded the decision to Douglas. He was presented with the gold medal by his father, who was President of the ABA between 1906 and 1924. After the Games, a tale went around that Douglas also fought the then professional world heavyweight champion Tommy Burns 'behind closed doors' in east London, though no real evidence of the bout exists. At a dinner in Australia he once said: 'I can't make a speech, but I will box any man in the room three rounds!'

John William Henry Taylor Douglas had his name immortalised on the cricket field when the J.W.H.T. was replaced by 'Johnny Won't Hit Today', a nickname adopted by the Australians during some dour batting displays for England. It is true, however, that his cramped style and limited stroke-play made him a difficult player to admire. His best Test figures were 119 against South Africa in 1913 and 5 for 46 against the Australians in 1912.

Douglas had joined his father's timber company and while his cricket career was winding down in the late 1920s he began to take a keener interest in the business. This often entailed travelling to Scandinavia with his father during the winter to buy timber. The winter of 1930 was a miserable one, with fog blanketing much of Northern Europe. On their way back from Finland, just before Christmas 1930, their ship the SS *Oberon* collided with another Finnish steamer in thick fog in the Kattegat. The *Oberon* sank within three minutes and eye-witnesses saw Douglas desperately trying to find his father as the ship went down. Neither was seen again.

Johnny Douglas, the all-round sportsman who became
Olympic middleweight boxing champion in 1908.

Britain's six-man clay pigeon team, gold medallists in 1908: (standing, left to right)
J.M. Postans, J.F. Pike, Philip Easte; (seated) Alex Maunder, F.W. Moore, Charles Palmer.

ARTHUR DOWNES

YACHTING

1908 London
Gold   12 Metres Class

Arthur Downes was the youngest of two brothers in the ten-man crew aboard the *Hera* which won the only Olympic event ever to take place in Scotland. Glasgow-born Downes was a member of the Royal Clyde Yacht Club – as were all the *Hera* crew – and was invited to take part in the Olympic event by owner Thomas Glen-Coats. The races were to be held on the Clyde because the organisers of the regatta, in Cowes, felt it would be easier for the two boats involved to race in Scotland rather than travel south to the Isle of Wight. The second boat was Liverpool's *Mouchette* and owner Charles McIvor agreed to sail north. But it was a wasted journey and the *Hera* comfortably won both races to take the gold medal.

Two weeks before the Games, Downes qualified as a doctor and went on to practise as a GP in Helensburgh for more than 40 years. He died in the town in 1956, aged 73.

HENRY DOWNES

YACHTING

1908 London
Gold   12 Metres Class

The elder of the two brothers aboard the *Hera* boat which won the gold medal in the 12 metres class, Henry Downes was also a member of the Royal Clyde Yacht Club. He and brother Arthur joined the ten-man crew, headed by *Hera* owner Thomas Glen-Coats. The race against Charles McIvor's *Mouchette* was held on the River Clyde and not at the Olympic Regatta, at Cowes, to avoid excessive travelling. McIvor's boat and crew were based in Liverpool. *Hera* won both the races, the first by a minute and 37 seconds, and the second by a minute and two seconds, to take the gold. Downes, an electrician by trade, died in Dunoon in 1943, aged 73.

DAVID DUNLOP

YACHTING

1908 London
Gold   12 Metres Class

Dunlop was a member of the ten-man crew of the *Hera*, a boat owned by Thomas Glen-Coats, who was a prominent figure at the Royal Clyde Yacht Club. He pulled together the useful members of the club to crew his boat at the 1908 Games. Intriguingly, the 12 metres event was held on his home waters, the Clyde, because the Olympic organisers had only two entries for the races – the *Hera* and a Liverpool-based boat, the *Mouchette*. Rather than force the two craft to sail down to Cowes, where the Olympic Regatta was taking place, they allowed the event to be staged in Scotland. The *Hera* won both races to take the gold.

PHILIP EASTE

SHOOTING

1908 London
Gold   Clay Pigeon Team

A disappointing performer in Britain's gold medal-winning six-man team at the London Games, Easte scored a lowly 55 points from a maximum 105 and was by some distance the lowest scorer. In fact, Britain also entered a second team for the competition and all six members of the B team scored more than Easte. Fortunately, the team around him performed better and they pipped the Canadians to the gold by just two points, with the British B team in bronze medal position.

GLADYS EASTLAKE-SMITH

LAWN TENNIS

1908 London
Gold   Indoor Women's Singles

Due to the lack of any top-class foreign players and all the major British stars playing in the outdoor tournament, Eastlake-Smith won the indoor gold without any significant opposition. Only seven women took part in the event and Eastlake-Smith found herself in the final after playing just two games. Her opponent was another average British player, Alice Greene, and after each player took a set, Eastlake-Smith stepped up a gear to win the decider 6–0 and take the gold.

Born in Lewisham, south London, in 1883, her first major title had been the All England indoor mixed doubles title, with the great Reggie Doherty, in 1905. She won this title again in 1908, with four-time Wimbledon singles champion Tony Wilding. As a singles player she won the 1907 All England title and lost in the 1908 final to the accomplished Dolly Lambert Chambers, who had decided to enter only the outdoor event at the Olympics, which she won.

Two days after her Olympic victory, Eastlake-Smith married tennis player Wharram Lamplough and in 1913 they won the now discontinued Married Doubles championship.

JUMBO EDWARDS

ROWING

1932 Los Angeles
Gold   Coxless Pairs
Gold   Coxless Fours

A larger-than-life character, Edwards was regarded by those within the sport as one of the greatest oarsmen of the 1930s. He put together an incredible series of major championship victories and then became an influential coach.

Born Hugh Robert Arthur Edwards, in Westcote Barton, Oxfordshire, in 1906, he earned the nickname 'Jumbo' at school because of his powerful build and amazing strength. He attended Westminster School and then Christ Church College, Oxford, where he made his debut in the Boat Race as a freshman. Sadly, he suffered a blackout after

two miles and Cambridge won by five lengths. He was not a great scholar and when he failed his exams in 1927 he spent two years as a schoolmaster before he joined the RAF. In the hope of getting a commission in the RAF he returned to Oxford in 1930 to get his degree. He rowed again for Oxford in the Boat Race, once more on the losing side, but won the Grand and the Stewards at Henley before travelling to Hamilton in Canada, where he took gold in the Empire Games coxless fours and eights. In 1931 he won three events at Henley on the same day, the Stewards, Grand and Silver Goblets – the last of which he repeated in 1932.

At the Los Angeles Games he was due to row only in the pairs with Lewis Clive, which they won comfortably, but when Tom Tyler, the number two in the crew, went down with flu a week before the regatta, Edwards was drafted in as a replacement. When the four came home for the gold, holding off the Germans, Edwards became the first man in Olympic history to win two gold medals on the same day. After the Games he became a well-known racing pilot and during the war served as a squadron leader with Coastal Command, winning the AFC and DFC. In 1943 he was forced to ditch his plane in the Atlantic and used his rowing skills to pilot his dinghy through a minefield to safety.

He retired from the RAF in 1946 and went back into rowing as a coach, quickly earning a reputation as a great innovator. He was once described by a team-mate: 'Out of the water he was an enigmatic character. Often he seemed to be in a dream, but experience showed that his brain was always at work on some new plan of action.' His two sons won silver medals in the 1962 Commonwealth Games coxless fours and he coached the Olympic eight in 1960. He died in Southampton in 1972.

MAXWELL ELEY

ROWING

1924 Paris
Gold   Coxless Fours

The winning crew in the coxless fours in Paris knew each other inside out, having rowed together since their schooldays at Eton. All four members then went up to Trinity College, Cambridge, where they continued their success. Eley, born in Samford, Suffolk, in 1902, along with Macnabb, Morrison and Sanders, maintained a thriving partnership for nearly six years.

At Henley in 1922 they won the Stewards under the name of Eton Vikings, then the Visitors, under the name of Third Trinity. They won the Stewards in

The winning coxless fours crew of 1924: (left to right) Terence Sanders, Robert Morrison, James Nacnabb and Maxwell Eley.

Launceston Elliot took two medals in the 1896 weightlifting competition in Athens: gold in the one-handed lift and silver in the two-handed event.

1923 and 1924 before travelling to Paris for the Olympics. Although the Canadians were confident of victory, the British team won comfortably on the River Seine course, the margin just under ten seconds. Eley had also been in the winning Cambridge crew in the Boat Race in 1924 and won the Goblets at Henley, with Macnabb, as well as joining the winning Leander crew in the Grand.

He worked all his life with ICI and then retired back to Suffolk, where he developed his father's estate at East Bergholt, near the home of the painter John Constable, into one of the finest private gardens in England. He died at the estate in 1983.

LAUNCESTON ELLIOT

WEIGHTLIFTING

1896 Athens
Gold   One-Handed Lift
Silver   Two-Handed Lift

Britain's first Olympic champion was actually born in India and went on to become a music hall star. Elliot did not see England until his father gave up his post as a magistrate in the colony in 1887 and returned home to his Essex farm. Born in 1874, the young man soon showed a flair for weightlifting and wrestling, using his size and strength to great effect. In 1891, at 16, he entered his first British weightlifting championship, under the personal coaching of Eugen Sandow, and performed well. He landed his first national title three years later and went to the first Olympics, in Athens in 1896, as one of the favourites for the two weightlifting competitions.

His good looks and impressive physique attracted the attention of the newspapers and sports fans – he even received a proposal of marriage from one mystery lady. Elliot won the one-handed lift event with 71kg, a huge margin over the second placed Viggo Jensen from Denmark. But in the two-handed lift he was placed second, even though he lifted the same weight – 111.5kg – as Jensen. The judge ruled that Elliot had moved a foot during his lift and awarded the gold to the Dane because of his greater style. The two athletes competed again in the rope climbing and Elliot also took part in the heavyweight Greco-Roman wrestling, where he finished fourth, and the 100 metres.

Back home he continued to increase his lifting records, setting four new national marks, and in 1905 he turned professional and joined circus strongman Montague Spencer in a speciality theatre double act. They performed mock battles in gladiator outfits and Elliot's *pièce de résistance* was to hold a metal pole across his shoulders, with a bicycle and rider at each end, then gradually spin them around. He married a vicar's daughter in 1897 and in 1923 they emigrated to Australia. He died seven years later in Melbourne after an operation for cancer of the spine.

ADRIAN ELLISON

ROWING

1984 Los Angeles
Gold   Coxed Fours

Britain were regarded as firm favourites for the gold in the absence of all the top Eastern Bloc countries, but as the final approached they were feeling the pressure. The Americans and New Zealanders were useful crews and anxious to upset the odds – particularly the American crew, who were keen to see a home victory.

The diminutive cox Adrian Ellison, born in Solihull in 1958, was an experienced campaigner, who had won a bronze in the 1981 World Championships and competed in two others. The four comprised Steven Redgrave, Andy Holmes, Martin Cross and Richard Budgett, and the plan was to establish domination in the early part of the race and then push right away in the second part. Unfortunately the plan went wrong and the Americans were half a length in front until the last 500 metres. But as the American crowd was beginning to cheer a home victory, the British crew picked up the pace and surged past the Americans to win the gold.

Ellison, a radiologist, coxed with the Tyrian Boat Club and at the end of the race was ceremonially hurled into the sea by the celebrating crew.

RAYMOND ETHERINGTON-SMITH

ROWING

1908 London
Gold   Eights

Etherington-Smith built an impressive record at Cambridge and Henley at the turn of the century before ending his career at the Olympics. Born in London in 1877, he went to Repton and then Trinity College, where he rowed in two successful Boat Races, in 1899 and 1900, the last as President of the Cambridge University Boat Club. A member of the Leander Club, he placed second on three occasions in the Grand at Henley, before finally winning the title in 1901, 1903 and 1905. He also won the Stewards with Leander in 1905 and 1906. Leander selected a strong, experienced crew for the 1908 Games, with the 31-year-old Etherington-Smith rowing at number seven. They were concerned about the strength of the Belgian crew from the Royal Club Nautique de Gand, but in the final Leander won reasonably comfortably by two lengths, in 7 minutes 52 seconds.

On leaving Cambridge, Etherington-Smith qualified as a surgeon, but he died tragically in 1913. Following an operation on a gangrenous lung at St Bartholomew's Hospital, both patient and surgeon contracted peritonitis and died.

WILLIAM EXSHAW

YACHTING

1900 Paris
Gold   2–3 Ton Class

A wealthy and cosmopolitan sportsman, Exshaw sailed his own yacht to victory in the Olympic Regatta held on the River Seine at Meulan. He won both races aboard the *Olle* ahead of two French entries and a German to score maximum points and clinch the gold medal. Exshaw was born at Arcachon, in the Bordeaux region of France, in 1866, where he ran the family's brandy production. His wealth made him a prominent socialite in France but he maintained contacts with Britain through sailing and his estate in Inverness. He died while cruising on his yacht in the Mediterranean in 1927.

DAVID FAULKNER

HOCKEY

1988 Seoul
Gold   Hockey Team

One of the rocks upon which Britain's gold medal-winning team in Seoul was built, Faulkner was voted hockey's Player of the Year in 1988, ahead of the goalscoring hero Sean Kerly. Faulkner, born in Portsmouth in 1963, made his England debut in 1982 and was in the silver medal-winning sides at the 1986 World Cup and 1987 European Championships. The Havant full-back then played in all seven matches during Britain's run for the gold in South Korea.

After a disappointing opening draw with the host nation and a defeat by West Germany, there was a chance the team would not even qualify from their group, let alone win a medal. But the side began to play and reached the semi-finals, where they beat favourites Australia 3–2, before avenging their only defeat in the Games by beating the Germans 3–1 in the final.

Faulkner was made captain of the side after the Olympics but has since given up the job because it was affecting his form. He works as a director of a south coast sports chain which specialises in sports shirts and sweatshirts.

JOHN FENNING

ROWING

1908 London
Gold   Coxless Pairs
Silver   Coxless Fours

Only four teams entered the 1908 Olympic coxless pairs competition, with two coming from the same British rowing club. Leander, the world's oldest and the most prestigious club of the day, could not choose between the two pairs – so they sent both into the Olympics.

Fenning, born in London in 1885, was a medical student at The London Hospital at the time of the Olympics, but rowed with the London Rowing Club. In the heats, Leander's two crews beat their foreign opposition, Canada and Germany, to meet each other in the final at Henley. Fenning, at bow, joined stroke Gordon Thomson in Leander I, while the Jesus College, Oxford, pair George Fairbairn and Philip Verdon crewed Leander II. But Fenning and

Thomson were far stronger and increased their halfway lead to a full two and a half lengths by the finish, to take the gold.

Thirteen years after starting medical school, Fenning finally qualified as a doctor in 1917, and after moving from the Home Counties established a practice in the Midlands just before the Second World War. He died in Coventry in 1955.

JOHN FIELD-RICHARDS

MOTOR BOATING

1908 London
Gold   8 Metres Class
Gold   Under 60-Foot Class

A degree of mystery shrouds the participation of Captain Field-Richards in this unlikely Olympic event. Although his name is conspicuous by its absence in the official report of the Games, compiled by the British Olympic Association, it certainly appears in many newspaper reports of the day. Whether or not he was actually awarded a gold medal as part of the crew of Tom Thornycroft's *Gyrinus II*, along with Bernard Redwood, is a matter of conjecture. Nonetheless it is reasonably clear he was on board the winning boat, which he and Redwood bought after the Games and raced on their own.

Motor boating was held as an Olympic sport in 1908 and only three classes existed – the Open class being won by a Frenchman and the British trio winning the other two. Poor weather conditions meant the only other entry in their classes failed to finish and as one sports historian succinctly put it, Redwood and Field-Richards won two gold medals each for their skills with a bucket!

The son of a vicar, Field-Richards was born in Penzance, Cornwall, in 1878 and went to Keble College, Oxford. During the war he served with the Hampshire and Yorkshire Regiments and received the OBE for his work as a staff officer. He left the army in 1920 and eventually retired to Hampshire, where he died in 1959, aged 70.

CHRIS FINNEGAN

BOXING

1968 Mexico City
Gold   Middleweight

'I'm just standing there wondering: "Could this be my day?" And all of a sudden, it's there. It hits me straight away. My whole life is gonna change. Bang! Christmas has come.' Chris Finnegan's face lights up at the memory of that distant evening in Mexico City, when they announced the name of the new Olympic middleweight champion and a marvellous awareness came crowding in. His life was indeed changed, and sometimes those changes took brutal and tragic forms. But even in the darkest days he would cherish the memory of Mexico, when he was 24 years old and the future was alive with glorious possibilities.

Finnegan arrived in Mexico by a typically circuitous route. He had learned his trade at Hayes Boxing Club, where the gifted trainer Dick Gunn had discerned a genuine talent, and he progressed along conventional amateur lines until he secured an ABA title in 1966.

By 1968 he was unquestionably the finest amateur middleweight in the country, and he was ready to prove the point until he met with a freak accident in the ABA North-West Divisional finals, when his eye was cut by an opponent's flying elbow. With selection apparently reserved for the ABA champion, Finnegan's Olympic dreams were shattered, and he drowned his disappointment in a succession of bars.

As the great-great-grandson of the 1908 Olympic featherweight champion, Dick Gunn understood the importance of the ultimate gold medal, and he sought the assistance of Jack Forse, chairman of the London ABA. Forse secured Finnegan a box-off to prove his credentials while Gunn rescued Finnegan from the ravages of two weeks' drinking, and his fighter recovered sufficiently to win the trial. Even then, there were many in the ABA who were opposed to Finnegan's selection, but he won his place on Forse's casting vote.

In truth, Finnegan could scarcely afford to attend those 1968 Games. He was a self-employed hod-carrier, with a wife, Cheryl, and two young children to support; money was tight and Dick Gunn helped organise raffles and auctions to offset his protégé's lost earnings. Moreover, the experts gave him only a slim chance of Olympic success. But his self-belief was typically strong: 'I fancied my chances,' he recalls. 'Dicky fancied them. And my missus fancied them. They were the only ones who were important to me.'

That belief was confirmed by a routine fitness

Chris Finnegan met with stiff opposition from American Al Jones (right) in the middleweight semi-final, but went on to beat Soviet boxer Alexei Kiselyov in the final to claim Olympic gold in Mexico City.

test, taken a few weeks before the Games. Finnegan was attached to a battery of wires and tubes while various readings were taken. At last, the doctor looked up and said: 'I don't believe it!' The boxer panicked: 'Don't tell me,' he said, 'I need to go to a health farm, not the Olympics.' The doctor put him at his ease, explaining that his pulse rate was astonishingly low and his general level of fitness remarkable. 'Blimey!' said Finnegan. 'And I'm only half-training. What the hell will I do when I really get myself in condition?'

So he worked harder than ever before and discovered, to his immense surprise, that he loved Mexico: 'As soon as I got off the plane, I knew it was my sort of place. I loved the heat, the sun. There was no Guinness, though. That was the only thing I missed.' The altitude of Mexico City held no terrors for him. 'I had great stamina. I was a hod-carrier, running up and down a ladder eight hours a day with half a hundredweight on my back. We were only boxing three three-minute rounds. No problem.'

He worked his comfortable way past some routine opponents, the only alarm arriving with the semi-finals, when he received two standing counts against the American Al Jones, before coming through for a points victory. Eventually, only the Soviet boxer Alexei Kiselyov stood between Finnegan and gold.

He had decided that Kiselyov was suffering from weight problems, that if he could be made to work hard in the opening round he would weaken as the fight progressed. The strategy demanded a frantic last round from the British boxer, and he delivered it to order. It was desperately close; Finnegan himself admits that he was fortunate to get the decision. But the judges voted for him 3–2. Chris Finnegan had become the first Briton since Harry Mallin in 1924 to take the Olympic middleweight title.

His life changed, as he knew it must. He was awarded the MBE for his Olympic achievement and, soon after returning from Mexico, he became a professional fighter.

He was, inevitably, an instant success, and his popularity with the crowds set him on a lucrative path. In January 1971 he became British and Commonwealth light-heavyweight champion. A year later he won the European title and in September 1972 he waged a memorable war against the extraordinary Bob Foster for the world title, pushing Foster to the limit before losing in the 14th round.

'It was Christmas every day, wasn't it?' he says. 'I didn't have to worry about a few quid. I had a car, my missus had a car, the money was there. As I always said: "Win or lose, drink your booze." I thought I'd go on forever. No plans, I just took every day as it came.'

The fights were hard; two defeats by John Conteh, brutal battles with Johnny Frankham. Then, suddenly, it was over, following the fight with Frankham in October 1975. 'I didn't get a lot of choice about finishing, did I?' he says. 'Me mince pie went up the creek, and that was that' — Finneganese for the detached retina which was to cost him the sight of his right eye.

He was hopelessly unprepared for life after boxing. He ran a pub, and it didn't work out. Other businesses suffered a similar fate. Unemployment claimed him: 'Boxing was the greatest thing,' he says. 'It was the only thing I seemed to be any good at.' The most savage blow arrived in the summer of 1991 when Cheryl died from cancer, leaving him to raise their two youngest children.

He still attends big fights, encourages the kids at the gym and helps his nephew, Tyrone, with his boxing ambitions. Amazingly, he manages to preserve a smiling public face. But the clouds arrive when he is asked about his future. 'I suppose,' he says, 'I suppose I'll take that like I took all the fights; one day at a time.' Then he gives a sad little shake of the head. 'Times change, don't they?' he says. 'It ain't Christmas every day now.'

JOHN FLEMING

SHOOTING

1908 London
Gold   Small-Bore Rifle – Moving Target

Four British marksmen were tied for the gold medal after the 25-yard moving target competition at a rain-soaked Bisley. Fleming, M.K. Matthews, William Marsden and Edward Newitt all scored 24 points from a possible 45 in the British-dominated event. The standard was poor and when the judges scrutinised the targets they awarded Fleming the gold outright on the count back.

Born in Keswick, in the Lake District, in 1881, Fleming was a lifelong civil servant and spent many years shooting at the City Rifle Club. During the First World War he was a firearms instructor and later he was made a life member of the National Rifle Association. He died in Surrey in 1965, aged 83.

PHILIP FLEMING

ROWING

1912 Stockholm
Gold   Eights

Almost a caricature of his age, Fleming came from a wealthy background, hunted big game in Africa, rowed for Eton and Oxford, ran a City merchant bank and was a leading light in Oxfordshire society.

Born in Scotland in 1889, he excelled at rowing at Eton, as well as at football and rackets. When he went up to Magdalen College his rowing career blossomed, the highlight of which was rowing in the winning crew in the 1910 Boat Race. In the same year he also became Oxford point-to-point steeplechase champion. In Stockholm he joined the Leander Club crew as stroke in the eights competition. Although 11 teams entered, the final was an all-British affair between Leander and New College, Oxford, with Leander winning by some four seconds.

During the First World War Fleming served with the Queen's Own Oxfordshire Hussars, as a subaltern, and at the end of hostilities took over the running of his father's bank, Robert Fleming & Co. He married Jean Hunloke, the daughter of a 1908 Olympic yachting medallist, and they became leading lights of Oxfordshire society, with Fleming riding in the Bicester, Heythrop and South Oxon hunts. In 1948 he was appointed High Sheriff of the County. He died at his home in Woodstock, Oxfordshire, in 1971, aged 82.

JENNIE FLETCHER

SWIMMING

1912 Stockholm
Gold   4 × 100 Metres Freestyle Relay
Bronze   100 Metres Freestyle

One of Britain's top women swimmers of the early part of the century, Fletcher was fortunate to live in the city where the great swimmer John Arthur Jarvis ran coaching sessions. The double Olympic gold medal winner took her under his wing and she developed into an exciting talent.

Born in Leicester in 1890, she was one of 11 children in a poor family. She worked 12 hours a day, six days a week in one of the city's many textile factories, managing to train only a few evenings a week. She joined the local swimming club, where she trained with Jarvis and the talented Henry Taylor, and became the country's fastest freestyle swimmer. Despite the family's poverty she turned down an offer to tour with the world-famous professional swimming attraction, Annette Kellerman.

Fletcher's first national 100 yards title came in 1906 and she won the event on six successive occasions – the last in 1912, the year of the Stockholm Olympics. Fletcher would certainly have been favourite for a gold had women's swimming events been part of the programme for the 1908 London Olympics. But the organisers decided against including them because of the lack of entries. Although her career was coming to an end in 1912 she was still among the favourites in the freestyle event. She had previously held the world 100 yards record, set in 1909, but her team-mate Daisy Curwen was now the one to beat. But when she fell ill and could only finish fifth in Stockholm, Australia's Fanny Durack came through to take the gold, with Fletcher some five seconds off the pace in third. She redeemed herself by anchoring the sprint relay team to victory in a world record time.

Interviewed just before her death she recalled: 'The crowning moment of my career was when King Gustav of Sweden placed the classic laurel wreath on my head, put the gold medal around my neck and said "well done England".' Shortly after her swimming career ended she emigrated to Canada, where she died in 1967.

CHARLIE FORSYTH

SWIMMING

1908 London
Gold   Water Polo Team

The scorer of a hat-trick in the Olympic final in London, Manchester-born Forsyth was one of Britain's twin strike force alongside the great George Wilkinson. The 23-year-old Salford SC star was a versatile swimmer and won national titles in 1904 while still a teenager. He beat the up and coming Henry Taylor in the 220 yards freestyle and won the 500 yards title. But water polo was his forte and he provided the goals that helped sink Belgium 9–2 in the London final. It was the only match Britain played after they drew a bye in the first round and Austria scratched from their semi-final encounter.

Forsyth died in Manchester in 1951.

BILL FOSTER

SWIMMING

1908 London
Gold   4 × 200 Metres Freestyle Relay

1912 Stockholm
Bronze   4 × 200 Metres Freestyle Relay

Foster learned to swim in the mill pond at the cotton factory where he worked as a boy in the Lancashire town of Bacup. He used to change into his swimming costume behind the great mill chimney before diving into the dirty, icy water. Born in 1890, he was just 18 when he took his place in the team which won the 4 × 200 metres relay at the London Games. He had earned selection alongside some of Britain's greatest swimming names after some amazing performances for Bacup Swimming Club in the 1907 national championships, where he finished second in the mile, third in the 440 yards and fifth in the 550 yards – while still only 17.

The 1908 Olympic swimming competition took place in a 100 metres outdoor pool, set in the middle of the White City stadium. Foster had already made the final of the 400 metres freestyle, where he finished last in a field of four, as well as the semi-finals of the 1500 metres freestyle. In the relay he was joined by the legendary Henry Taylor, multi-medal winner Paul Radmilovic and four-time national champion Rob Derbyshire. Foster held his own on the third leg, coming home in 8:15, behind the American and Hungarian teams. Taylor swam the last leg and soon caught the American, but the favourites Hungary were well in front, when suddenly their top swimmer, multi Olympic medal winner Zoltan Halmay, began to lose consciousness during the last 50 metres and had to be dragged from the pool before he drowned. Taylor came home to claim a new world record for the relay of 10:55.6 – to guarantee the team gold medals.

Foster joined the nearby Hyde Seal Swimming Club after the London Games and went on to win a bronze in the same relay in Stockholm. Though he always did well in relays he never won an individual swimming title at national level. He was for many years the coach and attendant at Lytham Baths and worked as a labourer at the gasworks in Lytham, until retirement at 70. He died at his home in the town three years later.

JIM FOX

MODERN PENTATHLON

1976 Montreal
Gold   Modern Pentathlon Team

Without doubt the most influential figure in the sport's development in Britain, Fox took the national title a staggering ten times and competed in four Olympics. Born in Pewsey, Wiltshire, in 1941, Fox joined the army on leaving school and made his Olympic debut in Tokyo in 1964, where he placed 29th in the individual event. Four years later he improved to eighth spot in Mexico, then fourth in Munich – just outside the medals – amid a cloud of suspicion over drug-taking surrounding some of the Eastern Bloc athletes who finished above him.

If controversy surrounded the 1972 event, then the Montreal modern pentathlon provided banner headlines for the world's press. It was in the fencing stage of the competition, against Britain, that the Soviet gold and silver medal winner from the Munich Games, Boris Onischenko, was found to have tampered with his foil so that it registered a hit even when he had made no contact with his opponent. The Soviet team was eliminated and Fox, Adrian Parker (who finished fifth in the individual event) and Danny Nightingale began their push for medals. After four events they were lying in fifth place, 547 points behind Czechoslovakia, but their running in the 4000-metre cross-country course was inspirational and brought them home to gold.

Fox was later commissioned in the REME and has since retired from the army. He is now a top event rider on the international circuit and runs a small farm in Oxfordshire, where he keeps horses and trains young riders. Fox remains a role model for young modern pentathletes in Britain and has been awarded both the MBE and OBE for his services to the sport.

HARRY FREEMAN

HOCKEY

1908 London
Gold   Hockey Team

Freeman captained England's Olympic team to success and then retired from international competition, though he went on to play a significant role as an administrator in the development of the sport.

Born in Staines, Middlesex, in 1876, Freeman did

not take up the game until he was 18, but showed such talent that he was soon playing for his home town club, then the county and, in 1903, made his England debut. Hockey was clearly the family forte: Freeman's four brothers also played for Staines and his son played for England. In the final of the 1908 Olympics, Freeman, in his familiar right-back role, led England to an 8–1 thrashing of Ireland to take the gold. It was the last of his ten caps.

He continued to play club hockey long after and then became a member of the International Hockey Board and was for many years an influential executive of the Hockey Association. Despite his prowess at hockey, Freeman's first love was water sports, particularly rowing, sailing and punting, in which he won the 1897 amateur doubles title. A solicitor by profession, he died in Bourne End, Buckinghamshire, in 1968.

RUSSELL GARCIA

HOCKEY

1988 Seoul
Gold   Hockey Team

An immensely talented midfield player, Garcia became the youngest man ever to play for Britain when he made his debut as an 18-year-old. Originally a hairdresser, Garcia was born in Portsmouth in 1970, and made three appearances in the British side during their triumphant run through the Seoul tournament. Although he did not play in the semi-final or final he made a significant contribution to the Olympic effort and is seen as a man for the future in hockey circles.

He became better known in 1991 when he made an appearance on ITV's prime-time weekend show *You Bet*, where he successfully completed a challenge to flick hockey balls at a specially built target, hitting the last ball in the last second of his allotted time. The Havant player has his own business as a sports consultant specialising in tuition in hockey and hopes to help Britain to a successive gold in Barcelona.

STANLEY GARTON

ROWING

1912 Stockholm
Gold   Eights

An outstanding oarsman at Eton, Garton won his rowing blue as a freshman at Oxford. He rowed in the winning Oxford crews at the 1909, 1910 and 1911 Boat Races. He was also in the Magdalen College boat that won the Grand at Henley in 1910 and 1911.

Garton, born in Epsom, Surrey, in 1889, made it a hat-trick of wins in the Grand in 1913 when he joined the Leander crew. It was in the club crew at the Stockholm Games that he won his Olympic gold, joining the eights to beat fellow Britons New College, Oxford, by some two and a half lengths. After retiring from competition he continued in the sport and coached Oxford until 1930.

Garton's daughter married 1948 rowing gold medallist Richard Burnell to carry on the family tradition, and their son Peter rowed for Oxford in the 1962 Boat Race. Sadly, Garton was not alive to see his grandson compete; he died in Surrey in 1960.

ROWLAND GEORGE

ROWING

1932 Los Angeles
Gold   Coxless Fours

The only British Olympic champion to command an active American unit during the Second World War, Rowland George is also the only 'wingless' member of the RAF to win the coveted DSO. An exceedingly modest man, he claims to have 'done nothing worthy of the distinction' despite the contrary official reports of his wartime heroics.

George was born in Bath, Avon, in 1905, and went to Wycliffe College, then Lincoln College, Oxford, where he learned to row after admitting defeat at other sports. He left Oxford in 1925 and joined a Bristol printing and packaging firm, who transferred him to London four years later. He joined the Thames Rowing Club and rapidly developed into one of the country's top oarsmen, rowing at Henley in the winning crews in the Wyfold Cup in 1931 and Stewards in 1932. He was also twice the losing finalist in the Grand in 1931 and 1932. The Stewards victory won him selection for the Olympics in Los Angeles and George joined John Badcock, Jumbo Edwards and Jack Beresford in the pursuit of gold. This tough crew won the final in Long Beach by two and a half lengths from Germany, Italy and the USA.

Shortly after returning from Los Angeles, George married the Hon Sylvia Norton, the daughter of Lord Rathcreedan, and they were together for more than 50 years before her death in 1984. They raised three sons and a daughter, who in turn provided nine grandchildren. Once married he gave up competitive rowing and when war broke out he served with the RAF's Equipment Branch, where he was about to be passed over for a commission when the interviewing officer noticed he had rowed in the Olympics and asked 'How did you get on?'

He specialised in explosives for the Norway campaign and served in the North Africa campaign, where he commanded a landing unit which saw action in the front line. After the Algiers landing he was promoted to Acting Wing Commander and given a role alongside US forces in planning the capture of Sicily from the Germans. When a plane carrying the American commanding officer of his unit was shot down, George was put in charge. In that Salerno campaign he was wounded and this prompted the award of the DSO, following an OBE for his services in North Africa. In 1944 he was involved in the Normandy landings, though this time from the safety of a planning bunker in Portsmouth. He then moved back to the front line to help supervise the push through Europe.

He was back in civvy street just before Christmas 1945 and returned to his old company, first in Ipswich and later in London. But keen to return to Bath he took early retirement in 1959 and became heavily involved in voluntary social work, spending 15 years at the Bath Centre for Voluntary Service before retiring at 70. He now lives in a small village near Salisbury, in Wiltshire, where he tends his allotment.

ANGUS GILLAN

ROWING

1908 London
Gold   Coxless Fours

1912 Stockholm
Gold   Eights

Gillan became the first oarsman from any country to win two Olympic rowing gold medals. Born in Aberdeen in 1885, Gillan went to Edinburgh Academy, then Magdalen College, Oxford, where his rowing career really took off. He was a member of the crack Magdalen crew that won the Visitors and Stewards trophies at Henley just before the 1908 Olympics. He then rowed in the same crew at the Games, when Magdalen beat fellow Britons Leander by two lengths in the final.

Four years later he had joined the Leander Club and was in their eights crew that held off the challenge of New College, Oxford, to win his second gold. He rowed in two Boat Races for Oxford, in 1907 and 1909, and was in Leander's winning eight at the Grand at Henley in 1911. This last Henley success and his second gold in Stockholm were won while on leave from his post with the Sudan Political Service, which he joined on leaving Oxford in 1909. Gillan served in the Sudan for 30 years and was knighted in 1939 for his work. After the war he helped organise the 1948 Olympics and the following year he left Britain again to become the British Council's representative in Australia. He returned in 1951 and worked as chairman of the Royal Overseas League until 1962, when he retired. He died in Surrey in 1981, aged 95.

ALBERT GLADSTONE

ROWING

1908 London
Gold   Eights

A relative of the nineteenth century British Prime Minister, Albert Gladstone also took the family's traditional educational route, via Eton, to Christ Church College, Oxford. He was born in Cheshire in 1886 and was the youngest member of the Leander crew which took the gold in the 1908 Olympic final. Gladstone rowed at bow and the

Kitty Godfree (*née* McKane), pictured here with the legendary Suzanne Lenglen (left), won a total of five Olympic tennis medals: gold, silver and bronze at the 1920 Antwerp Games, and silver and bronze in Paris in 1924.

British team won comfortably against the much vaunted Belgian Royal Club Nautique de Gand. He rowed in four Boat Races for Oxford, but only in his last race, in 1909, did he come home a winner. A few weeks before the 1908 Games he sharpened his form by helping the Christ Church eight to victory in the Grand at Henley.

He served in Mesopotamia and at Gallipoli during the First World War, where he was mentioned in despatches three times and awarded the MBE in 1919. After the war he developed a successful business career in the financial world and was a director of the Bank of England for 23 years. In 1929 Gladstone was made Deputy Lieutenant of Flintshire and in 1935 Chief Constable of Flint Castle. In 1945 he inherited the family baronetcy and died, Sir Albert Gladstone, in Hampshire in 1967.

THOMAS GLEN-COATS

YACHTING

1908 London
Gold   12 Metres Class

The owner of the winning boat in the 12 metres class, Glen-Coats was able to sail to victory on his own territory. There were just two entries for the event, Glen-Coats' *Hera* and Charles McIvor's *Mouchette*, from Liverpool. The Olympic organisers refused to bring the boats all the way down to Cowes and decided to stage the race on the River Clyde. This suited Glen-Coats perfectly as he and his entire crew were members of the Royal Clyde Yacht Club and knew the course intimately. *Hera* predictably won the first two races, the third being unnecessary, to take the gold medal.

Glen-Coats, born in Paisley in 1878, was the eldest of four sons of Sir Thomas Glen-Coats, who was a wealthy spinning merchant. He was sent to Eton and Merton College, Oxford, and enjoyed a life of leisure. He inherited the family baronetcy on his father's death in 1922, married in 1935 and died in 1954.

KITTY GODFREE

LAWN TENNIS

1920 Antwerp
Gold   Women's Doubles
Silver   Mixed Doubles
Bronze   Women's Singles

1924 Paris
Silver   Women's Doubles
Bronze   Women's Singles

When Kitty McKane was nine years old, her father was obliged to travel to Berlin on business. As a family man, he was reluctant to leave his wife and children. As an active man, he was equally reluctant to cross Europe in the idleness of a ship's cabin or a train compartment. The problem was solved in a moment of inspiration. Kitty remembers it well: 'He said: "We'll all go. And we'll go on our bikes." And so we did, and it was great fun.'

Now when a girl of nine can take on a 600-mile bicycle journey, it requires no great prescience to assume that she is destined for a sporting career. And Kitty's cycling prowess was merely one indication of her destiny. The sporting family McKane was in the habit of spending a month in Switzerland each winter. Kitty became a keen skater, and when she was ten she received the bronze medal of the National Skating Association. In later years she took up badminton, winning a total of eight All-England titles, and in 1914 she was selected to play for England against Scotland at lacrosse in a match which was cancelled owing to the outbreak of war.

And then there was tennis. Like so many well-bred, middle-class girls of her era, she just drifted towards the game. 'We lived near Henley-on-Thames,' she says, 'and we had a largish lawn which was turned into a tennis lawn. And when our relatives and friends came to visit, they would play a little friendly tennis and my sister and I would join in. We weren't terribly good, but it was great fun.' But, in time, she discovered that she had real ability. She improved her game at St Leonard's School in Scotland and she made her tournament debut at Roehampton in the spring of 1919. A few weeks later, she was reaching the quarter-finals of Wimbledon at her first attempt and she swiftly became a prime candidate for Olympic selection for the Antwerp Games in 1920.

'There wasn't quite the fuss about the Olympics that there is today,' she says. 'In fact, what I was really looking forward to was the chance to travel. It was only when I arrived in Antwerp that I realised what was involved; that it really was something very important. One lives and learns, doesn't one?' In fact, she learned with remarkable speed. She reached the semi-final of the singles, but conceded a walkover as she wanted to be at her freshest for the women's doubles. However, she had qualified for the play-off for third place, which she won by defeating Sigrid Fick of Sweden to take the bronze medal. In the mixed doubles, she was partnered with a remarkable athlete named Max Woosnam, and together they secured the silver medal.

But her real triumph was reserved for her main target: the women's doubles. The British partnership of McKane and Winifred McNair was drawn against Elisabeth D'Ayen and the legendary Suzanne Lenglen of France in the semi-final. Mlle Lenglen, says Kitty, was: 'Easily the greatest player of her era. She really was so much better than the rest of us, but we gave it a jolly good go.' Indeed they did, coming through from a set down to secure a final place against their fellow Britons Geraldine Beamish and Dorothy Holman.

'Now they were good,' says Kitty, 'but they were from the old school. In fact, I'm not at all sure that they didn't serve under-arm. Winifred was a fine athlete and we both enjoyed running to the net. It was a battle, but we were very pleased to win.'

Her achievements in Antwerp confirmed her place among the world's most gifted players, and she reinforced that status in 1924, when she came back from a set and 1–4 down to defeat the great American Helen Wills in the Wimbledon final. With her form and her competitive experience, she was established as one of the favourites for the Olympic title at the Paris Games in that same year. She duly won a silver medal when she partnered Edith Covell in the women's doubles, but she was the hapless victim of an extraordinary singles semi-final against Julie Vlasto of France. Kitty was leading 6–0, 3–0 when the crowd surrounding the court demanded that the scores be announced in French. 'It quite put me off,' recalls Kitty. 'I was absolutely disgusted with them and with myself. I mean, there's no reason why they shouldn't have had it in French if they wanted to. But they shouldn't have demanded it in the middle of a rally!' In the end, she was forced to settle for bronze.

In January 1926, Kitty married the tennis player Leslie Godfree, and at that year's Wimbledon she reached the peak of her dazzling career. She won her second singles title by defeating Lili d'Alvarez of Spain in three sets; she reached her third women's doubles final and the Godfrees became the only husband and wife partnership ever to win the Wimbledon mixed doubles. And yet, despite her successes at the All England Club, it was the Olympics which claimed the warmest place in her heart. 'I'd say the Olympics were more appealing,' she says. 'After all, there's a long gap between Olympics, and when you've won that title, you've got it for the next four years. Whereas, if you win at Wimbledon, somebody can come along and take your title in the very next summer.'

When Mrs Kitty Godfree, born in May 1896, looks back down the decades, she believes that she played tennis when the game was at its most enjoyable. 'It was a game, and we played it as a game,' she says. 'These days, they seem to play it in a rather different spirit. I think I should have found it an awful strain.'

Occasionally, she remembers her Olympic adventures, and recalls the five medals she won in Antwerp and Paris all those years ago. 'When the Olympic talk comes up, I'm very pleased that I can join in,' she says. 'I always say that I was lucky, that I played with a nice partner; that sort of thing. But I always stress that we had a lot of fun. We took it seriously . . . but not too seriously.'

FRED GOODFELLOW

TUG OF WAR

1908 London
Gold   Tug of War Team

The victorious City of London police team were caught up in one of the many protests that marred the London Games. This time it was the Americans complaining about the British teams using cleats on their heavy boots to gain an unfair advantage. The Olympic Jury of Appeal did not uphold the complaint and after the competition had ended the City team offered to face the Americans in stockinged feet. The highly trained City team beat the Liverpool Police team in the final to win the gold. Goodfellow, then a 34-year-old City officer, died in Croydon, in 1960.

DUNCAN GOODHEW

SWIMMING

1980 Moscow
Gold   100 Metres Breaststroke
Bronze   4 × 100 Metres Medley Relay

Goodhew considered himself a 'stupid oddity' at school thanks to the twin misfortunes of losing all his hair after an accident when he was ten and being dyslexic. Subsequently he had a history of

The women's 4 x 100 metres freestyle relay team which won gold in Stockholm in 1912.

Seen here in action in the 1977 European Championships, Duncan Goodhew went on to capture Olympic gold in the 100 metres breaststroke in Moscow in 1980.

rebellious behaviour and only as he got older did he begin to realise that swimming, for which he had a natural talent, could be the way to rebuild his self-esteem. From that moment he decided to become the best in the world – and that meant an Olympic gold medal.

Born in London in 1957, Goodhew was among the top breaststrokers by the time he was 18 and was spotted by the coach of North Carolina State University, where he was offered a scholarship. He studied business management at NCSU and after just nine months in the USA made the British team for the Montreal Games, finishing seventh in the 100 metres breaststroke final. He then improved steadily, using the American facilities and his own competitive ability. He took two silvers at the 1978 Commonwealth Games and followed those with fourth place in two individual events and a bronze in the relay at the World Championships. But his preparation was for Moscow and there he won the gold comfortably from the Soviet Arsen Miskarov in 1:03.44. American criticism of the events, because of the boycott, made little impression on the swimming world, as Goodhew was always a racer rather than a clock man and he had beaten world record-holder Gerald Morken and reigning Olympic champion John Hencken before the Games.

He retired from swimming after Moscow and took part in the British bobsleigh effort at the 1982 European Championships, before returning to the pool in 1982 to win five events in the Masters Olympics in Philadelphia. Since then he has become a well-known TV and media figure, as well as a tireless charity worker. He is perhaps now best known as the face on TV commercials for Heineken beer, eggs and shampoo! He is currently a director of the Barbican Health and Fitness Centre and along with two of his brothers owns a French restaurant in Kent.

MARY GORDON-WATSON

EQUESTRIAN

1972 Munich
Gold   Three-Day Event Team

Mary Gordon-Watson, at just 24, confounded the sceptics in Munich by helping Britain to a team gold in a sport where experience is counted a prerequisite for international success. She paid handsome tribute to her horse Cornishman V, which Richard Meade had borrowed to win a team gold four years earlier in Mexico. Mary's father bought the horse for

himself to use for hunting and possibly racing. He was eight years old before he competed in the Olympics and although he was too big for her she began riding him in the late 1960s and turned him into one of the best event horses of the decade. His temperament was questionable at first and his jumping technique, even at the Olympics, was unorthodox to say the least.

A year after Mexico, Mary won the European title on Cornishman V and in 1970 won the individual title and helped Britain to the team gold. In Munich she finished fourth in the individual event, won by Meade, and with Bridget Parker riding well Britain won the team gold. Mary continued to compete for another ten years and then retired in the early 1980s for financial reasons. The horse had his own career on screen, appearing in the movies *Dead Cert* and *International Velvet*, as well as having his own documentary, called *When Cornishman was King*, with TV personality Angela Rippon.

Mary now works as a freelance journalist, mainly for magazines, and has written seven 'how to do it' books on dressage and eventing. She also teaches, was appointed as a member of Britain's senior selection committee for the equestrian team and stewards at race meetings.

ARTHUR GORE

LAWN TENNIS

1908 London
Gold   Indoor Men's Singles
Gold   Indoor Men's Doubles

Arthur Gore was already 40 when he competed in the London Games, but he still had three more Wimbledon finals to play. He was a hard working and successful Victorian businessman who played the game for fun. But he was also extremely fit for his age and used his strength to play power tennis from the baseline, often running round his poor backhand to hit a fierce forehand.

Born in Lyndhurst, Hampshire, in 1868, Gore played in eight Wimbledon singles finals – winning three. After captaining Britain's first Davis Cup team, in the USA in 1900, Gore's first Wimbledon success came in 1901 and interrupted the Doherty reign of singles titles. In 1908 he won the title for a second time, beating fellow Olympian Roper Barrett in a five-set final. At the Olympics he took the indoor singles title, beating fellow Briton George Caridia in the final in straight sets, before adding a second gold in the doubles with Roper Barrett as his partner. With Barrett he also made the Wimbledon doubles final three times, winning in 1909.

Arthur Gore, who took two indoor tennis titles at the 1908 London Olympics.

Fred Grace, surprise winner of the 1908 lightweight boxing competition.

The 50km walk at the 1932 Los Angeles Olympics was won by Britain's Tommy Green (198), aged 38.

Gore's place in tennis history is assured because of the extraordinary length of his career. He played Wimbledon every year from 1888 to 1927 – 39 unbroken years. The record books show him to be the oldest winner of the singles title – 41 when he beat Major Ritchie in the 1909 final. He was also the oldest finalist – well over 44 when he lost to Tony Wilding in 1912. He died in Kensington in 1928.

WILLIAM GOSLING

ASSOCIATION FOOTBALL

1900 Paris
Gold   Soccer Team

Born in Bishop's Stortford, Essex, in 1869, William Gosling had a distinguished early sporting record. An accomplished high jumper, he was also a member of Eton's cricket and football sides, following in the footsteps of older brother Robert, a Cambridge blue and England international at football and a talented cricketer with Eton, Cambridge and Essex. The youngest Gosling brother, Thomas, completed the sporting tradition, winning a football blue at Cambridge.

Unlike his brothers, William chose a military commission rather than a place at university, serving with the Scots Guards. However, he remained a keen sportsman and, military duties permitting, made regular appearances for Chelmsford football club. The Chelmsford connection made William a well-known figure in Essex sporting circles and he was invited to join the Upton Park Football Club on tour in September 1900.

After three games in the West Country, Upton Park crossed the Channel to take part in a match at the Paris Exhibition, a game which doubled as the first Olympic soccer final. Gosling began the game at the back, but sustained an injury early in the first half and was forced to retire. Undeterred, his teammates went on to beat the Parisian XI 4–0, securing Gosling's gold in his absence.

William returned to his regiment and tasted military action in the Boer War, which ended in 1902. The following year he married Victoria, daughter of the Marquess of Lothian. More than a decade later Gosling was back in action, again with the Scots Guards, in the First World War. He returned to England and in 1922 inherited the family seat at Hassiobury, Bishop's Stortford, following the death of his older brother. Five years later he again followed in Robert's footsteps, being appointed High Sheriff of Essex.

William Gosling died at Hassiobury in October 1952, at the age of 83.

FRED GRACE

BOXING

1908 London
Gold   Lightweight

The lightweight competition was an all-British affair and Fred Grace was not among the favourites to win a medal, far less the gold. Gainsford AC's Fred Spiller and Matt Wells were the fancied boxers for the Olympic title. Born in Edmonton, north-east London, in 1884, Grace boxed for the Eton Mission club and had never won a major title going into the Games. But in the quarter-finals he scored a remarkable victory over Matt Wells, who went on to become British and European champion in the professional ranks. This success seemed to galvanise Grace and in a closely-fought final with Spiller he managed to win the judges' verdict over the three rounds with a clever display of boxing skills. The bout was marked by one farcical moment when both Spiller and Grace threw right hands, missed and fell forward onto the canvas, amid laughter from the crowd.

Grace went on to further amateur success, winning four ABA lightweight titles, including a final victory in 1920. He was unable to defend his Olympic title in 1912 because the Games were held in Sweden, where boxing was illegal. At the age of 36 he made one more Olympic bid, in Antwerp, but was beaten by the eventual winner, Sam Mosberg of the United States, in the second round.

Grace worked as a heating engineer and retired just after the war. He died after being hit by a car near his home in Ilford, Essex, in 1964.

ERIC GREEN

HOCKEY

1908 London
Gold   Hockey Team

Probably better known as the hockey correspondent of *The Times* for many years, Green was a handy left-winger in the English side that took the first-ever Olympic hockey title. The home nations were represented separately at the London Games and in the final England trounced Ireland 8–1 to win the gold.

Green, born in Epsom, Surrey, in 1878, went to St Mark's School, Windsor, and joined fellow Olympian Harry Freeman at the Staines club, the country's premier hockey side of the day. He played 16 times for England and made his last appearance in the Olympic final before moving into the field of journalism. He died in Berkshire in 1972, aged 94.

TOMMY GREEN

ATHLETICS

1932 Los Angeles
Gold   50km Walk

It was nothing short of a miracle that Tommy Green should have been involved in competitive sport at all, far less win an Olympic title. He could not even walk until he was five because of rickets; he then faked his age to join the army and was invalided out when a horse fell on him. If that did not put an end to any sporting notions he may have had, he was wounded three times and badly gassed in France during the First World War.

Green was born in Fareham, Hampshire, in 1894, and left the local Ringwood School at 12 to join the army, where two years later, while serving in the Royal Hussars, he suffered the accident which ended his career. But when war broke out he was recalled to the Reserves and sailed to France with the British Expeditionary Force, serving with the King's Own Hussars. In 1917, after his gassing, Corporal Green was sent home and warned not to undertake any physical endeavour. This was a disappointment as he was a keen boxer, but he was advised to walk for exercise. He joined the local Eastleigh Railway Service, working in the wheel shop, and had little thought of the sporting career that awaited him.

His introduction to road walking came after he helped a blind friend train for the London to Brighton Walk. His friend suggested he could have a future as a walker in his own right. Green decided to have a go and in 1926 entered his first race, a 12-mile event from Worthing to Brighton, and won hands down. Fuelled by this success he joined Belgrave Harriers and built an amazing walking record, winning every major race of his career except one – the national 20 miles. His victories included four London to Brightons; six Manchester to Blackpools and Nottingham to Birminghams, the latter six times in a row; and the Milan 100km. In Los Angeles, then aged 38, he seemed to be in trouble early on, visibly wilting in the Californian heat, but he came back strongly in the last half of the race and finished in 4:50:10, more than seven minutes clear of Latvia's Janis Dalinsch. He made a second Olympic bid in 1936 but could finish only fourth in the British trials and did not make the trip to Berlin. Green continued race-walking until he was 54, winning his last race, the Poole to Wareham, before putting an end to an amazing career.

In 1934 he had left the railway to become the landlord of a local inn, which he ran until moving to a bigger hotel in 1953, before retiring in 1960. A prominent figure in south-coast sporting circles, Green was president of the local cricket association and held various posts in the Southampton and Eastleigh Athletic Club. A father of four girls, Green died in 1975 in Eastleigh, the day before his 81st birthday, after a long illness prompted by a collapse during a reunion of the Old Contemptibles.

JOHN GRETTON

YACHTING

1900 Paris
Gold   Open Class
Gold   0.5–1 Ton Class

The only Member of Parliament to win an Olympic gold medal while still in office, Gretton's political and sporting life was underpinned by the family's vast brewing empire. He joined Lorne Currie aboard the *Scotia*, which they co-owned, though a question mark hangs over the identity of the helmsman on the boat. Some historians insist it was Linton Hope, who designed the boat, while new research suggests it was Algernon Maudslay, a prominent yachtsman of the day. Gretton and Currie were certainly on board and won their first gold in the Open class, beating three French boats to the gold. They then won the 0.5–1 ton class, edging out a German crew by two minutes.

Gretton's millions enabled him to sail all over the world and his political career certainly appears not to have suffered. He was an MP for 48 years, between 1895 and 1943. He was awarded the CBE in 1919, became a Privy Councillor in 1926, and a year after he left the House of Commons was created 1st Baron of Stapleford. He died three years later in Melton Mowbray, aged 79.

CECIL GRIFFITHS

ATHLETICS

1920 Antwerp
Gold   4 × 400 Metres Relay

At 19, Griffiths' extraordinary performances as a junior earned him the selectors' vote for the Olympic team in Antwerp, and he fully justified their faith. More than a few eyebrows had been raised at the wisdom of sending the untried Surrey AC quarter-miler into the cauldron of Olympic competition. But in the relay he ran a stunning opening leg, coming home yards clear of a world-class field that included the USA's Ted Meredith, to hand over to Robert Lindsay and avoid the change-over pile-up that followed behind him. The team, which also included John Ainsworth-Davis and anchorman Guy Butler, then cruised to victory, beating the South Africans by two seconds.

Born in Worcester in 1901, Griffiths could never repeat his relay successes in the individual event, although he finished third on three occasions in the AAA 440 yards. He decided to move up to 880 yards and twice won the AAA title, in 1923 and 1925. His greatest race was probably the 1926 AAA 880 yards, where Douglas Lowe and Germany's Otto Peltzer each broke Ted Meredith's world record of 1:52.2. Griffiths had to settle for third place in 1:53.4 – the second fastest ever time by a British athlete.

MARTYN GRIMLEY

HOCKEY

1988 Seoul
Gold   Hockey Team

Midfielder Grimley played in all seven of Britain's matches in the Seoul Olympics and was a key figure in helping the team to the gold. Born in Halifax in 1963, Grimley made his international debut in 1984 and was in the silver medal-winning sides at the 1986 World Cup and 1987 European Championships. By the time Seoul came around Grimley was firmly established in the heart of the team, though few people felt Britain could win the competition.

After a disappointing opening draw against South Korea, Britain beat Canada 3–1, then lost to the Germans to leave them under pressure to qualify from their group. But successive defeats of the Soviet Union and India gave them a semi-final showdown with favourites Australia. In a thrilling match Britain ran out 3–2 winners and then gained revenge for their group defeat by beating the Germans 3–1 in the final. At the time of the Games, Grimley was playing for the Hounslow side and teaching at Dulwich College. He then left both; he joined Neston, and made a distinct career change to become a financial advisor for Allied Dunbar. He is now back at Hounslow.

JUDY GRINHAM

SWIMMING

1956 Melbourne
Gold   100 Metres Backstroke

It had been 32 barren years since Lucy Morton's success in the Paris Games and Britain had almost forgotten what it was like to have an Olympic swimming champion before Judy Grinham's triumph in Melbourne. She helped inspire a wave of interest in swimming in Britain.

Born in Hampstead in 1939, her first success came in the Middlesex girls 100 yards backstroke and she won the first of her seven national titles two years later in 1955. She retained the title in 1956 and earned selection for Melbourne, where three British women made the 100 metres backstroke final. Shaken by pre-race nerves she got a poor start and was fifth at the turn, but fighting back. She drew level with ten metres left and touched first ahead of America's Carin Cone, although the judges gave them both the same time of 1:12.9 – a new world record.

After a brief flirtation with freestyle, winning the national 220 yards title in 1957, she returned to backstroke and went on to become the first swimmer to hold Olympic, European and Empire titles at the same time, taking the European title in Budapest in 1958 and in the same year the Empire title in Cardiff, in another world record of 1:11.9. She won a second Empire gold and shared another world mark in the 4 × 110 yard medley relay, in which Britain beat the highly fancied Australian team which had the great Dawn Fraser at anchor. Asked to name her most pleasurable swimming moment, she feels this relay in Cardiff, rather than her own gold in Melbourne, was her best.

At the height of her fame she decided she could achieve little more in the sport and with the training growing ever more demanding she quit at the top, in 1959, shortly after her 20th birthday. On retiring she was offered the post of *Daily Express* swimming correspondent and spent a couple of years in the job until she decided journalism was not for her. She had met and married hockey journalist Pat Rowley and they had two children, both keen hockey players. In fact, son Keith played for England indoors and then fought back to play first-class hockey after fracturing his spine in a coach crash in France.

Judy was divorced in 1979 but married chartered surveyor Mike Roe in 1982. She has been working with the charity organisation Barnardos for 15 years and until recently was Head of Appeals Training. Already a grandmother at just past 50, she lives in Abbots Langley, in Hertfordshire.

DICK GUNN

BOXING

1908 London
Gold   Featherweight

One of the most formidable amateur boxers of the late nineteenth century, Gunn was asked to retire by the authorities because he was too good. Born in London in 1871, Gunn joined his father's tailoring business as a teenager and took up boxing at the Surrey Docks club, in Bermondsey, in 1893. He took the ABA featherweight title in 1894, 1895 and 1896, by which time the mere presence of his name on a tournament entry sheet caused would-be opponents to drop out. Such was his pre-eminence in the division that the ABA asked if he would step down for the benefit of the sport so that new talent would be encouraged to come through. Ever the sportsman, Gunn agreed and although he still trained and kept a keen interest in the sport, he went back to his business having decided not to fight again.

No British boxers went to the 1904 St Louis Games, so the first chance for British amateurs to shine at the Olympics was in London. Gunn decided it was too good an opportunity to miss and despite his age – 37 years and 354 days, making him the oldest Olympic boxing champion – he decided to come out of retirement. He beat a Frenchman and an Englishman to reach the final, where he met fellow Briton Charlie Morris. Gunn gave Morris a boxing lesson in the first round, but the younger man fought back in the second, so Gunn needed to call on all his ringcraft to take the verdict after the third. After receiving his gold medal he retired again, finally this time. He had lost just one fight in 15 years of competitive boxing. He ran his tailoring business until his death in Lambeth, south London, in 1961, aged 90. But the family tradition carried on. His great-grandson, also called Dickie Gunn,

was the man who trained Chris Finnegan to Olympic gold in 1968 and still coaches young amateurs today.

WYNDHAM HALSWELLE

ATHLETICS

1908 London
Gold   400 Metres

In the furore that erupted over the famous 'Halswelle Incident' at the 1908 Olympics, one thing is always forgotten – that Wyndham Halswelle was a remarkably fine athlete and would probably have won the gold medal even if the Americans had been in the race. Although the extraordinary affair of the 400 metres was largely overshadowed by events in the marathon, Halswelle's gold medal was tainted by the controversy and it caused the athlete to retire from the sport.

Halswelle was born into a wealthy Scottish family, in Mayfair in 1882, and was educated at Charterhouse and the Royal Military College, Sandhurst, where his athletic prowess was first noticed. He was commissioned into the Highland Light Infantry in 1901 and ran several races while serving in the Boer War, where he was spotted by Jimmy Curran, a professional coach, who persuaded Halswelle to take his athletics seriously when he returned home. He won his first major event, the 1904 Army 880 yards.

The following year he came down to the quarter-mile and took the AAA and Scottish titles, before taking part in the renegade 'Olympic' event in Athens in 1906, where he took silver in the 400 metres and bronze in the 800. When he came home he attended the Scottish Championships and won the 100, 220, 440 and 880 yards – all on the same afternoon! He also took the 1906 AAA 440 yards and in the following year added the 100 and 200 yards in the Scottish Championships before injury curtailed his season.

In Olympic year he was among the favourites for the 400 metres, especially having set a new world record for 300 metres and a British 440 yards record. But in London things went wrong. He strolled to victory in the 15th of 16 first-round heats, then easily won the second of the 'semi-final' heats. He lined up against three Americans in the final – Robbins, Taylor and Carpenter – and as the final was not run in lanes, Halswelle made his move for the front on the final bend. It was there that Carpenter shoved him so far sideways that he was

Dick Gunn, who lost just one fight in 15 years of competitive boxing, took the Olympic featherweight title in 1908.

Middle-distance runner Tommy Hampson set a new world record of 1:49.7 to take gold in the 1932 800 metres final in Los Angeles.

Wyndham Halswelle, Olympic 400 metres champion in 1908, having just received his medal from Queen Alexandra.

almost on the other side of the track. Before Taylor crossed the line, the judges broke the tape and declared the final a 'no race'. Carpenter was then disqualified and the final ordered to be rerun two days later, with strings separating the lanes. So infuriated were the Americans that the remaining two athletes refused to take part and Halswelle had to canter round the White City track on his own, still running 50 seconds flat, to take the gold.

Although disgusted by the events, Halswelle agreed to make one final appearance a few weeks later at the Glasgow Rangers Sports at Ibrox Stadium. Then one of Britain's greatest quarter-miling talents retired at the age of just 26. He returned to his regiment and was killed by a sniper at Neuve Chapelle, France, in 1915, aged 32.

TOMMY HAMPSON

ATHLETICS

1932 Los Angeles
Gold   800 Metres
Silver   4 × 400 Metres Relay

In the space of just three years Tommy Hampson went from a below-average college half-miler to the world-class athlete who would increase Britain's domination of the Olympic 800 metres to 12 years. The son of a middle-distance runner, Hampson was born in south London in 1907, and showed scant interest in athletics during schooling at Bancroft's and St Catherine's, Oxford. It was in his last year at Oxford that he began to dabble in the sport, running fourth in the 1929 Oxford–Cambridge half-mile. But he began to improve rapidly and ran well for the Combined Universities in the United States, then contributed to the British relay team which smashed the 4 × 880 yards mark.

He began teaching at St Albans School in 1930, the year which saw his incredible rise to world prominence, when he won the AAA and Empire Games 880 yards. The following season he again fared well against foreign competition and added a second AAA title, completing a hat-trick in 1932. He had also spent the winter adding speed to his strength and stamina, which was shown in his second place in the 1932 AAA 440 yards.

Hampson was regarded as a medal chance in the Los Angeles Olympics. In the event, he ran a near perfect race, letting Canada's Guyanese-born Phil Edwards roar off into a 20-metre lead and then reeling everyone in on the last lap, finally overhauling Alex Wilson with just a few feet left to take the gold in a new world record of 1:49.7 – an improvement of nearly seven seconds in three years! In his diary, written during the Games, Hampson gave all the credit for his victory to his fiancée Winnie. 'I can truly say that but for her I would never have got where I am. A runner perhaps, for they can be made by diligence and hard work; a racer possibly, for they are born of experience in running; but a world beater must, like a great artist, be inspired – and what greater inspiration can anyone have than the love of such a beautiful, kind, gentle, sweet, good creature.' This diary note may go some way to explaining the rapid improvement in Hampson's athletic career, although coaches may well frown at the idea of a 'love' factor in his world record time!

Five days after the final Hampson added a silver in the 4 × 400 metres relay and ended his career with a run in the 4 × 880 yards at the Empire v USA match, a few weeks after the Games, in San Francisco. In 1935 he gave up teaching and joined the RAF, which he left after the Second World War. He worked for a variety of welfare organisations and continued in athletics as coach to the AAA. He died in Stevenage in 1965.

EDITH HANNAM

LAWN TENNIS

1912 Stockholm
Gold   Indoor Women's Singles
Gold   Indoor Mixed Doubles

Had the Swedish organisers staged a women's doubles event at the Stockholm Games, Edith Hannam may well have returned with three gold medals rather than two. Curiously, they staged indoor and outdoor events for men and women, but not a women's doubles. They also decided to hold the outdoor tournament in the same week as the Wimbledon Championships, with the result that no British competitors took part outdoors at the 1912 Games.

Born Edith Boucher, in Bristol in 1878, she came from a prominent Gloucestershire family and learned to play tennis with her four older brothers. In 1909 she married timber merchant Francis Hannam and they lived in Canada for a while before returning home. At the Olympics she comfortably beat Denmark's Thora Castenschiold in straight sets to take the gold, while in the doubles she played alongside Charles Dixon and they won the title, beating Britain's Helen Aitchison and Roper Barrett in three sets.

Hannam had an outstanding record at the Welsh Championships, which she won ten times, and had some success at Wimbledon, where she reached the semi-finals of the singles in 1911 and the final of the doubles in 1914. Two years later her husband, now Captain Hannam, was killed in action in France while serving with the Gloucestershire Regiment. She died in Bristol in 1951.

TED HANNEY

ASSOCIATION FOOTBALL

1912 Stockholm
Gold   Soccer Team

Centre-half Hanney played in the opening match of the 1912 Olympic soccer tournament, but injury ruined his chances of playing any further part in Britain's side. Hanney turned professional after the Games and was one of the sport's rare big-money transfers.

Born in Reading, Berkshire, in 1889, Hanney graduated from non-League Wokingham Town to Reading and won two amateur caps with England. He was replaced in the Stockholm Games first by Harry Stamper and then Henry Littlewort, and despite the switching of such a key position Britain maintained a 100 per cent record in their three games, beating Denmark 4–2 in the final. Hanney signed for Manchester City in 1912 for the consider-able sum of £1250 – only seven years after the first four-figure transfer had staggered the soccer world – and played nearly 80 times for the side. It would have been considerably more had the war not interrupted his career and in 1919 he joined Coventry City before ending his career in the lower divisions as captain of his home town team Reading. He later took over a pub in the town after coaching in Germany.

HARRY HARDMAN

ASSOCIATION FOOTBALL

1908 London
Gold   Soccer Team

A diminutive but tricky left-winger, Hardman played in two FA Cup finals and four times for England, as well as in the Olympic final in London. He became a leading light in the game as a director and later chairman of Manchester United, and as President of the Lancashire Football Association.

Born in Blackpool in 1882, Hardman first played with the Northern Nomads before joining Everton

in 1903. He remained an amateur because he wanted to train as a solicitor rather than make the game his career. He was a great success at Goodison Park and stayed there for five years. He won an FA Cup winners' medal in 1906 after their 1–0 victory over Newcastle and just missed out on a double when Everton were beaten 2–1 by Sheffield Wednesday in the following season at Crystal Palace. He played ten times for the England amateur side and four times for the full international XI, his last appearance coming against Wales in 1908. In that year he helped Britain to the gold medal; they won all three games, including the final against Denmark, 2–0.

After the Games he joined Manchester United, then Bradford City and Stoke before retiring in 1913 to concentrate full-time on his legal business. He became a director of Manchester United in 1912 and chairman in 1950. He was responsible for allowing manager Matt Busby to ignore official disdain and take United into European football. Unlike Busby, he was not on the plane that claimed the lives of so many great United figures in the Munich Disaster of 1958, because he had remained in Manchester to attend the funeral of fellow director George Whittaker. But it fell to Hardman and his board to rebuild the club, and when Busby finally recovered from his injuries the task began in earnest. He was still chairman when he died at his home in Cheshire in 1965, aged 83.

RUSSELL HARMER

YACHTING

1936 Berlin
Gold   6 Metres Class

Harmer was a keen sailor from a very early age, building his first boat when he was just seven. Born in Cambridge in 1896, he attended Uppingham School and the RMA Woolwich before he was commissioned into the Royal Signals. During the war he was shot in the thigh and miraculously recovered from gangrene before he was invalided out as a captain. He began work with the family's clothing business in Norwich and eventually suc-ceeded his father Sir Sidney Harmer as managing director.

A member of the Royal Corinthian Yacht Club, he was one of the five-man crew who sailed *Lalage* to victory at the 1936 Games, beating a stiff challenge from the Norwegians and Swedes. The winches on board the boat were designed by Harmer and he maintained a keen interest in sailing all his life. A keen pilot, he was for many years President of the

Norwich & Norfolk Aero Club and also enjoyed shooting and carpentry. He died of cancer in 1940, leaving a wife and three children.

A. HASLAM

ASSOCIATION FOOTBALL

1900 Paris
Gold   Soccer Team

Haslam was both inside-left and captain of the Upton Park side which won the 1900 Olympic title. The match which gave Great Britain the gold was played against a Parisian XI, in fine conditions, at the municipal cycling track. The game began badly for the English team as they lost a defender early in the first half. Haslam played a true captain's role, rallying his depleted side with the crucial opening goal. Upton Park added another three, winning 4–0 and continuing their September tour as Olympic champions.

HARRY HASLAM

HOCKEY

1920 Antwerp
Gold   Hockey Team

Haslam holds a place in hockey history as the man who toured Britain with the nation's first-ever film about playing the game. It was part of the sales pitch he used in his work for a sports manufacturing company.

Born in Aston, Worcestershire, in 1883, Haslam moved south to the then rural London suburb of Ilford in Essex. A keen hockey player, Haslam kept goal for Ilford and Essex and won nine England caps. He conceded only two goals during the 1920 Olympic competition as England defeated Denmark, Belgium and France. It was a good year for Haslam; after the Games he was awarded the OBE for his work with the Special Constabulary. He maintained strong links with the sport as a senior administrator and his name often appeared on newspaper articles about the sport, particularly in the *News Chronicle*. He died in Ilford on his 72nd birthday, in 1955.

ROBERT HAWKES

ASSOCIATION FOOTBALL

1908 London
Gold   Soccer Team

Slight in stature and lacking natural strength, Robert Hawkes was nevertheless a thoughtful, skilful left-half whose abilities thoroughly merited a place in the gold medal side of 1908. Born in Hertfordshire in 1880, Hawkes attended Luton Higher Grade School and became a well-known figure in Bedfordshire football. After serving a football apprenticeship with several local sides he joined Luton Town in his early twenties, maturing enough to become club captain inside five years. While still an amateur he won five full England caps, as well as appearing for the amateur side in 22 internationals. In 1911 he turned professional, his career with Luton ending after the war.

A straw hat manufacturer by trade, Hawkes made a few appearances for Bedford Town in the 1919–20 season before retiring from football altogether and concentrating on his business. Hawkes died in Luton, at the age of 64, in 1945.

DAVID HEMERY

ATHLETICS

1968 Mexico City
Gold   400 Metres Hurdles

1972 Munich
Silver   4 × 400 Metres Relay
Bronze   400 Metres Hurdles

The nation sat up late that night, staring in wonder at black and white television screens as he skimmed across the final hurdles. David Hemery first, the rest nowhere. An Olympic title in a world record time; the ultimate athletic performance. Hemery seemed remarkably underwhelmed by his achievement. 'It wasn't a surprise to have won,' he said. 'I'd have been very disappointed if I hadn't won.' Then, typically, he wondered if his remarks might be considered a touch immodest.

Hemery, of course, has never been vulnerable to such a charge. His reaction simply reflected the depth of his talent and the quality of his mental and physical preparation. Nobody can guarantee that they will win an Olympic gold medal, but when Hemery walked to his blocks on 15 October 1968,

David Hemery on his way to gold in the 400 metres hurdles in Mexico City in 1968.

there was a curious inevitability about the performance which followed. In a sense, his entire life had been a preparation for this one race. The idea of competition, of measuring his progress, had fascinated him from an early age. At first, as an under-sized youngster, he competed against himself: 'Just knowing that I could improve on the number of times I could jump on a pogo stick, or how long I could hold my breath, they were all good yardsticks for self-improvement,' he recalls.

By the age of 18, he had grown beyond six feet and had started to show promise at the high hurdles, winning the AAA Junior title in 1963 under the guidance of a 70-year-old Harrow maths master named Fred Housden, who was to prove a critical influence on Hemery's career. Hemery's early education had been divided between Britain and America, and he took a BSc course in management at Boston University, where he met his other great mentor, the Boston athletics coach Billy Smith. He decided to commit himself to athletics and his sprint hurdling brought him the AAA and Commonwealth titles in 1966, but he reasoned that his sprinting speed would not allow him a real chance of Olympic success over the high hurdles. Smith suggested an experiment with the one-lap hurdles, and the early results were enough to convince athlete and coach that they were on the correct course.

A badly-torn hamstring wrote off the 1967 season and, with the Olympics just 13 months away, Hemery dedicated himself to learning and perfecting his new event. 'Fred Housden taught me how to hurdle, Billy Smith taught me how to work, and I added the third component, which is what's going on in the mind,' says Hemery. Progress was swift and impressive, as he lowered the British record at both the American Collegiate Championships (49.8 seconds) and at the AAA Championships (49.6). Yet he was all too aware of the gathering American challenge. In the US Olympic trials, Geoff Vanderstock had run a world record of 48.8, while the other American Olympians, Boyd Gittins (49.1) and Ron Whitney (49.2) were also ahead of Hemery in the world ratings.

He worked at focusing his mind on all the different possibilities of the race ahead; how he would run if his lane draw were inside, middle or outside; how he would cope with various weather conditions; how he would set himself at breaking the world record, which ought to deliver him the gold medal. 'I was there in the greatest sensory detail I could imagine,' he says. 'So much so that my heart-rate and breathing-rate went up as I ran the event in my mind. I thought that if I ran my perfect race, I could finish ahead of everyone.'

Both Hemery and his colleague John Sherwood had broken the British record in their semi-finals with identical times of 49.3 seconds, but the Americans had performed stunningly to form, while the Germans Rainer Schubert and Gerhard Hennige had run European records of 49.1. Only the perfect race would deliver Hemery his gold. History records how well he responded to the challenge, blasting out of lane six, breaking the field by halfway, maintaining his pace to the line and destroying the world record with an incredible 48.12 seconds, ahead of Hennige (49.0) and Sherwood (49.0). He was presented with his medal by the Marquess of Exeter, who had won the event for Britain in the Games of 1928. 'It was like putting the last piece into a giant jigsaw,' says Hemery. 'I was delighted that it was completed successfully, that there weren't any pieces missing, that I hadn't let anybody down.'

Within days, he was assessing the next challenge. For a while, he flirted with the decathlon, but he returned to his gold medal event for the 1972 Munich Olympics. This time the motivation was less urgent, less compelling. 'In '68, it was the desire to see how far I could go. In '72, I just thought I ought to go on,' he says. 'I was there on an "ought", rather than a personal desire to prove myself. I rehearsed negative images, imagining being beaten and saying: "It's okay, you're just going to try your hardest to do your best." As I walked into the stadium, I was biting the nails into my hands and saying: "For God's sake, wake up. This is the Olympic final!" And the programmed voice said: "It's okay, you're just going to try your hardest . . ."'

The natural talent, along with the work he had done, brought him a bronze medal, but he refuses to regret the defeat. Instead, he regards it as an opportunity to demonstrate to those he now teaches that: 'If you rehearse self-doubt, it can kill you.'

Like so many of his generation, Hemery left athletics earlier than he might have done, thanks to the absence of sponsorship or real financial reward. He found a degree of success when he competed in the BBC Television *Superstars* series, but his real fulfilment came in the field of education. He obtained a Certificate of Education at Oxford and taught at Millfield School. He moved on to Harvard for an MA in Education and coached for seven years at his old university in Boston.

The question 'Why me?' had always fascinated him. What were the factors which had allowed him to fulfil his potential? It led to a PhD thesis which became a book: *The Pursuit of Sporting Excellence*. The conclusions it contains form the basis of the Performance Coaching seminars he now runs, teaching the value of self-awareness and personal responsibility and drawing on the analogies between sport and business. He believes that the mental attitude which brought him an Olympic gold medal can be applied, literally, to any walk of life.

David Hemery now lives the life of a contented family man, with two young sons whom he helps search for a sport which will offer them the kind of enjoyment which he once found. Occasionally, he looks back to those days of 1968; not simply to that extraordinary performance but to the entire, daunting enterprise. 'I truly believe,' he says, 'that if I had not been able to compete in Mexico, if I had broken my leg a week before, I would have found the whole training experience worthwhile, because each day was intrinsically worthwhile. I loved bettering the times I'd done, and challenging myself against the other people in practice. Or against the sand dunes or the hills in the distance. It was in itself an enjoyable challenge. And I love challenges.'

ALBERT HILL

ATHLETICS

1920 Antwerp
Gold   800 Metres
Gold   1500 Metres
Silver   3000 Metres Team Race

One of the greatest figures in British athletic history, Albert Hill is now a largely forgotten hero despite his Olympic achievements. The son of a keen rower, he was born in Tooting, south London, in March 1889 and worked for much of his life on the railways, both in Brighton and at London Bridge. He began his sporting career at 15, competing for the now defunct Gainsford AC as a swimmer and cyclist. His interest in athletics was pricked by taking second place in a local half-mile race. Soon he was achieving more regular athletic success, winning the North London Junior Cross-country five-mile title three years on the run between 1907 and 1909. In 1909 he ran well in the AAA four-mile championship at Stamford Bridge, but faded to fourth place. The following year he took the title, his first major track success, and continued to thrive on the cross-country circuit. He did not defend his AAA title in 1911 and made no attempt to qualify for the Olympic team for Stockholm in 1912. Mystery still surrounds his lack of competition; it is possible he was injured.

He married Lily Wood in July 1912 – they were together for 56 years – and in the following year he changed allegiance to the country's leading athletic club, the Polytechnic Harriers, where he enjoyed continued good fortune on and off the track. At the Poly, Hill's coach was Sam Mussabini, who would go on to bring lasting fame to Harold Abrahams. The war robbed Hill, and others, of the chance to shine at the 1916 Olympics and he spent the bulk of his war years as a wireless operator in France. Demobbed in the spring of 1919, he immediately returned to full-scale athletics and, at the age of 30, won the Poly's half-mile; then the AAA 880 yards, mile and medley relay – all in the same afternoon.

At the 1920 Olympics in Belgium, Hill was widely considered to be past his prime. However, he had been working hard through the winter, missing his usual cross-country season and concentrating on speed work in the spring. Even so, the AAA did not want Hill to double up in the 800 and 1500 metres, particularly after his defeat in the 1920 AAA 880 yards by Bevil Rudd. But after vociferous representations from the athlete, the authorities relented.

In Antwerp he confounded the critics, running a tactically near-perfect race, before blasting past his great rival Rudd in the last 20 metres to take the 800 in 1:53.4 and beat Frank Cross's 32-year-old British record. Hill later described it as his most satisfying victory. The weather was awful for the final of the 1500 – driving rain on a heavy, chopped-up cinder track. At the bell fellow countryman Philip Noel Baker moved on to his shoulder and, with the rest of the field nowhere, Hill had a clear run for the line, coming home in 4:01.8 – his fastest-ever metric mile. He remains the oldest Olympian to win either event. The following year, under the aegis of the old professional runner Walter George, he brought down the curtain on a fine track career by winning a classic AAA mile in 4:13.8, beating the British record by more than three seconds.

Hill was a runner steeped in the purest amateur traditions. After the Antwerp Olympics he was asked by the famous professional athlete Joe Binks if he would go for a world three-quarter-mile record, with expenses and prize money on offer. He declined, preferring instead to run in the London Division of the London and North Western Railway AC 28th Annual Sports! After 1921, Hill turned to coaching, first with Blackheath Harriers and, after the death of Mussabini, at the Poly. Living in Northwood, with his wife and two daughters, Hill left the railways, joining W.H. Smith, where he worked overnight sorting newspapers for the van deliveries. Unlike some of the Oxbridge athletes of the time, Olympic success brought Hill no financial comfort.

His coaching helped sprinter Jack London to a silver in the 1928 Olympics and he was the mentor of the legendary miler Sydney Wooderson, who described him as a 'kind uncle'. After the Second World War and the end of Wooderson's career, Hill's coaching faded and he was asked by one of his daughters, who had married a Canadian, to emigrate with her. He never returned to Britain, helping his daughter's family in their market garden business. He died in January 1969.

Albert Hill achieved a remarkable 800 and 1500 metres double at the 1920 Antwerp Games.

Britain's victorious 1956 three-day event team: (left to right) Frank Weldon on Kilbarry, Bertie Hill on Countryman and Laurence Rook on Wild Venture.

ARTHUR HILL

SWIMMING

1912 Stockholm
Gold   Water Polo Team

Centre-half Hill was the linchpin of Britain's successful water polo side in Sweden. The Birmingham-born swimmer played in all three of Britain's games in which they secured a 100 per cent record, scoring 21 goals and conceding just eight. Twenty-four-year-old Hill, from Aston SC, was outstanding in the final, in which Austria were routed 8–0 to ensure the Olympic title remained in Britain.

BERTIE HILL

EQUESTRIAN

1956 Melbourne
Gold   Three-Day Event Team

Bertie Hill grew up on an isolated Devonshire farm where the only means of getting to and from school was on horseback. Born in 1927, on the outskirts of Swimbridge, Hill began riding competitively during the war, in local gymkhanas and horse shows, to help raise money for the Red Cross. After the war he began to establish a reputation as one of the West Country's leading horsemen, particularly in point-to-points.

In the early 1950s he was selected to train for the 1952 Olympic team, where he was the top Briton, finishing seventh on Stella. Hill took the individual European title in Basle in 1954, as well as a gold in the team event, this time riding Crispin. He won a third European gold in the team event in the following year and in 1956 he was again selected for the Olympic eventing team and travelled to Stockholm (the main Games were in Melbourne, but the equestrian events were held in Sweden because of the strict Australian quarantine laws) with his mount Countryman, which belonged to the Queen. The trio of Hill, Frank Weldon and Laurence Rook rode well enough to hold off the Germans for the team gold, with Weldon claiming the individual bronze. The same trio rode together as an unbeaten international team for six years.

In 1960, Hill became the first rider to compete in three Olympics, this time with Weldon and Mike Bullen, but missed out on a team bronze medal by a fraction to the French. Hill continued in the sport, training the successful event teams that went to both Mexico and Munich, and by 1968 he had established his own riding academy and has helped produce a string of top-class riders and horses. Today, with son Tony, he continues this work and for 14 years has been mastering the Dulverton West Foxhounds.

GEORGE HILLYARD

LAWN TENNIS

1908 London
Gold   Men's Doubles

Hillyard began to take tennis seriously only after marrying six-time Wimbledon singles champion Blanche Bingley. Until then he had played the game socially and purely for enjoyment. He was far better known as a stylish county cricketer with Leicestershire and Middlesex than as a tennis player. He was also a top amateur golfer and once had the honour of defeating the twice British Open champion Harry Hilton.

Born in Hanwell, Middlesex, in 1864, he joined the navy as a young man and served on the same ship as the Prince of Wales, the future King George V. They became firm friends and it is said this friendship began the close alliance between the royal family and tennis. Hillyard married Blanche Bingley in 1887 and at that time she had only captured one of her six Wimbledon titles. They practised together and soon Hillyard was among the best tennis players in the country. He won the English covered courts doubles with Harry Scrivener in 1890 and 1891, and again in 1904 and 1905 with Laurie Doherty, although his major singles successes came abroad, with two German Championships in 1897 and 1898.

At the 1908 Olympics he teamed up with Reggie Doherty in the doubles and they took the gold in a tough three-setter, 9–7, 7–5, 9–7, from Major Ritchie and James Parke. A year before the Games Hillyard took over as Secretary of the All England Club, a post he held until 1924. He died in Pulborough, Sussex, in 1943, aged 79.

The final of the 1908 men's doubles competition was won by Reggie Doherty and George Hillyard, who beat Major Ritchie and James Parke in a tough three-set match.

Percy Hodge, winner of the 1920 3000 metres steeplechase, was renowned for his unusual but effective hurdling style.

Fred Holman, Olympic 200 metres breaststroke champion in 1908.

BILL HIRONS

TUG OF WAR

1908 London
Gold   Tug of War Team

At 36, Hirons was the oldest member of the tough City of London police team that took the gold. They had trained for five months for the event, unheard-of in those days, under the supervision of their trainer Inspector Harry Duke. Duke, a cross-Channel swimmer and police wrestling champion, clearly got his preparation right. The City team were far ahead of the other teams, disposing of Britain III – the Metropolitan Police K Division team – before meeting Liverpool Police in the final. They pulled them off their feet in both 'tugs' to win 2–0 and take the gold.

Hirons, born in Wolston, Warwickshire, in 1871, weighed in at 15 stone, one of the lightest men in the team. He died in Nottingham in 1958.

GORDON HOARE

ASSOCIATION FOOTBALL

1912 Stockholm
Gold   Soccer Team

The hero of the Olympic final in Stockholm, Hoare scored twice to drive the British side to a 4–2 win over Denmark. A clever inside-left with a thundering shot, Hoare also scored in the opening match against Sweden and helped Britain to maintain a 100 per cent record in their three matches. Born in south London in 1884, Hoare was a key member of the Glossop side and won 13 England amateur caps, ending his playing career with Woolwich Arsenal. He died in London in 1973, aged 89.

PERCY HODGE

ATHLETICS

1920 Antwerp
Gold   3000 Metres Steeplechase

Percy Hodge won one of the most extraordinary steeplechase races to qualify for the 1920 Olympics. He was among the favourites to win the AAA title in Olympic year and to take one of the three British team places. But in the second lap he was badly spiked and his shoe was ripped off. Hodge stopped, discovered the heel had been torn off, adjusted it as best he could, put it back on and set off in pursuit of the leading group who were now some 100 yards away. The stunned crowd watched as he inched back into the race, caught the pack and roared away to win by an incredible 70 yards.

Born in Guernsey in 1890, Hodge moved to England to find work and began running before the war. He might well have made his mark on the athletics world sooner had it not been for the war, and he had to wait until he was 28 before he enjoyed his first major victory. But after that the titles kept coming, including four AAA steeplechases in the space of five years.

After his astonishing victory in 1920 Hodge sailed to Antwerp as one of the main contenders for a medal. He ran well throughout the competition and cantered away from a quality international field in the final to win by over 100 yards from America's Pat Flynn in a new Olympic record time of 10:00.4. One of Hodge's claims to fame was his extraordinary hurdling style, upright and perfectly balanced. He often demonstrated it to good effect at sports meetings and exhibitions by hurdling while carrying a tray of glasses! He died in retirement in Bexhill-on-Sea in 1967.

FRED HOLMAN

SWIMMING

1908 London
Gold   200 Metres Breaststroke

Fred Holman had an outstanding swimming career despite his casual approach to training, and friends had to cajole him into entering the Olympic trials. But such was his natural ability in the water that he easily made the British team and then set the inaugural world record in the event to win the gold.

Holman, the son of a hotelier and one of ten

children, was born in Dawlish, Devon, in 1885. There were seven boys and together they made a formidable water polo team, as well as a useful contribution to local cricket and soccer sides. Holman worked during the day and spent the evening at the local baths, where he developed a stroke that was based on powerful leg movements, perfect for breaststroking. It was said that he only needed a few strokes to complete a length at Exeter Baths. He began winning titles as an 11-year-old and pulled together an impressive list of county awards.

At the London Games he devoured the opposition at the White City's open pool and took the gold more than three seconds clear of team-mate Bill Robinson, in 3:09.2. Crowds gathered in Exeter to welcome him home after the Games and when he finally arrived in Dawlish the local council laid on a horse-drawn carriage for him to head a parade and then presented him with a gold watch and chain. Sadly, he died of typhoid in 1913, aged just 29, and it is believed he probably contracted the disease at Exeter Baths.

ANDY HOLMES

ROWING

1984 Los Angeles
Gold   Coxed Fours

1988 Seoul
Gold   Coxless Pairs
Bronze   Coxed Pairs

One of Britain's greatest oarsmen of the modern era, Holmes took two gold medals in the heat of the fiercest Olympic competition. His victory in the coxed fours in Los Angeles was tempered by the fact that the strong Eastern Bloc nations were not present due to the Soviet boycott. But if he had anything to prove it was achieved in the coxless pairs in Seoul, where after a summer of nagging injury, Holmes and Steven Redgrave destroyed the best the world had to offer.

Born in Uxbridge, Middlesex, in 1959, his first major success came in the Grand at Henley in 1982 when he was in the winning Leander crew. After disappointments at the World Championships in 1982 and 1983, he took gold in the Los Angeles coxed fours, beating off a determined American challenge in the final. Holmes summed up his feelings thus: 'My dearest recollection of the race was drifting across the line with one arm raised just mumbling to myself, "We've done it, by Christ we've done it." Even though I'd spent hours contem-

plating what it would be like to be Olympic champion it took a long time to sink in.

'Unpacking my case at home I pulled out the winner's certificate and for the first time I really looked at it hard. It had Olympic rings at the top and below the words: "For excellence in sport – Andrew Holmes." I stood there for a full five minutes, tears streaming down my face.

'Since then much time has passed, but I know that whatever happens in my life from now on, I will always be an Olympic gold medallist.'

In the 1987 World Championships Holmes and Redgrave took gold and silver in the coxless and coxed pairs, in preparation for repeating the feat in Seoul. There, they took the coxless title, but could only take bronze in the coxed. But the television images of Holmes striking the water with his hand as they crossed the line to take another gold made Holmes and Redgrave household names in Britain during the Seoul Games.

He now works in the interior design, antique and architectural salvage business and lives in Surrey.

FRED HOLMES

TUG OF WAR

1920 Antwerp
Gold   Tug of War Team

Britain won the last-ever Olympic tug of war competition at the 1920 Games in Antwerp, and were represented, as usual, by the tough City of London police team. Holmes, born in Cosford, Shropshire, in 1886, was part of the team that fought its way past Holland, Belgium and the United States to take the gold.

On retiring from the police he moved out to Hadleigh in Suffolk, but died in St Bartholomew's Hospital, London, in 1944.

EWART HORSFALL

ROWING

1912 Stockholm
Gold   Eights

1920 Antwerp
Silver   Eights

Five months after leaving Eton, Ewart Horsfall was in a winning Oxford crew in the Boat Race. His rapid rise to rowing fame was due to his superb natural talent, which had been nurtured at Eton and finely honed at Magdalen College. That first Boat Race was in 1911 and he was in a second winning crew in 1913.

Horsfall, born in Liverpool in 1892, was a natural sportsman and gained honours at football and cricket, and was a junior swimmer of some note. He was the youngest member of the Leander eight that took the gold at the 1912 Stockholm Olympics, comfortably holding off the challenge of fellow Britons from New College, Oxford. He was regarded as one of the finest strokes in rowing history and in the 1913 Boat Race became the only stroke to win when behind at Barnes Bridge.

At Henley his record was outstanding, stroking four Grand winners and two Stewards before the First World War interrupted an amazing career. During the war he served first with the Rifle Brigade, then the RAF, where he became a squadron leader. He also achieved the rare distinction of being awarded the Military Cross as well as the DFC. He returned to Oxford after the war to coach rowing and took part in the 1920 Olympics, where he stroked the Leander crew to a silver, half a length behind the US Naval Academy.

He worked in the banking world in Liverpool and kept up his hobby of long-distance running, but always maintained his interest in rowing. He coached throughout the 1930s and was manager of the 1948 Olympic team that won two gold medals. He died in Wiltshire in 1974.

HARRY HUMBY

SHOOTING

1908 London
Gold   Small-Bore Rifle Team
Silver   Small-Bore Rifle

1912 Stockholm
Silver   Clay Pigeon Team

Widely recognised as one of the best shots in London, Humby came from an enthusiastic and talented shooting family. Both his father and elder brother won dozens of competitions towards the end of the nineteenth century and Harry was no exception to the family rule.

Born in west London in 1879, he began competitive shooting in 1905 when he joined the Alexandra Palace Rifle Club and he won the club's championship in the following year. He had the unusual talent of being able to shoot just as well using open sights, orthoptics or peep sights. He won his first major National Rifle Association competitions in 1908 and this performance earned him selection for the Olympics. At Bisley he was beaten by just three points by Arthur Carnell in the individual small-bore rifle event and with Carnell deciding not to take part in the team event the pressure was on Britain to keep up their excellent standards in the shooting events. Humby's score of 194 was the second best in the four-man British team and enough to defeat Sweden, who took silver, and France, who took the bronze.

In 1912 he concentrated on clay pigeon shooting and took a silver medal in the British team that finished behind the United States. He was joint fourth in the individual event. He served as a captain in the Middlesex Regiment during the First World War and, after the hostilities had ended, he made one more Olympic appearance, in Antwerp in 1920. He was again in Britain's clay pigeon team, which finished just outside the medals in fourth place. Humby died in north London, less than three years after his Olympic farewell.

FRED HUMPHREYS

TUG OF WAR

1908 London
Gold   Tug of War Team

1912 Stockholm
Silver   Tug of War Team

1920 Antwerp
Gold   Tug of War Team

One of only three men to represent the City of London police team in all three Olympic tug of war competitions, Humphreys was born in London in 1878. At the London Games he also took part in the freestyle and Greco-Roman wrestling competitions, but was eliminated in the early rounds.

Humphreys, weighing in at 15st 9lb, helped the City team to victory over Liverpool Police in the 1908 Olympic final, was in the team that lost to the Swedes in the 1912 final and joined the City team in the last-ever Olympic tug of war competition in Antwerp to claim his second gold. He was 42 years old at the 1920 Games and remains the oldest man ever to win a tug of war gold. He died in Brentford, Middlesex, in 1954.

KENNETH HUNT

ASSOCIATION FOOTBALL

1908 London
Gold   Soccer Team

A courageous and speedy wing-half, Kenneth Hunt was not only a member of Great Britain's gold medal-winning side in 1908 but returned, at the age of 36, to play in the 1920 Olympic tournament in Antwerp. This great Olympic footballer was born in 1884 in Oxford; he attended Trent College and went on to Queen's College, Oxford, where he was a mainstay of the University team. 1908 was a busy year for Hunt. Not only did he win an Olympic gold medal, but he also played in his fourth (and final) Varsity game and then went on to score a goal for Wolverhampton Wanderers in their 3–1 FA Cup final win over Newcastle United. It was also during this year that he embarked on a career in teaching at Highgate School.

The teacher continued to play football at the highest levels, turning out in the League for Leyton and Crystal Palace and at amateur level for Oxford City. In 1913, Oxford lost to South Shields in the FA Amateur Cup final. This defeat meant Hunt just missed out on being the third man in history to have both an FA Cup and FA Amateur Cup winners' medal. During his impressive career Hunt won two full international caps and appeared 20 times for the amateur side, making his final appearance for England in 1921.

Ordained in 1911, Hunt continued teaching at Highgate until his retirement in 1945. He died four years later in Sussex, at the age of 65.

ALBERT IRETON

TUG OF WAR

1908 London
Gold   Tug of War Team

Ireton's Olympic Games included the joy of winning a gold medal in the tug of war competition and the indignity of lasting less than a minute in the boxing. Fourteen stone Ireton, born in Baldock, Hertfordshire, in 1879, was a City of London policeman and joined the force's team for the Games. They had been in training for five months for the Olympics and trounced both Britain's third team, Metropolitan Police K Division, and Liverpool Police to win the final.

Ireton was also a keen amateur boxer, but in the heavyweight competition he was unfortunate to be drawn in the first round against the ferocious punching Sid Evans, the reigning ABA champion. He was knocked out inside a minute of the first round. He died in Stevenage, Hertfordshire, in 1947.

DAVID JACOBS

ATHLETICS

1912 Stockholm
Gold   4 × 100 Metres Relay

Jacobs' athletic career was inspired by watching the great sprinters in action at the 1908 London Olympics. He saw himself as another Reg Walker or Bobbie Kerr and set himself to become the next Olympic sprint champion. Born in Cardiff in 1888, he joined the Herne Hill Harriers after the 1908 Games and began to make progress as a sprinter.

Andy Holmes (right), pictured here with partner Steven Redgrave, added to his 1984 coxed fours triumph by taking gold in the coxless pairs event in Seoul four years later.

Double Olympic gold medallist in 1900, John Arthur Jarvis collected an amazing 108 swimming titles in his career.

Victor Johnson, who took the one-lap cycling title at the 1908 Games.

He was good enough to merit selection for both individual sprints and the relay in Stockholm, site of the 1912 Olympics. The standard of sprinting was excellent and Jacobs, though performing well, went out in the semi-finals of both the 100 and 200 metres. But he made up for the disappointment by combining with Britain's number one sprinter Willie Applegarth, Henry Macintosh and Vic D'Arcy in the relay. With the Americans disqualified in the semi-finals, the Germans were the only real danger and Jacobs ran a controlled third leg to give Applegarth a clear run in for the gold. The Germans were beaten by a few feet, but were then disqualified for a faulty baton change. The British squad's time of 42.4 was a new Olympic record.

Jacobs never won an AAA title, though he placed second in the 1912 220 yards and 1913 440 yards. He might have gone on to better things, but the outbreak of the First World War put paid to his career and he never returned to the track when the hostilities were over. His home was in London but he died on holiday in Aberconwy, Wales, in 1976, aged 88.

JOHN ARTHUR JARVIS

SWIMMING

1900 Paris
Gold 1000 Metres Freestyle
Gold 4000 Metres Freestyle

One of the sport's legendary figures and the self-styled amateur swimming champion of the world, Jarvis collected an astonishing 108 titles during a glittering career around the turn of the century. He went on to become a top coach and, under the name 'Professor Jarvis', taught life-saving all over Europe.

He was born in Leicester in 1872, and his wholesale assault on the national swimming scene began in 1897 when he won the one mile in east London's West India Dock. He completed 24 national titles at distances including 440, 500, 880 yards, the mile and long distance. He also won medals for plunging and captained the English water polo team. At the Paris Games the events were held in the River Seine, with the current, so times were fast. In the 1000 metres he beat the second-placed Austrian Otto Wahle by a staggering 73 seconds to take the gold medal in 13:40.2. He then completed a golden double by winning the 4000 metres in 58 minutes 24 seconds, more than ten minutes ahead of the highly-rated Hungarian Zoltan Halmay.

He took part in the 1906 'renegade' Games, where he won a bronze and silver medal, and his international successes had a regal ring to them. They included the Kaiser's Championship of Europe, the King of Italy's World Long Distance Championship, Queen of the Netherlands 4000 Metres and Emperor of Austria's World Championship in Vienna. A non-smoker, teetotaller and fitness fanatic, Jarvis took part in the 1908 London Olympics, but by then he was 36 and did not make it past the 1500 metres semi-finals.

He was able to help other swimmers of the day train, and funded their travelling expenses thanks to a painting and decorating business he ran in Leicester. He often trained with a road-walking friend; each Sunday they would walk the 26 miles to Nottingham, and Jarvis would swim in the Trent and then catch the train back. Having written an instructional book in 1902, called *The Art of Swimming*, and collected more trophies and medals than practically any other swimmer, he was well placed to start a career in coaching. With professional swimmer Joey Nuttall he developed a special kick to go along with his special side-stroke – the two together made him an awesome swimmer. One newspaper described him during the 1907 World Championships swimming 'with a regularity so perfect as to seem absolutely mechanical'. His three daughters all became swimming teachers and his sister chaperoned the women's gold medal-winning Olympic relay team in 1912.

Jarvis remained involved in the sport until his death in London in 1933, and was inducted in the International Swimming Hall of Fame in the United States in 1968.

VICTOR JOHNSON

CYCLING

1908 London
Gold One-Lap Race

The fastest British cyclist of his day, Johnson won an extraordinary number of sprint races during his career, including six national titles and a world championship. Born in Erdington, Warwickshire, in 1883, Johnson had the perfect family background for a future champion – his father built bicycles for a living and had held numerous national and world records in the late nineteenth century.

Johnson sprang to national attention in 1907 when he won 24 of his 72 races with the famous Rover Racing Club in Birmingham, and set a speed record over a mile of 2 minutes 3.1 seconds, from a standing start, at Crystal Palace. The following year he won the national quarter-mile title in London and was among the favourites for the Olympics. No fewer than 46 riders entered the one-lap event at the Games, over a distance of 603 metres, and after two rounds of heats four men lined up for the final – Johnson, fellow Briton Danny Flynn, Germany's Karl Neumer and the French ace Emile Demangel. Johnson drew the inside station and they crawled around the first 100 yards before Neumer made a break and the race was on. Johnson managed to pass the German on the final bend and hold off the fast-finishing Frenchman by the width of a tyre to win in 51.2 seconds.

Less than a fortnight after the Games he travelled to Leipzig in Germany and won the world sprint title. In the following year he set a speed record of 28 seconds for a quarter-mile – again from a standing start – which remained unbroken for more than 20 years. In 1910 he won the national mile title and in the following year won three British titles in one day at Manchester's Fallowfield – the quarter, one mile and five miles. A carpenter by trade, Johnson won his last national title in Leeds in 1912 before retiring from competition. He died in Sutton Coldfield, Warwickshire, in 1951.

BANNER JOHNSTONE

ROWING

1908 London
Gold   Eights

A successful oarsman at Cambridge and Henley, Johnstone was for many years the rowing correspondent of the *Daily Telegraph*. Born in Bebington, Cheshire, in 1882, Johnstone went to Eton and Trinity College, where he excelled on the water. He rowed in the Boat Race for four years, winning three, and in his last year, 1907, he was made President of the Cambridge University Boat Club.

The following year, at the London Olympics, he was a member of the Leander eight which defeated the crack Belgian crew from the Royal Club Nautique de Gand by two lengths. His Henley record was superb, with two wins in the Grand and three in the Goblets, the last in 1909. In the same year he joined the Government Survey Department in Ceylon, but moved to Zanzibar in 1913, as an administrator. When war broke out he served in East Africa, then in France and Belgium with the Black Watch, where he was awarded the OBE. After working for the *Telegraph* for many years he died in Bournemouth in 1964.

BEN JONES

CYCLING

1908 London
Gold   5000 Metres Track Race
Gold   Three-Lap Pursuit
Silver   20km Track Race

One of the most successful cyclists of the day, Jones rode in no fewer than five events in London, including one of the greatest cycling fiascos in Olympic history. The final of the 1000 metres sprint was ridden at a crawl by the four finalists and when two of the British riders, Clarrie Kingsbury and Victor Johnson, both suffered punctures, the spectacle grew even more ridiculous. Officials had been waving red flags at the competitors throughout the race to make them ride properly, but only when Johnson dropped out did the two remaining riders, Jones and Frenchman Maurice Schilles, sprint for the line. Schilles won the battle by a hair's breadth but both riders were hopelessly outside the one minute 45 seconds time limit and the final was declared void. The organisers were so outraged by the 'loafing tactics' employed by the riders that they refused to allow the race to be rerun.

Jones, born in Wigan in 1882, had more luck in his other races, particularly the 5000 metres. Two weeks before the Games he had won the national five-mile title and started this event as favourite. He did not disappoint, sprinting off the last bend to pip Schilles by six inches on the line. There was more controversy after the race when the Frenchman protested, claiming Jones had collided with him on the last lap, but the objection was not upheld. Jones had earlier taken second place behind Kingsbury in the 20km race and then joined his team-mate, along with Leon Meredith and Ernie Payne, to win the three-lap pursuit, over a distance of 1810 metres.

By the end of the Games Jones had ridden in 11 races, won two golds and a silver and missed out on another medal in the 1000-metre fiasco. After the Games he placed second in the world amateur sprint championships in Leipzig, and in 1910 he again won the national five-mile title in Newcastle. A coal miner in his native Lancashire, Jones quit competitive cycling on the outbreak of the First World War.

BEN JONES

EQUESTRIAN

1968 Mexico City
Gold   Three-Day Event Team

Sergeant Ben Jones became the first non-commissioned officer to represent Britain in Olympic equestrian events. Born in Newport, Shropshire, in 1932, he joined the Royal Veterinary Corps on leaving school and was selected for the British team at the 1964 Tokyo Games. He finished in ninth place in the individual competition, just behind Richard Meade, and four years later came home in fifth place, riding The Poacher. With Derek Allhusen finishing second and Meade fourth, the British trio were well clear of the field to take the team gold.

A regular international, Jones was in the British team that won gold in the European Championships in 1967 and 1969. He was for some time the staff sergeant in charge of riding and horsemanship at the King's Troop of the Royal Horse Artillery in St John's Wood, north-west London. On his commission he became Captain Jones and moved to Melton Mowbray to run the horse-training depot, where, in January 1990, he died while schooling a horse.

CHRIS JONES

SWIMMING

1920 Antwerp
Gold   Water Polo Team

When Britain defeated the host nation Belgium in the Olympic final the team had to be led from the poolside by armed police. It had been a stormy match which the British side had won 3–2, but the partisan crowd were unhappy with the competitive tactics and some of the refereeing decisions. The Welsh international Jones played in defence during the Games. It was his last major competition. At 34 he was a veteran, having won his first international cap in 1904.

Born in Pontypridd, Glamorgan, he played for the successful Weston-super-Mare team that claimed the national title three times. He was also a fine rugby player and was a regular in the Penarth first XV until the First World War interrupted his career. After the war he returned to water polo, made the Antwerp Games and then retired from competition. He was a successful coal merchant in South Wales and died in Penarth in 1937.

J.H. JONES

ASSOCIATION FOOTBALL

1900 Paris
Gold   Soccer Team

Administrator, organiser and goalkeeper, Jones was a leading figure in the team which became the first-ever Olympic soccer champions. As player-secretary of Upton Park FC he led a tour of the West Country, Channel Islands and France, during which the East End club defeated a Parisian XI. In so doing, they won the Olympic title. As dangerous French attacks peppered the Upton Park goal, the Londoners' keeper was equal to anything they could throw at him.

After this triumph, Upton Park had to interrupt their tour, return to England and take part in an Essex cup tie. It was a depleted side which made the journey and Jones appears to have shown some ingenuity in making up the numbers. Reports of the time suggest he sought aid from the services — 'the eleven being completed by some gentlemen in khaki'. However, the new faces proved of little help. After a gold medal three days earlier and despite another fine performance, Jones was beaten six times as Upton Park crashed to defeat. Ironically, the team which doled out this 6–0 thrashing went under the name of Olympic!

FOXHALL KEENE

POLO

1900 Paris
Gold   Polo Team

One of just a handful of Americans ever to win a gold medal for Britain, Keene played in the first-ever international polo match for the United States against Britain! This bizarre situation says everything about the relaxed sporting atmosphere surrounding the Paris Games, where many of the competitors did not know they were competing in an Olympics. Some thought it was an informal sports gala tacked on to the Exposition that was running in the city at the time.

Keene, born in Oakland, California, in 1867, played in the inaugural USA v GB Westchester Cup game in Rhode Island in 1886, where he also scored the first-ever goal. He was educated at Harvard before joining his father's business empire, but there seemed to be enough time to play polo and hunt on both sides of the Atlantic. It was during a stay in England in 1900 that he was asked to play for the Foxhunters team which travelled to the Paris Games and won the final by beating another Anglo-American side 3–1.

A talented golfer, Keene once reached the quarter-finals of the US Amateur Golf Championship and also played in the US Open. He also enjoyed motor racing and rackets. He died in Canada in 1941, where he had lived for many years with his sister.

FRED KELLY

ROWING

1908 London
Gold   Eights

A remarkably versatile oarsman, Kelly won major championships at almost every rowing event from single sculls to the eights. Had he not been killed during the First World War it is likely he would have gone on to become a concert pianist and composer. Born in Sydney, Australia, in 1881, Kelly went to Eton and Balliol College, Oxford, and he won the Diamond Sculls, his first major title, at Henley in 1902. He won this event twice more, and added the Wingfield and three Grands.

In 1908 he concluded his rowing career as part of the Leander crew that defeated the tough Belgian Royal Club Nautique de Gand in the final by two lengths. He had left Balliol in 1903 to put his musical talent to the test, studying for five years in Frankfurt at the Dr Hoch Conservatory. He made his concert debut in Australia in 1911 to great critical acclaim. The following year he made his debut in London, but when the war interrupted his career he joined the navy and served aboard HMS *Hood*, where he met and became great friends with the poet Rupert Brooke. Indeed, his best work is believed to be a 1915 memorial piece dedicated to the memory of Brooke. Kelly won the DSC at Gallipoli, but when he was transferred to France in the following year he was killed as his unit tried to storm a German machine gun post.

PETER KEMP

SWIMMING

1900 Paris
Gold   Water Polo Team
Bronze   Obstacle Race

Apart from winning a gold in Britain's successful water polo team, Kemp featured in one of the most curious events ever held at an Olympic Games. The 200 metres obstacle race was held in the River Seine, fortunately with the current, and the swimmers had to negotiate three obstacles. First they had to scramble over a pole, then a row of boats and finally under a second row of boats before swimming to the finish. The details of the race are vague – some sources even suggest the swimmers had to swim underwater through barrels – but Kemp managed to finish third in a time of 2:47.4, nine seconds behind the Australian winner Freddie Lane.

In the water polo event, which was held on the same day, the 22-year-old Manchester swimmer represented his own Osborne club and they won both their matches, beating Belgium 7–2 in the final.

SEAN KERLY

HOCKEY

1984 Los Angeles
Bronze   Hockey Team

1988 Seoul
Gold   Hockey Team

Millions of sports fans tuned into the exploits of Britain's 1988 Olympic hockey team and their success turned striker Sean Kerly into a celebrity. Kerly was the undoubted star of the tournament for Britain and even the tabloid press began to follow his story, dubbing him hockey's Gary Lineker.

Born in Herne Bay, Kent, in 1960, Kerly first sprang to prominence in the bronze medal-winning side at the 1984 Games, where he scored seven goals. He then played in the silver medal-winning sides of the 1986 World Cup and 1987 European Cup, while his Southgate club won the national title in 1987 and 1988. But his finest hour came in Seoul, where he scored eight goals during the tournament and became a national hero.

After a spluttering start the side made it through

Ben Jones, who competed in five cycling events at the London Games of 1908 and won medals in three.

Clarrie Kingsbury, winner of two cycling gold medals at the 1908 Olympics in London.

Sean Kerly, the hero of Britain's gold medal-winning hockey team of 1988.

to the semi-final against the favourites Australia. Kerly scored two goals, but Australia hit back and equalised, and with just over a minute on the clock and extra time looming Kerly completed an outstanding personal performance with his hat-trick and a place in the final for Britain. The West German side, who had already beaten them in a group match, were ominously strong, but Kerly again provided the decisive contribution, setting up one and scoring another in a famous 3–1 victory to secure the Olympic title.

Just before the Games he had lost his job as a buyer for a men's fashion chain, due partly to the demands of training for this truly amateur sport. The British success gave a massive boost to the sport and when Kerly and his Southgate team travelled to Devon for their first club match after the Games they were stunned to find a crowd of 1100 waiting to see them when normally no more than the odd relative and friend would be present.

He now has two young daughters to support and has been forced to step back from international hockey, though he still plays for Southgate. He works as a salesman for a company specialising in synthetic hockey pitches and tennis courts near Hampton Court.

CLARRIE KINGSBURY

CYCLING

1908 London
Gold   20km Track Race
Gold   Three-Lap Pursuit

Kingsbury was an incredibly talented cyclist able to peak at a variety of distances. Over a five-year period he won the national title for the quarter-mile and 50 miles, as well as many in between. Born in Portsea Island, Hampshire, in 1882, he started racing as a 12-year-old and won his first title at just 16. Britain's selectors regarded him as a safe bet at any distance between a mile and ten miles and he rode in four events at the London Games.

The year before the Games, racing for his local Portsmouth North End Cycling Club, he won his first national title — over five miles — in Exeter. A fortnight before the Games he took the national mile title and when the final of the 20km race began he was among the favourites. One of the others, Britain's Leon Meredith, was out of the race within 100 yards thanks to a puncture. With a lap to go it was still anybody's race. Kingsbury was in the lead, with team-mate Jones second, and a phalanx of

European and American riders alongside. Kingsbury sprinted for the line and in the rush at the finish was judged to have just edged out Jones by three inches. Three days later Kingsbury joined Jones, Meredith and Ernie Payne to defeat the Germans in the three-lap pursuit to take a second gold.

After winning the invitation race at the World Amateur Championships in Leipzig just after the Games, he returned home to Portsmouth to a hero's welcome, with thousands of locals lining the streets, and a civic reception was held in his honour. In the same year he capitalised on his fame by publishing a training book called *Text Book of Cycling – For Beginner and Expert*.

At the London Games his medals were collected from the Queen by his two young daughters, who went on to become top-class badminton players in the 1930s. Kingsbury continued to thrive on the national scene, winning six more British titles, the last two at 25 and 50 miles, in the 1912 championships.

On retiring from racing, he became a prominent publican in Portsmouth and locals still remember that he displayed dozens of his trophies around the pub. He died in Southsea in 1949, but a memorial trophy, the Kingsbury Cup, is presented each year to the winner of the five-mile race in Portsmouth.

WALLY KINNEAR

ROWING

1912 Stockholm
Gold   Single Sculls

A working-class Scot, Kinnear decided that if he was going to better himself he had to move south. Born in Laurencekirk in 1880, he left home at 18 to seek his fortune in London. His job in the drapery trade in Scotland landed him employment as a rep in the south London suburbs with Debenhams. It is there that friends introduced him to rowing, for which he showed immediate enthusiasm and talent. He first joined the Cavendish Rowing Club and won a variety of local titles before joining the bigger Kensington Rowing Club in 1910. In that time he had earned a reputation as a tremendous sculler and superb sportsman, and after joining Kensington he had a very successful five years, making an immediate impact by winning Henley's Diamond Sculls and Wingfield Sculls in 1910, a feat he repeated in 1911.

With these wins under his belt he was now regarded as one of the world's top oarsmen and the Olympics in Stockholm beckoned. Before the Games he won an invitation race in Paris but was surprisingly beaten in the Diamond Sculls, with the press suggesting it was because his favourite boat had already been shipped to Sweden. When Kinnear arrived in Stockholm he was in supreme condition and moved easily into the final against Belgium's Polydore Vierman, in which he stormed to victory. After winning the gold he returned to Henley and claimed his third successive Wingfield Sculls.

His career was ended abruptly by the First World War and after seeing service with the Royal Naval Air Service he returned both to Debenhams and to the rowing scene, where he devoted his energies to coaching, which he continued throughout his life. A father of seven, Kinnear became a familiar face at major meetings well into his eighties and worked for many years raising money for the Royal Hospital of Richmond. He died in 1974, aged 93, still happy to boast that he was the first working-class 'laddie' to win an Olympic gold rowing medal.

ALISTER KIRBY

ROWING

1912 Stockholm
Gold   Eights

Yet another gold medal-winning oarsman from Eton and Magdalen College, Oxford, Kirby was also captain of the crew that retained the Olympic eights title in Stockholm. Born in London in 1886, Kirby rowed in the Oxford crew in four consecutive Boat Races – only winning the last, in 1909, when he was President of the Oxford University Boat Club.

Leander faced a familiar foe in the final of the eights in the 1912 Games – another British crew. New College, Oxford, had battled through the opposite side of the draw, but as Leander had won four years earlier they were keen to retain the title for the club, the college and Britain. In the event they won rather more easily than had been expected, with a margin of some four seconds at the finishing line. When war broke out Kirby was commissioned into the Rifle Brigade and died in France in 1917.

JIMMY KIRKWOOD

HOCKEY

1988 Seoul
Gold   Hockey Team

Kirkwood missed out on any chance of repeating his gold medal success in Barcelona when he opted to play for Ireland in the qualifying tournament for the 1992 Games. Ireland then failed to qualify and although the British selectors did not name him among their preliminary 25 names for Barcelona, he cannot now be picked.

Born in Lisburn, County Antrim, in 1962, Kirkwood played as a striker with the Lisnagarvey club, and for both Ireland and Britain at international level. He came on twice during the Seoul Games, against South Korea in the opening game, which ended in a 2–2 draw, and against India, the final group game, which Britain won 3–0 to book their passage into the semi-finals. The side then took the gold by beating their great rivals West Germany 3–1 in the final.

Kirkwood works as a financial adviser in Ulster, specialising in investment.

ARTHUR KNIGHT

ASSOCIATION FOOTBALL

1912 Stockholm
Gold   Soccer Team

A tough tackling full-back, Knight was a regular with Portsmouth when he played in the Olympic tournament. Born in Godalming, Surrey, in 1887, he always remained an amateur player despite offers to turn professional. He won 30 England amateur caps in a 13-year international career and played once for the full England side, against Northern Ireland in 1920.

His performances for Portsmouth earned him selection for the Olympic side and Britain won the three-match tournament comfortably, beating Denmark 4–2 in the final. The First World War interrupted his soccer career and he saw service in Egypt, India and France, rising to the rank of captain. He continued to play for Portsmouth after the war and his full England cap was won while the club was still in the Third Division. His form earned the veteran full-back an Olympic recall for the Antwerp Games in 1920, but Britain's domination of the title ended with an embarrassing defeat in their first game against Norway.

Knight ran an insurance business in Portsmouth, played cricket for Hampshire and served as a squadron leader in the RAF during the Second World War. He died in retirement in Hampshire in 1956.

DOLLY LAMBERT CHAMBERS

LAWN TENNIS

1908 London
Gold   Women's Singles

One of the great figures of women's tennis at the start of the century, Lambert Chambers won Wimbledon on no fewer than seven occasions. Her first appearance in the final was in 1903, which she won, while her last final came in 1920 when she was 41 years old, a record unlikely to be beaten. She also holds the record for the quickest Wimbledon final, when she despatched the unfortunate Dora Boothby in just 12 games in 1911.

A vicar's daughter, Dorothea Douglass was born in Ealing, Middlesex, in 1878, and learned to play tennis at her local school. Before the Olympics she had claimed three of her Wimbledon singles titles and in 1907 married Robert Lambert Chambers. At the Games only five women took part and Lambert Chambers beat Boothby in the final 6–1, 7–5. Only two women have surpassed her total of Wimbledon wins, Helen Wills-Moody and Martina Navratilova. Moreover, had it not been for the First World War, when Wimbledon was suspended for four years, she would almost certainly have added to her total. She came close in a classic encounter in 1919 when she had two match points against Suzanne Lenglen, but the French star managed to claw the game back and run out a 10–8, 4–6, 9–7 winner.

Lambert Chambers returned for her last final appearance in 1920, but was again beaten by Lenglen. She played her last-ever match at the championships in 1927, aged 48, before retiring from competitive tennis to concentrate on a career as a professional coach.

Lambert Chambers was an all-round sportswoman, winning two All England badminton titles and playing hockey for Middlesex. She died in London in 1960, aged 81.

TOMMY LANCE

CYCLING

1920 Antwerp
Gold   2000 Metres Tandem

Born in Paddington in 1891, Lance was the only British Olympic cycling gold medallist never to have won a national title. He partnered the hugely successful Harry Ryan to victory in Antwerp.

Lance and Ryan started competing for their Polytechnic Cycling Club at the start of the 1920 season. With Ryan steering and Lance behind, they set a new British quarter-mile record in June and were selected for the tandem event at the Olympics, which were to be held less than two months later. In Antwerp they overcame the Dutch pair Frans de Vreng and Piet Ikelaar in a 1200-metre semi-final and in the final, over the full 2000-metre distance, they sprinted to victory to snatch the gold from the South African team, Jimmy Walker and Bill Smith, in 2:49.4. They covered the last 200 metres in an astonishing 11.6 seconds.

Like Ryan, who won bronze, Lance took part in the sprint event in Antwerp, but was eliminated in the early rounds. When he retired from competitive cycling he established a small bookmaking business in Brighton, where he died in 1976, aged 84.

JOHN LANDER

ROWING

1928 Amsterdam
Gold   Coxless Fours

An Olympic gold medal was the first and last major rowing trophy won by John Lander, who could not even win a blue at Cambridge. Born in Liverpool in 1907, he went to Shrewsbury School before Trinity College, and was just 20 when he earned selection for the coxless fours. Rowing at stroke he performed brilliantly in Amsterdam as Britain fought through to the final. In the semis they were fortunate to win, as Germany were leading by half a length with just 50 metres to go when one of their crew blacked out and collapsed over his oars. The stunned British crew powered past to win and secure a place in the final against the Americans and Italians. The Trinity team trailed the Americans for most of the race before putting on an astonishing burst of speed and catching them with 20 metres to go. They roared off to win by half a length.

Winner of seven Wimbledon singles titles, Dolly Lambert Chambers (left) became Olympic champion in 1908, beating Dora Boothby in the final.

Tommy Lance (rear) partnered Harry Ryan to success in the 2000 metres tandem event at the 1920 Antwerp Games.

Despite this success, Lander was still not selected for the Boat Race in 1929 – and the man doing the selecting was Cambridge University Boat Club President Richard Beesly, who was in Lander's coxless four at the Olympics.

Lander left Britain to start a business career in Hong Kong after leaving Cambridge and was killed in the colony in 1941 during the Japanese invasion. He was the only British Olympic gold medal winner to be killed in action during the Second World War.

GEORGE LARNER

ATHLETICS

1908 London
Gold   3500 Metres Walk
Gold   Ten Miles Walk

George Larner, a Brighton policeman, had been retired from the track for two years when the London Games opened in 1908. But the Chief Constable decided that a gold medal would reflect well on the Force and allowed him time off to train specifically for the Olympics.

Born in Langley, Buckinghamshire, in 1875, Larner did not actually take up walking until 1903, when he was already 28. A year later he took two AAA titles and went back the next year to complete a second double. However, despite winning four AAA titles and setting nine world records, he felt the training and competition were interfering with his police duties and decided to retire in 1905. During his short career he completely rewrote the record books, setting a mile walking record of 6:26 in only his second season – a mark that remained unbeaten for 66 years.

When his superiors allowed him a brief return, he went straight back to winning ways, taking the 1908 AAA two-mile title just before the Olympics. There were two walking events – the 3500 metres and ten miles – and Larner took both titles. He won the shorter distance from Hackney's Ernie Webb by some 45 yards, in 14:55; while in the longer event, he came home in 1:15:57.4, ahead of an all-British field.

Having taken two gold medals back to Brighton and impressed the Chief Constable, Larner duly retired for a second time, though he was seen in occasional cross-country runs. He remained in the sport as a judge, particularly after retiring from the police. He died in Brighton in 1949, with most of his walking records still unbroken.

RAN LAURIE

ROWING

1948 London
Gold   Coxless Pairs

A leading British oarsman of the 1930s, Laurie's chances of Olympic glory seemed to have gone with the war, but ten years after climbing out of a boat he returned to the Games in London – and won. Laurie's story is one of the most fascinating tales from Olympic rowing.

Born in Grantchester, Cambridgeshire, in 1915, he went to Monkton Combe and Selwyn College, Cambridge, where he established his credentials as an oarsman. He appeared in three winning Cambridge eights and stroked the Leander eight to victory at the 1934 Grand at Henley. In 1936 he stroked the British eight in Berlin, but they finished fourth. He later said that had his great friend and rowing partner Jack Wilson been in the crew they would have won. After Berlin, Laurie joined the Sudan Political Service, where Wilson was already working, and they took leave to make a final appearance at Henley, winning the Goblets in 1938. In 1948, they persuaded the Sudan Government Service to grant them leave to compete at the London Olympics, aided considerably by the influence of the then Chief Secretary Angus Gillan, who had won two rowing golds at the 1908 and 1912 Olympics.

Despite their advancing years and the fact that Wilson had been injured by a spear a few years earlier, the two arrived in good health and began training. It went horribly wrong until their coach suggested they should change places in the boat – then it all began to work. The duo, dubbed the Desert Rats by the press, were allowed heavy industrial rations in austere post-war Britain and they took the Goblets at Henley before going on to the Games, where they won an historic battle with the Swiss Kalt brothers. A week after the event they were back at work in the Sudan. Laurie remained there until retirement brought him back to England, where he qualified as a doctor and ran a practice in the Home Counties, where he still lives.

GILBERT LAWS

YACHTING

1908 London
Gold 6 Metres Class

Laws was the designer and helmsman of the winning boat in the 6 metres class at the Olympic Regatta at Cowes. The owner of the *Dormy*, Tom McMeekin, decided that Laws knew the boat better than anyone and should steer her in the Games. The decision turned out to be correct: *Dormy* won two of the three 13-mile races to take the gold medal, ahead of Belgian and French boats.

The son of a shipbroker, Laws was born in Tynemouth, Northumberland, in 1870. Boats and boat building were his life and he started his own business at Burnham in Essex. It grew to be one of the biggest in the country and he ran it until the outbreak of the First World War, when he was commissioned into the RNVR, where he saw service in the Mediterranean. The experience told on his health and he died in 1918 in an officers' nursing home on the Isle of Wight.

CHARLES LEAF

YACHTING

1936 Berlin
Gold 6 Metres Class

The owner of the winning boat in the 6 metres class at the Olympic Regatta at Kiel, Leaf was one of the country's leading yachtsmen at the time of the Games. Born in 1895 into a wealthy Cambridge family, he attended Harrow and Trinity College, but he had been at Cambridge for only a few months when the First World War began. He was commissioned as a lieutenant into the East Kent Regiment and served with the Machine Gun Corps in France. He survived the hostilities and returned to Trinity in 1919 to complete his education, skippering the university team in regattas against Oxford.

A member of the Royal Corinthian Yacht Club at Burnham, Leaf was also a keen archaeologist and wrote papers on the subject. At the 1936 Olympics he joined forces with Trinity contemporary Chris Boardman, Miles Belville, Russell Harmer and Leonard Martin on board the *Lalage*. The crew just pipped the Norwegians for the gold medal, with Sweden in third place.

During the Second World War he served as a lieutenant in the Royal Marines and died in Reading in 1947, aged 51.

ARTHUR LEIGHTON

HOCKEY

1920 Antwerp
Gold Hockey Team

Despite being gassed in the trenches during the First World War, Australian-born Leighton made a full recovery and went on to great hockey success with England.

Educated at Bishop's Stortford College and Caius College, Cambridge, where he won his hockey blue, Leighton made his international debut in 1909 and went on to win 27 England caps. During the war he served as an officer in the Royal Field Artillery and was awarded the Military Cross. A regular striker with the Walsall club, he won selection for the Olympic side for Antwerp, which comfortably won the gold by crushing Denmark, Belgium and France. He made his last England appearance a year after the Games and later became a selector for the national side, while building a career with a Midlands hardware firm. He died in Walsall in 1939, aged 50.

RICHARD LEMAN

HOCKEY

1984 Los Angeles
Bronze Hockey Team

1988 Seoul
Gold Hockey Team

An outstanding forward and England's most-capped player, Leman retired from the international scene after the 1990 World Cup with a peerless record.

Born in East Grinstead, Sussex, in 1959, he attended Gresham School in Norfolk, and joined his local hockey club. After helping Britain to a surprise bronze medal at the Los Angeles Games in 1984, Leman was also in the silver medal-winning sides from the 1986 World Cup and 1987 European Cup. But his real success came in Seoul, when Britain exceeded all expectations by winning the tournament, beating favourites Australia in the semi-finals and West Germany 3–1 in the final.

After leading Britain to fifth place at the 1990 World Cup in Lahore, Leman decided to retire, having accumulated a record 225 caps. He still plays for the East Grinstead side and works as a personnel manager for a computer recruitment agency.

EDWARD LESSIMORE

SHOOTING

1912 Stockholm
Gold   Small-Bore Rifle Team – 50 Metres

Lessimore was a member of Britain's four-man team which took the gold in the small-bore team event in Sweden, over 50 metres. Britain sent two small-bore teams to the Stockholm Games to tackle two events, 25 and 50 metres. Lessimore, born in Clifton, Gloucestershire, in 1881, joined William Pimm, Joseph Pepé and Robert Murray in the 50-metre event. They scored a total of 762 points to take the gold by some 14 points from Sweden, with the USA in third place. Lessimore just missed out on a medal in the individual small-bore event, scoring 192 points – two off the gold medal – and missing out on a bronze only on the count back. He died in Bristol in 1960.

ERIC LIDDELL

ATHLETICS

1924 Paris
Gold   400 Metres
Bronze   200 Metres

One of the greatest figures in British athletics, Liddell was immortalised in the film *Chariots of Fire*. However, some of the 'facts' in the film were at odds with reality – a strange situation as Liddell's real life hardly needed to be fictionalised. For example, Liddell knew for months before the Games that he could not run in the 100 metres because it was to be held on a Sunday; he did not find out as he was climbing aboard the team's boat. There was no 'swap' with the Lord Burghley figure to run in the 400 metres, as Liddell had won the AAA 440 yards in the run-up to the Games and was among the favourites. He also never ran against Harold Abrahams over 100 metres, although he twice beat him over 200.

The film did capture his strong religious beliefs and it was this Christian zeal that drove his life. Born in Tientsin, China, in 1902, the son of a missionary, Liddell grew up in Scotland and went to Eltham College, where his obvious sporting talents first surfaced. They flourished at Edinburgh University and in 1921, aged just 19, he won the first of five successive Scottish 100- and 220-yard titles. He also went out to the quarter and won the Scottish title in 1924 and 1925, as well as taking AAA titles at 100 and 220 yards in 1923 and the 440 in 1924.

During this time he also thrilled the sporting public as a flying winger in Scotland's rugby team, winning seven caps. He gave up the game to concentrate on training for the Paris Olympics and when it became clear the 100 metres final was to be held on a Sunday, he declared he would not race on the 'Lord's day' and would run just the 200 and 400. He also missed the 4×400 relay because that too was staged on a Sunday.

In the 200 he claimed a bronze behind the two great US sprinters Jackson Scholz and Charlie Paddock, with Abrahams trailing in last. But in the 400, with his familiar head-back style, he moved into the final with some unspectacular times. In the final, however, Liddell roared around the outside lane of the cinder track, passing the 200-metre mark in 22.2 seconds and then actually increasing his lead down the home straight to win by a staggering five metres, in a new Olympic, British and European record of 47.6 – he had never before beaten the 49-second mark.

After the Olympics the athletic fire seemed to wane in Liddell and he began to spend more time on his religious duties. He returned to China in 1925 to begin work in the mission and made just one more major track appearance, in China in 1929, when he beat Germany's great Otto Peltzer in 49.1. Liddell decided not to run in the 1928 or 1932 Olympics and ran his last race in 1930, winning the North China 400 metres title. He stayed in China for the rest of his life, working as a missionary, but when the Japanese invasion was at its height he was interned in a concentration camp in Weihsien, where he died in 1945, aged 43.

Flying Scot Eric Liddell, winner of the 400 metres in Paris in 1924, was immortalised in the film *Chariots of Fire*.

Vivian Lockett captained Britain's polo team to success at the 1920 Antwerp Games.

Ran Laurie (right) and Jack Wilson, coxless pairs champions in 1948.

Harry Llewellyn and Foxhunter competing in the 1948 London Olympics where Britain took team bronze in the Prix des Nations. Four years later in Helsinki bronze turned to gold.

ROBERT LINDSAY

ATHLETICS

1920 Antwerp
Gold   4 × 400 Metres Relay

One of the many athletes whose career was ruined by the First World War, Lindsay had been steadily improving over the quarter-mile and was a double Scottish champion in 1914. Though of Scottish descent he was born in south London in 1890 and ran for the Blackheath Harriers club. His first major success was a fourth place in the AAA 440 yards in 1911 and he claimed the Scottish title in 1912, 1913 and 1914. He also took the 220 yards in the year the war began.

He was 30 when the Olympics opened in Antwerp, but was still running respectable times. He made the relay team after running well in the AAA 440 yards. He did not compete in the individual race but performed well in the relay, running the second leg in a team that included Cecil Griffiths, Jack Ainsworth-Davis and the great Guy Butler. Britain took the gold in 3:22.2, two seconds ahead of the South Africans, who had AAA champion Bevil Rudd on the anchor leg. It was against Rudd that Lindsay enjoyed probably his finest moment on the track. In the AAA Championships the year after the Games, he beat the South African to win the 440 yards title.

He died in Battersea in 1958.

BILL LISTER

SWIMMING

1900 Paris
Gold   Water Polo Team

The junior member of the Manchester Osborne Swimming Club team which represented Britain at the Games, 18-year-old Lister remains the youngest Briton to have won a water polo gold at any Olympics. He played in both Britain's games in Paris, the first against the French Libellule de Paris Club, which they won 10–1, then the final against Belgium's Swimming et Water Polo Club, which they comfortably won 7–2 to take the gold.

HENRY LITTLEWORT

ASSOCIATION FOOTBALL

1912 Stockholm
Gold   Soccer Team

Henry Littlewort was Britain's saviour in the Olympic final, plugging the gap left by their influential but injured centre-half Ted Hanney. Littlewort had played right-half in the previous two games, yet his performance in the centre of defence earned him rave reviews from watching sports writers and helped Britain to a 4–2 win over Denmark to retain the Olympic title.

Born in Ipswich in 1882, Littlewort was one of the key men at Glossop, where he won nine England amateur caps. After retiring from the game he became a soccer reporter with the *News Chronicle* and died at his home in north London in 1934 after suffering a heart attack.

SIR HARRY LLEWELLYN

EQUESTRIAN

1948 London
Bronze   Prix Des Nations Team

1952 Helsinki
Gold   Prix Des Nations Team

When they came to the final event of the 1952 Olympics, Britain's cupboard was almost bare. There was a sprinkling of silver and a smattering of bronze, but the gold medals which the nation expected had failed to materialise. It followed, therefore, that anybody who could break that barren sequence was destined to secure a special place in the public's affection.

Enter Wilf White on Nizefella. Enter Colonel Douglas Stewart on Aherlow. Enter, finally and most dramatically, Colonel Harry Llewellyn on Foxhunter, whose final, impeccable tour of the show jumping fences gave Britain the Prix des Nations and ensured that the Games of Helsinki would be remembered for something other than gallant failure.

The British habit of elevating horses to the status of national heroes was relatively undeveloped in 1952, but on that afternoon in the Finnish capital, Foxhunter took his place in an exclusive club which later would accommodate the likes of Red Rum,

Dawn Run and Desert Orchid. Colonel Llewellyn had acquired the horse as a six-year-old in 1946. 'Paid a lot of money for those days,' he recalls. '£1500. I was rather ashamed of paying so much for a show jumper. But within a year I was offered around £30,000 for him. A little while later, he was priceless. Splendid animal, Foxhunter. A real character.'

In fact, Sir Harry – he was knighted for services to Wales in 1977 – was something of a character himself. Born in 1911, the second son of a coal-owner and Master of Foxhounds, he learned to ride as a child. He was less than happy at his public school, Oundle, as few of the other pupils were interested in horses or fox-hunting, but Trinity College, Cambridge, was a quite different matter. 'Great fun,' he says. 'In those days it wasn't absolutely vital to do very well academically. As long as you were healthy and enjoyed yourself and applied yourself reasonably, it was very easy to get through the exams.' His books were not allowed to interfere with his pleasures. He owned racehorses while at Cambridge and a typical Christmas vacation would involve hunting on 17 out of a possible 18 days and an average of four hunt balls a week.

After Cambridge, he turned with relish to steeple-chasing and rode Ego in the 1936 and 1937 Grand Nationals. In 1936, as a rank outsider, he finished second and one of his post-race telegrams read: 'Congratulations. Winston and I both backed you. Clementine Churchill.' In 1937 he was overnight favourite for the National, but Ego finished fourth after being baulked by a loose horse.

His robust frame was ill-suited to steeplechasing and he was forced to adopt drastic measures to reduce his weight, plunging from 14 stone to 10st 3lb before the 1936 National. The effort of sweating off pounds and stones became increasingly intoler-able and by the outbreak of war he was already moving into the world of show jumping.

When war began, he went to Palestine with the 1st Cavalry Division. 'Great fun,' he says. 'We had 550 horses in our regiment. You did your little cavalry drill, then you went show jumping or hunting jackals. Wasn't a proper war at all.' Later he joined up with the 8th Armoured Brigade, on General Montgomery's staff. He was wounded when an American station he was visiting came under fire and the Americans offered him a Purple Heart. He declined. 'Absolute nonsense,' he told them. 'It was only a scratch. You can't get a medal for a scratch.' But he later accepted the Legion of Merit from General Omar Bradley. 'Not sure what it was for,' he says, 'but apparently it's a pretty good medal to have.' He was twice mentioned in despatches and in 1944 received the OBE for his war efforts.

Foxhunter was one of several horses he bought to work and train at his new home Gobion Manor, near Abergavenny. 'He was such an athlete,' says Sir Harry. 'A fantastic jumper, particularly over the very big fences. And he liked human beings. He used to accompany my wife when she went black-berry-picking. He'd graze nearby, or even stretch out and lie down. He was a companionable horse.'

The partnership developed at a great pace and they were selected to compete at the 1948 London Olympics. Sadly, Foxhunter was daunted by the huge arena at Wembley and the result was a team bronze medal and equal seventh place in the individual rankings. But, a few months after the Games, they won the King George V Gold Cup at the White City, the first of three such victories. Foxhunter remains the only horse to have scored a hat-trick in that event.

Progress continued through the next few years, and the strong British team carried high expectations to the Games at Helsinki. Yet the opening round brought disappointment. Foxhunter totted up 16.75 faults and almost unseated his rider. Britain was marooned in fifth place. It was close to disaster.

Colonel Llewellyn returned to his hotel for a short sleep. Foxhunter also slept, watched over by the family groom. Thoroughly rested, they returned to the arena where events were acquiring a quite different shape. Wilf White repeated his first-round performance for a combined total of eight faults. Douglas Stewart made just one mistake for a total of 16. Foxhunter could afford to put down one fence if the team was to win the gold. In fact, he was fault-less, sailing over fence after fence and assembling the clear round which brought home the British with points to spare over Chile and the United States.

The public reaction was astonishing. Foxhunter began to receive a flow of cards, letters and presents from all over the country. A national newspaper ran a story that the horse had perfected the knack of signing his own name, and the Llewellyn home was inundated with requests for autographs. On one occasion, his owner gave him a mild slap for refusing a fence. The next day he received a chastising letter which said: 'You must not hit Foxhunter, for he does not belong to you. He belongs to the nation.'

Foxhunter, the hero of Helsinki, had ceased to be a mere horse. He had become a well-loved institution.

He died on 19 November 1959, and Sir Harry delayed the announcement for almost two weeks: 'Until I could talk about him without a lump in my throat.' Foxhunter's hide is buried on Blorenge Mountain, overlooking Gobion Manor. 'I could see his tomb from my house,' says Sir Harry. 'We'd been for some very pleasant rides on the moun-tain, and I thought this was a nice place for him to be buried. I'm always glad I did that. A lot of people still come to visit him there. He deserves a bit of adulation, I think. He was quite a hero in his time.'

The name lives on in the competition Sir Harry

devised, the Foxhunter Jumping Championship. It was originally introduced to help him dispose of trophies which he had won and which his wife refused to clean, but it has had the effect of introducing young riders to high-level competition.

Sir Harry remains President of the Royal International Horse Show and chairman of the British Show Jumping team. Over the years, he has played a major part in helping to popularise his sport. But he could not have done it alone. He needed the help of a brave, gifted and eternally amiable horse; a horse who cleared a series of fences one afternoon in 1952. And brought a smile to the face of a nation.

VIVIAN LOCKETT

POLO

1920 Antwerp
Gold   Polo Team

Another army-trained polo player, Lockett was able to perfect his sporting talents on the regimental fields of the 17th Lancers. Born in New Brighton, Cheshire, in 1880, he trained at Sandhurst RMC after Wellington School and Trinity College, Cambridge, and enjoyed an excellent record in the Britain v USA Westchester Cup matches. He also excelled in regimental polo and played right up until three years before his retirement. He was selected for the 1920 Antwerp Games after some sterling performances in the army and helped steer Britain to a 13–11 victory over Spain in the final which delivered the gold medal.

He took over command of his Lancer regiment in 1927, by chance succeeding his 1920 Olympic polo team-mate Tim Melvill. Colonel Lockett retired in 1933 but was recalled in 1940 to run the Cavalry Training Unit in Edinburgh. He retired to an estate in Norfolk, where he died in 1962.

GERALD LOGAN

HOCKEY

1908 London
Gold   Hockey Team

England won the inaugural Olympic hockey tournament in London where the home nations represented themselves independently. In the final,

England crushed Ireland 8–1 to take the gold. They won all their matches, scoring 24 goals and conceding just three.

Logan, born in Wimbledon in 1879, attended Kingston Grammar School, where he played for the hockey first XI, then the successful Hampstead side, Surrey and finally England. This progression was mirrored by his striking partner Stanley Shoveller and together they scored half England's 24 goals in the Olympics, Logan netting five. Logan played nine times for England and emigrated in 1909.

ANITA LONSBROUGH

SWIMMING

1960 Rome
Gold   200 Metres Breaststroke

When the boilerman arrived at the swimming baths at dawn, he would find young Anita Lonsbrough waiting on the doorstep. Together they would walk through to the pool, switching on the lights and keeping watch for the cockroaches which swarmed out from the wooden cubicles. Anita recalls those mornings with a shudder. 'My first job was to pick the cockroaches out of the water,' she says. 'When I warmed up, I kept thinking: "Have I missed any? Is there another one? Am I going to swallow it?" Ugh!'

Those are the moments which remain in an athlete's memory when the great Olympic day arrives, a band plays, a flag flies and they reach out to accept the medal of gold. Certainly, Anita Lonsbrough never forgot.

Born in York, she learned to swim as a young child in India, where her father had been posted as a regimental sergeant major with the Coldstream Guards. But she did not begin to swim seriously until she was a 15-year-old schoolgirl in Yorkshire. In 1957 she won the English schools title at Bournemouth, opting reluctantly for the breaststroke when a friend took her place at the butterfly. She was training three times a day, improving at a dramatic rate and in 1958 she confirmed her progress with a Commonwealth gold medal as well as a gold in the medley relay, in which the English squad lowered the world record.

The 1958 European Championships also yielded her silver at breaststroke and bronze in the relay, and when she followed this with a world record at 200 metres breaststroke in 1959, the Olympic title seemed to be at the mercy of her talent.

But the road to Rome was littered with obstacles.

At the start of her winter's training, she contracted gastric flu. She then picked up shingles and finally went down with gastric enteritis. 'People said I would never even swim at the Olympic trials, never mind go to the Games,' she recalls. 'And of course it was a long haul. But I think it made me even more determined.'

By now, she was working in the Borough Treasurer's department of Huddersfield Corporation. 'They were very good to me,' she says, 'but when I had time off for training or competition, they stopped my pay. We really were amateurs then. After Rome, the media got hold of that fact, and from then on I got all the time off I wanted.'

Anita fell in love with Rome. 'I enjoyed everything about it; the heat, the city, the superb open-air pool. Everything. I go back there quite a lot now, and the memories always flood back.'

She had learned from her experience at the European Championships that she was not at her best in the morning, so she set her alarm for 5am and wandered around for almost five hours to make sure she was wide awake before the heats began. Her chief rival was Wiltrud Urselmann, who had taken her world record a few weeks before the Games. Urselmann was, in fact, the fastest qualifier for the final, and this suited Anita: 'She was the favourite. So far as I was concerned, the pressure was off me.'

On the afternoon of finals day, she sat in her room and varnished her fingernails: 'Because that's something people say you can't do if you're nervous.' She carried that calm assurance all the way to the changing room. The breaststroke final was the second race of the evening, but it was delayed by 15 minutes after a controversial decision in the men's 100 metres freestyle final. 'I can always remember lying on one of the rest beds in the room and watching Urselmann prowling up and down and thinking: "You're wasting your energy. This is doing you no good at all,"' says Anita.

She anticipated that the German girl would go out fast, but in the past she had always been able to come back at her in the second half of the race. She describes the swim which brought her gold: 'I just hoped that I could turn fourth or fifth, make a move up the third length, then pass her on the last length. Well, she went off very, very fast, and to my surprise I was second at halfway. I closed a lot on the third length and we were actually level with 25 metres to go. Then I passed her, and for the first time in her life she came back at me. But I had enough strength to hang on and win.'

Anita won by half a second; close, but leaving no room for doubt. It was not simply an Olympic title, but a world record of 2 minutes 49.5 seconds. She turned to wave to her mother in the stands, then she started to wonder: 'Is this a dream? Am I going to wake up in a minute and find I've still got to swim the race?' Her doubts dissolved when she returned to the athletes' village: 'We'd all been given red towels, and they laid them out for me to walk on. A real red-carpet welcome, it was wonderful.'

When she returned home to Huddersfield, she realised what she had achieved. 'There were a couple of civic receptions, and the town collected and presented me with a silver tea service,' she says. 'I had to make a speech, and when I looked down, there were four old ladies sitting in the front row, crying. It's a marvellous feeling; you compete for your own satisfaction, but when it means so much to other people, it really is gratifying.'

Over the next three years, Anita Lonsbrough revealed the true range of her ability. She won gold, silver and bronze at the European Championships of 1962. At the Commonwealth Games in Australia she won two breaststroke medals as well as a medley gold. In the same extraordinary year, she twice broke the 220 yards breaststroke world record.

In 1963, she actually won a national title on front crawl, which gave her immense satisfaction, and she decided to desert breaststroke and opt for the medleys at the Tokyo Games of 1964. Competitively, Tokyo was not a success for Britain's finest swimmer: 'I broke an Olympic record, but I didn't win a medal. Yet I became the first woman to carry the flag for the British team, which was an honour to remember.' There were other consolations. On the flight to Japan, she met Hugh Porter, the promising young cyclist who was to become world professional pursuit champion on four occasions. They were married in June 1965.

She retired after Tokyo, no longer able to commit herself to the workload of an international swimmer. Almost immediately, she became a swimming journalist with the *Sunday Telegraph*, a position she still holds. She also works with BBC Radio and assists the Sports Aid Foundation in its work for Britain's athletes.

'I often feel as if I've had two lives,' she says. 'I enjoyed swimming, and all the hard work that went into it. But I enjoy my life now, because I'm still involved with the sport. I didn't just retire and walk away. I really did try to put something back.'

Anita Lonsbrough, gold medallist in the 200 metres breaststroke at the
Rome Olympics of 1960.

In 1928 Douglas Lowe became the first man
successfully to defend the Olympic 800 metres title.

DOUGLAS LOWE

ATHLETICS

1924 Paris
Gold   800 Metres

1928 Amsterdam
Gold   800 Metres

One of the greatest British middle-distance runners, Douglas Lowe was the first man successfully to defend the Olympic 800 metres title. He was also involved in arguably the greatest middle-distance race staged in Britain between the wars.

Born in Manchester in 1902, he attended Highgate School, where he won the Public Schools half-mile title, and then went up to Pembroke College, Cambridge, where he won blues for both soccer and athletics. He was in the British team for both 800 and 1500 metres for the Paris Olympics, but Henry Stallard was the favourite for the 800, having beaten Lowe in the trials a few months earlier. But Stallard was carrying a foot injury and in the final he faded to fourth place, allowing Lowe to battle past Switzerland's Paul Martin to take the gold by a yard in 1:52.4 – a new British record. Two days later he finished a creditable fourth in the 1500 metres, a distance with which he was not familiar.

His greatest race was probably the 1926 AAA 880 yards final, in which he was narrowly beaten in a titanic struggle with Germany's Otto Peltzer. A 25,000 crowd witnessed the race at Stamford Bridge, where Peltzer just pipped Lowe to win in a new world record 1:51.6, with Lowe unofficially clocked at 1:52.0, which also beat the previous record. In 1927, after a surprisingly long wait, he claimed his first AAA title at 880 yards, adding the 440 yards and 4 × 440 relay and making up for previous disappointments.

He retained the 440 and 880 yards in 1928 in the run-up to the Amsterdam Olympics, where he was among the favourites for a medal, although the new world record-holder, Seraphin Martin of France, and America's Lloyd Hahn were rated better prospects. With Peltzer taken ill and eliminated in the semi-finals, Lowe turned the final into a one-man show, sweeping past Martin and Hahn on the final bend and sprinting home by eight yards to win in a new Olympic record of 1:51.8 and to take his second gold. He then ran in the 4 × 400 relay squad which finished fifth. Then, after running a magnificent British record of 1:51.2 in Berlin at the end of the 1928 season, beating Peltzer in the process, he decided to retire.

Lowe had been called to the Bar of the Inner Temple in 1928; he then served as secretary to the AAA between 1931 and 1938, before retiring from the sport completely to concentrate on his legal career. He became a bencher in 1957, took silk in 1964 and was deputy chairman of Warwick quarter sessions and a Recorder of Lincoln and the Crown Court. He died in retirement in Cranbrook, Kent, in 1981.

JACK McBRYAN

HOCKEY

1920 Antwerp
Gold   Hockey Team

An extraordinary character, McBryan was a first-class cricketer, emerged from four years in a German PoW camp to win an Olympic gold medal, made a fortune on the stock exchange and then lost everything at the age of 80. Born in Box, Wiltshire, in 1892, McBryan attended Exeter School, then RMC Sandhurst, where he excelled at sport, especially cricket, rugby and hockey. He actually made his first-class cricket debut for Somerset in 1911, while still at the military academy. He took a commission in Prince Albert's Somerset Light Infantry but resigned it a year later having decided to follow his father into the medical profession. But the war interrupted his career plan and he rejoined his old regiment only to be captured in France with the war just three weeks old.

When he eventually returned home he went to Jesus College, Cambridge, and won a cricket blue. He continued to play hockey for the college, where he was spotted and selected for the English squad for Antwerp. The team won the Olympic title comfortably, beating Denmark, Belgium and France for the gold. McBryan did not feature on the international scene again. He left Cambridge and eventually decided on a career in the City, broking shares, which gave him time to play for Somerset and continue to play golf and rugby.

A key figure for Somerset until he retired in 1931, McBryan played for England in 1924 against South Africa and in the same year went to South Africa with an MCC side. *Wisden* named him among their cricketers of the year in 1925 and on five occasions he scored more than 1000 runs in a season. After retiring from the stockbrokers for whom he had worked for most of his life, he was persuaded to join a rival firm, which then collapsed. He lost everything and spent the last years of his life in circumstances to which he had certainly never been previously accustomed.

He died in Cambridge in 1983, aged 91.

IAIN MacDONALD-SMITH

YACHTING

1968 Mexico City
Gold   Flying Dutchman Class

MacDonald-Smith and Rodney Pattisson were the dominant small-boat sailing force of the day, and they forged such a successful partnership that their competitors were content to fight for second place. They started sailing together in 1967 after Pattisson had unsuccessfully advertised for a crew. MacDonald-Smith was introduced by Pattisson's younger brother and in their first year they finished second in both the British and European competitions.

They were remarkably fit and trained hard for Mexico, paying meticulous attention to their boat *Superdocious*. In Olympic year they won the British title, then the European event in Hungary before returning home to sweep the board at the trials. Their domination of the Olympic Regatta at Acapulco is legendary; they spent three weeks acclimatising and training before the event began. There were seven races and they won the first, only to be disqualified for a starting infringement. With six of the seven races to be scored, the pair were immediately under enormous pressure but they responded with a string of five successive wins, and were able to sit back and finish second in the final race to win the gold by a massive margin. For the following two years the pair won the World Championships before splitting at the end of 1970.

MacDonald-Smith, born in 1945, turned to the Finn class and won the British and German Championships. He was a reserve for Munich and competed in the Soling event at Montreal, where he finished 13th. He was awarded the MBE for his services to sailing and he maintains a keen interest in the sport. A solicitor by profession, he currently lives in Hampshire.

GEORGE McGRATH

HOCKEY

1920 Antwerp
Gold   Hockey Team

Selected as an inside-forward for the Antwerp Olympics, McGrath was an experienced hockey player. As captain of Wimbledon he attracted international attention and was a useful squad member for the English side. In truth, the competition was undemanding and Denmark, Belgium and France were crushed by substantial margins. McGrath did not play for England after the Olympics but was well known as an administrator, serving as secretary to his own Wimbledon club and the Southern Counties Hockey Association.

HENRY MACINTOSH

ATHLETICS

1912 Stockholm
Gold   4 × 100 Metres Relay

The greatest Scottish sprinter of the early part of the century, Henry Macintosh had scarcely set foot on a track until he went to Cambridge University. The son of an Episcopal clergyman, he was born in Kelso in 1892 and was educated at Trinity College, Glenalmond, where he excelled as a rugby player. It was when he went up to Corpus Christi that his love affair with the track began and he won the Freshman's 100 yards in 1912 in a modest 10.8.

He soon became secretary to the University Athletic Club, but his form in the national championships was poor, and he finished last in the 100 yards. However, he was selected for the Olympic team and was quickly eliminated in both sprints before joining the relay team – Willie Applegarth, Vic D'Arcy and David Jacobs – to take the gold. The Americans had been favourites but they were disqualified in the semi-finals. Britain then pipped Germany in the final – though the Germans were also later disqualified – coming home in 42.4 seconds.

Macintosh continued to improve after the Olympics and won the Oxbridge and Scottish 100 yards titles in 1913, when he was also made President of the Cambridge UAC. He then went abroad and equalled the British 100 yards record of 9.8 in

Vienna and won a race in Budapest, for which he was awarded an enormous Italian statue which he had to haul home on the train. He also set all-comers records for the 100 and 200 metres in Austria.

In 1914 he again took the Oxbridge and Scottish 100 yards titles before leaving Britain to work as an Assistant District Commissioner in South Africa. But he returned home after a few months and was commissioned into the Argyll & Sutherland Highlanders. In the summer of 1918 he died of wounds received in action on the Somme, in France, just a month past his 26th birthday.

MIKE McINTYRE

YACHTING

1988 Seoul
Gold   Star Class

Hopes were high for medals when the yachting team left for the Seoul Olympics, but few felt the Star class pairing of McIntyre and Bryn Vaile stood a chance. Their victory was set against a background of personal sacrifice, an accident during the competition and a thrilling final-day race for gold.

McIntyre had made his Olympic debut in Los Angeles four years earlier and finished a creditable seventh in the Finn class, in which he had been three times British champion. In the interim he teamed up with Vaile and they decided to attack the Star class at the regatta in Pusan. A sales manager in Salisbury, McIntyre had to give up valuable work time to train for the Games and in Korea they made only a modest start.

Their first win came on the second day, but while still in contention on day five disaster struck when Vaile was hit on the head in an accident on shore. The injury needed stitches but Vaile decided to carry on. They finished a below-par 14th and looked like going out of the medals completely. After finishing seventh in the penultimate race they knew exactly what was required to win the gold. Nothing but first place for them would do and the Americans had to finish sixth or worse. On a day of high winds and big seas McIntyre drove the boat brilliantly to win by 11 seconds. Only when he stepped ashore did he realise that the Americans had retired with a broken mast. The gold was theirs!

Glaswegian McIntyre, born in 1956, still lives and works in Salisbury and hopes for more Olympic success in Barcelona.

JOHN McKENZIE

YACHTING

1908 London
Gold   12 Metres Class

McKenzie was an outstanding Scottish sailor and a leading member of the Royal Clyde Yacht Club. He was selected to represent the club at the 1908 Games, joining the ten-man crew of the boat *Hera*, owned by club-mate Thomas Glen-Coats. They had only one opposition boat, the *Mouchette* from Liverpool, and the Olympic organisers decided to allow the competition to be staged on the Clyde rather than at Cowes. On home water the *Hera* won both 26-mile races by more than a minute to take the gold medal.

FRANK MACKEY

POLO

1900 Paris
Gold   Polo Team

One of two Americans to play under the British banner in the Paris Games, Mackey did not even play the game until he was 40. Born in Chicago, Mackey was playing in England around the time of the Olympic tournament with the Foxhunters team and was asked to take part. He joined fellow American Foxhall Keene on the team that beat another Anglo-US side, Wanderers, 3–1 in the Olympic final. After the Games, which many competitors thought to be an adjunct to the Paris Exposition and not an Olympics, Mackey played successfully for the US polo team against Britain in the Westchester Cup.

Background Judy Grinham, winner of the 100 metres backstroke at the 1956 Melbourne Games.

Below Left David Wilkie on his way to gold in the 200 metres breaststroke in Montreal in 1976.

Below Adrian Moorhouse celebrates his victory in the 100 metres breaststroke at the 1988 Seoul Olympics.

Background Queenie Newall, who won the 1908 archery title in London.

Below Malcolm Cooper, gold medallist in the small-bore rifle (three positions) shooting event at both the Los Angeles and Seoul Olympics.

Background Wally Kinnear, who took the single sculls title at the 1912 Stockholm Games.

Left Rodney Pattisson (left), winner of two golds (1968 and 1972) and a silver (1976) in the Flying Dutchman class.

Below 1988 coxless pairs champions Andy Holmes (right) and Steven Redgrave, who won a bronze in the coxed pairs event at the same Games.

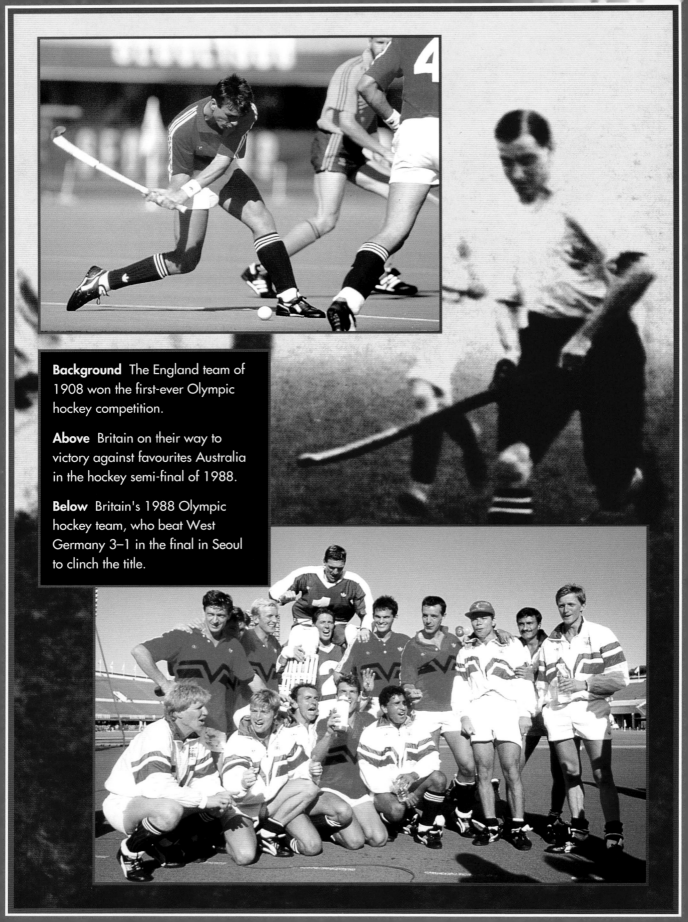

Background The England team of 1908 won the first-ever Olympic hockey competition.

Above Britain on their way to victory against favourites Australia in the hockey semi-final of 1988.

Below Britain's 1988 Olympic hockey team, who beat West Germany 3–1 in the final in Seoul to clinch the title.

Background Ann Packer adds Olympic gold in the 800 metres to her silver medal in the 400 metres at the Tokyo Games of 1964.

Above Tessa Sanderson, whose throw of 69.56 metres secured her the Olympic javelin title in Los Angeles in 1984.

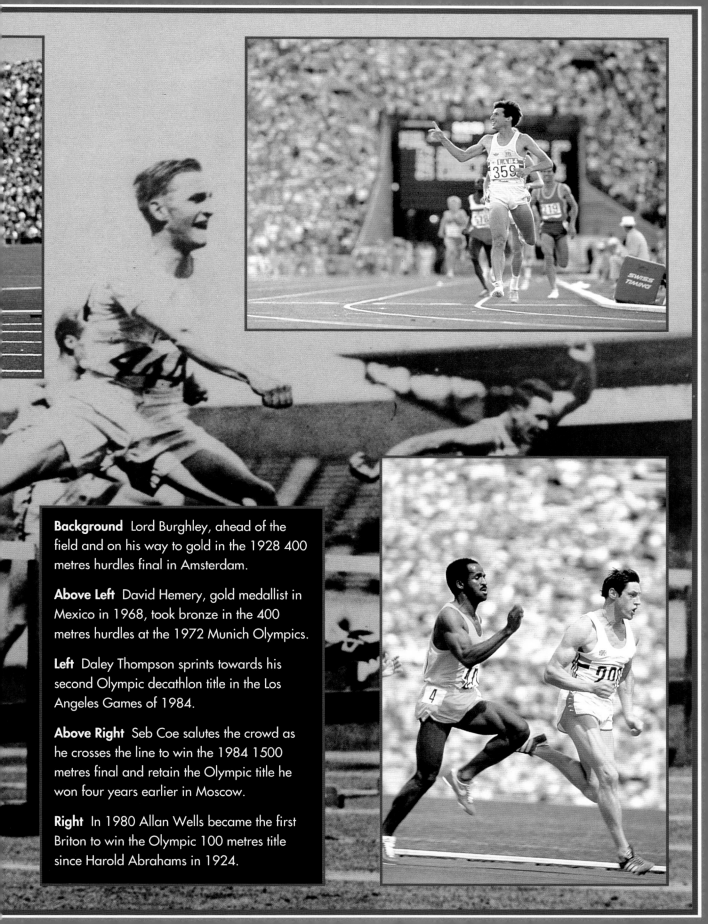

Background Lord Burghley, ahead of the field and on his way to gold in the 1928 400 metres hurdles final in Amsterdam.

Above Left David Hemery, gold medallist in Mexico in 1968, took bronze in the 400 metres hurdles at the 1972 Munich Olympics.

Left Daley Thompson sprints towards his second Olympic decathlon title in the Los Angeles Games of 1984.

Above Right Seb Coe salutes the crowd as he crosses the line to win the 1984 1500 metres final and retain the Olympic title he won four years earlier in Moscow.

Right In 1980 Allan Wells became the first Briton to win the Olympic 100 metres title since Harold Abrahams in 1924.

Background The smooth baton-change between Bill Roberts and Godfrey Brown set the British squad up for victory in the final of the 1936 4 x 400 metres relay.

Above Left On the victory rostrum with Seb Coe are Jurgen Straub of East Germany and great rival Steve Ovett, who won silver and bronze behind Coe in the 1500 metres in 1980.

Above Right The 1500 metres at the 1984 Los Angeles Olympics. Seb Coe, here leading from Steve Cram and Steve Ovett, went on to achieve a successful defence of his title.

DUNCAN MacKINNON

ROWING

1908 London
Gold   Coxless Fours

In five years of stiff competition at Henley, Mac-Kinnon lost only two races and won six major titles. Born in London in 1887, he went to Rugby and Magdalen College, Oxford, which had a long-standing tradition of rowing excellence. He was just 20 when the London Games were held and had not even won his blue, but he joined the college's coxless four at Henley which beat Canada in the semi-final. Leander took the other semi against Holland, leaving an all-British final, which Magdalen won comfortably by two lengths in eight minutes and 34 seconds.

After the Games, MacKinnon rowed for Cambridge in the Boat Races of 1909, 1910 and 1911. His Henley title haul included two Grands, two Visitors, the Stewards and the Wyfold. He left Oxford in 1911 to join the family business in Calcutta, but came home when the First World War began and was commissioned into the Royal North Devon Hussars. He was serving with the Scots Guards when he was killed in action at Ypres in 1917.

CYRIL MACKWORTH-PRAED

SHOOTING

1924 Paris
Gold   Running Deer Double Shot Team
Silver   Running Deer Single Shot
Silver   Running Deer Double Shot

One of Britain's great marksmen, Mackworth-Praed was a significant ornithologist and spent his entire life compiling a six-volume work on African birds. He published the last volume in 1973 less than a year before his death and remains one of the country's most revered naturalists.

He was born in Surrey in 1891, and spent a lonely childhood in Herefordshire, where he developed an interest in shooting, fishing and natural history.

His shooting talents grew at Eton and Trinity College, Cambridge, and during the war he served with the Scots Guards in East Africa and France. Returning from the war he married an African naturalist's daughter and began helping him identify the continent's birds. He worked as a broker on the stock exchange, which allowed him the necessary time and money to pursue his shooting. He put together the British team that travelled to the Paris Games.

He was hugely successful at the Olympics, winning a gold and two silvers in the various Running Deer competitions. The gold came in the team event, alongside Whitty, Perry and Neame. He took part in several other events, including the clay pigeon, in which he was also a useful shot. In Paris he finished eighth, but he went on to win the World Clay Pigeon Shooting Championship in the 1930s.

He began the *African Handbook of Birds* project in 1932 and it became a major reference source as it took shape over the ensuing 40 years. During the Second World War he ran the Commando Training School in Scotland, and was later made a life member of the National Rifle Association.

He made a second Olympic appearance in 1952, then well past 60, and finished 11th in the clay pigeon shooting in Helsinki. In addition to his pet subject, African birds, he was also keenly involved in wildfowl preservation in Britain and invented the original adopt-a-duck scheme to raise money for ringing birds. He was awarded the OBE for his services to ornithology, as well as the Zoological Society's Stamford Raffles Award and the Union Medal.

He died in retirement in Hampshire in 1974, aged 82.

GILCHRIST MacLAGEN

ROWING

1908 London
Gold   Eights

An outstanding cox of the early Olympic era and the holder of an impressive array of Henley titles, MacLagen was born in London in 1879, the son of a doctor. He was educated at Eton, where he excelled at fives and soccer, before going up to Magdalen College, Oxford. He coxed the Oxford boat for four consecutive years and the Leander eight from 1899 to 1908, amassing six titles at Henley. The Olympics rounded off a fine career, when he again coxed the Leander crew to victory over the

Belgian Royal Club Nautique de Gand in the final.

He was commissioned as a lieutenant in the Royal Warwickshire Regiment on the outbreak of the First World War and was killed in action at Pilken Wood, France, in 1915.

TOM McMEEKIN

YACHTING

1908 London
Gold 6 Metres Class

McMeekin was the owner of the *Dormy* which won the 1908 6 metres class event at the London Games. He handed over the job of helmsman to the designer of the craft Gilbert Laws and joined Charles Crichton as a crewman. The *Dormy* won the first two 13-mile races of the series at the Cowes regatta and came home a comfortable third in the final race to take the gold ahead of the Belgians and France.

JAMES MACNABB

ROWING

1924 Paris
Gold Coxless Fours

Macnabb and his coxless four team-mates almost did not get to take part at the Paris Olympics after their boat and oars mysteriously disappeared en route to the rowing HQ on the Seine. They eventually turned up, three days later, in packing cases on a cart drawn by a team of donkeys.

Macnabb, born in Keighley, Yorkshire, in 1901, went to Eton and then Trinity College, Cambridge, and made his Henley debut in 1920. His first successes there came two years later in the Stewards and the Visitors, with his coxless four from Trinity called the Eton Vikings. The famous Trinity four of Macnabb, Eley, Morrison and Sanders were a formidable outfit, having grown up together at Eton and stayed together at Trinity. They scored more successes at Henley, but for Macnabb 1924 was the year to remember. He was a member of the Cambridge crew that won the Boat Race; he then won the Goblets with Eley, before taking the Stewards with his Trinity colleagues and repeating the feat in Paris.

Macnabb recalled that after sailing to France

they never saw the rest of the team or the stadium and were housed in a noisy hotel above the Gare St Lazare. But the crew used all their years of experience to win the final comfortably from the Canadians and cap a perfect year. After retiring from competitive rowing he maintained his interest in the sport, as honorary treasurer of the Amateur Rowing Association for 20 years, a steward at Henley and a Leander treasurer. He also enjoyed the rare privilege of coaching both Cambridge and Oxford crews for the Boat Race, pre- and post-war.

During the war he commanded a regiment of the Royal Artillery in Burma before returning to his accountancy practice and charitable work in housing, for which he was awarded the OBE in 1972. He was for many years the Chief of the Clan Macnabb and later President of the Clan Society. He was still coaching well into his eighties and died at his London home in 1990, aged 89.

WINIFRED McNAIR

LAWN TENNIS

1920 Antwerp
Gold Women's Doubles

McNair benefited enormously from the demonstration of faith shown by her partner Kitty McKane in Antwerp. McKane was a favourite at least to reach the final of the singles but withdrew in the semis to concentrate on the doubles. The tactic clearly paid off as the pair then defeated the much-favoured French pair Elisabeth D'Ayen and the great Suzanne Lenglen in a tough three-setter. Lenglen easily won the singles against Britain's Dorothy Holman, who then joined Geraldine Beamish to face McNair and McKane in the doubles final. McNair and McKane won reasonably comfortably 8–6, 6–4 to take the gold – just a few days after McNair had celebrated her 43rd birthday.

Although McKane was clearly the better player McNair had enjoyed considerable successes on her own. She reached the 1913 Wimbledon singles final, which she lost to the great Dolly Lambert Chambers, yet secured a doubles victory alongside Dora Boothby at the championships that same year, when Lambert Chambers and Chattie Sterry were forced to retire.

A year after the Antwerp Games she returned to golf and played for England, as well as finishing runner-up in the English Ladies Championship. She married Roderick McNair in 1908 and he went on to become the first President of the International Lawn Tennis Federation. Born in Newbury, Berkshire, in 1877, she died in London in 1954.

Britain's 1924 Running Deer team, gold medallists in the double shot competition: (seated, left to right, holding rifles) Allen Whitty, Cyril Mackworth-Praed, Herbert Perry and Philip Neame.

In 1924 Harry Mallin retained the middleweight title he won in Antwerp to become the most successful British boxer in Olympic history.

Dundee-born Dick McTaggart (standing), the lightweight boxer who won two Olympic medals – gold in 1956 and bronze in 1960. He is the only British boxer to compete in three Games.

DICK McTAGGART

BOXING

1956 Melbourne
Gold   Lightweight

1960 Rome
Bronze   Lightweight

The way Dick McTaggart tells it, boxing is the most uncomplicated of sports. 'I was always taught to hit and not be hit,' he says. 'That's all there is to it, really.' It is a simple philosophy, one which he practised throughout a career which spanned almost two decades, three Olympic Games and countless contests against men who carried far heavier artillery than the slim southpaw from Dundee.

Yet if it really were that easy, as somebody once said, then everybody would be doing it. The truth is that McTaggart's success was made possible by a remarkable combination of boxing's virtues. He possessed the courage to back his skills against intimidating strength, the brain to devise the safest yet most punishing strategy and the technique to implement his schemes with a shuffle of the feet or a swift, sniping jab. To a degree which was probably unique in the history of British amateur boxing, Dick McTaggart had class.

He came from the kind of background which traditionally has produced the best fighters; born in Dundee in the hungry 1930s into a family of 18 children. 'We struggled by somehow,' he says. 'We shared everything; clothes, shoes, things like that. And because there were so many of us, we got a lot of things free, like bus fares and meals. It wasn't that bad, really.'

His oldest brother, Peter, was becoming a successful amateur boxer when Dick took up the sport at the age of ten. Boxing became his hobby through his teens, then he started to take it seriously when he joined the RAF as a national serviceman. It was as a services boxer that he suffered his first heavy defeat in the final of the ABA championships, against Dave Charnley, who was later to become one of Britain's finest professionals.

But McTaggart learned from failure as well as success. He won the ABA title in the Olympic year of 1956 and such was his talent that he was regarded as a genuine prospect for a medal of some metal in Melbourne. He began his Olympic preparations a year before the Games, undertaking special training and working harder than he had ever done to reach a peak for the trip to Australia; circuit training, running, sparring and a strict regime of early nights.

By now, he had developed a taste for foreign travel: 'The terrific thing was that it didn't cost you anything,' he says. 'Sure, they only gave you seven and sixpence a day spending money, which is something like 35p in today's money, but we managed on that. I was always aware that I'd never have seen such places if it hadn't been for amateur boxing.'

He loved everything about Melbourne; the weather, the people, the Olympic Village, the feeling that there was nothing to do but prepare for the fights of his life. He enjoyed the two easy contests which carried him into the semi-final, and he felt he was reaching a new level of fitness and performance when he overcame the Soviet boxer Anatoli Lagetko to win a place in the final. 'As soon as I reached the final, I just relaxed,' he says. 'All the hard training was done, now I had to conserve all my energy. I didn't know too much about Harry Kurschat, the German I'd be meeting in the final, but he was the European champion, so I guessed he'd be no push-over. Most important, I knew he'd had a lot of hard contests in getting to the final, and I was hoping that he'd taken a lot out of himself along the way.'

His coach told him that if he boxed just as he had been boxing all the week, then the gold medal would be his. But McTaggart knew that he would have to be more aggressive, that he was growing tired after a heavy programme, that his legs would not allow him to dance as freely as he had done in his earlier contests.

In the event, things worked even better than he had dared to hope. 'Kurschat was a strong man, hellish strong,' says Dick. 'I put him down twice and I heard myself saying: "Please stay down. Please don't get up." But he just came on as strong as if I'd never touched him. We were both very tired in the last round but I just tried to keep out of trouble because I thought I'd won it. And when they gave me the decision, well, I nearly broke down then. People jumped into the ring and lifted me up on their shoulders. I felt like a king.'

Yet even the gold medal ceremony did not prove the final coronation for Dick McTaggart. He was asked by officials to remain in the arena until all the finals were over. Then he was awarded the Val Barker trophy, the coveted award for the most stylish boxer of the Olympics. Britain's seven-man team had emerged from Melbourne with two gold, one silver and two bronze medals, but McTaggart was the pick of the bunch; the pick, indeed, of the entire Games.

They lined the streets in their thousands upon his return to Dundee and the mayor sent him off to the shops to select a gold watch as the city's gesture of appreciation. He was also paraded around the Dundee football ground in an open-top bus. 'Treated like a king again,' he says.

Inevitably, the professional managers came calling with open cheque books. McTaggart listened, and turned them down. 'To turn pro, you've got to be dedicated,' he explains. 'I was dedicated to boxing, but not for seven days a week. I like a social life as well. I've no regrets at all about my decision. I mean, money isn't everything. And when I think of some of the injuries you can pick up in professional boxing, well, I'm glad I was clever enough to stay away from those dangers.' Not that life was easy for him outside the ring. He tended to take jobs which allowed him time off for training and competing. When he entered the RAF, he was a butcher. When he came out, he went into a sweet factory, then worked with a brother as a joiner's mate. He moved to Glasgow to work as a rat catcher, to the great delight of the headline writers, and for the past 24 years he has worked as an oil technician for Rolls Royce.

Melbourne was to prove the peak of his boxing career, yet that career carried on for a further nine years. He won a bronze medal at the Rome Olympics of 1960, losing to the eventual winner, Kazimierz Pazdzior of Poland, and at the 1964 Tokyo Games — when he became the only British boxer to compete in three Olympics — he lost in the quarter-finals, again to the eventual gold medallist. There were also gold medals at the Commonwealth Games and European Championships, and no fewer than five ABA titles, after the last of which, in 1965, he decided to retire. 'I was 30 years old and I was starting to get hit,' he says. 'I realised that it really could be a rough game.'

McTaggart continued in the sport, coaching the skills which he had possessed to such an extravagant degree. He became a national coach and, in that capacity, worked at the Los Angeles Olympics and at the Edinburgh and Auckland Commonwealth Games. He confesses that he grew more excited when coaching than he had ever done as a competitor. Now, at least for a while, he has decided to take a rest from the sport which has dominated his life.

He was asked how he would like to be remembered a hundred years hence, and he thought for a while about his answer. 'Just say I was a gold medal winner,' he said. 'And a long time from now, well, my grandchildren would know all about it. That'd be great . . .'

DOUGLAS McWHIRTER

ASSOCIATION FOOTBALL

1912 Stockholm
Gold   Soccer Team

McWhirter had travelled to Stockholm in hope rather than in expectation of a game. But injury to first-choice centre-half Ted Hanney meant a shake-up in the British side and the selectors brought him in for the final against Denmark. The team had won their two previous games comfortably and the changes did not seem to affect the side as they ran out 4–2 winners against Denmark, who were reduced to ten men during the second half.

Born in Kent in 1886, McWhirter played for Leicester Fosse and won four England amateur caps. His greatest moment, apart from the Olympics, came in 1911 when he played for Bromley in the FA Amateur Cup final side that beat Bishop Auckland by a single goal at Herne Hill.

He died in Plumstead, Kent, in 1966, aged 80.

W.J. MADDISON

YACHTING

1920 Antwerp
Gold   7 Metres Class

Maddison was among the four-man crew of the *Ancora* which took the 7 metres class Olympic title in Ostend. He was recruited by the boat's owner Cyril Wright who was a friend and fellow member of the Royal Burnham Yacht Club in Essex. The *Ancora* came from a race down to beat the Norwegian boat *Fornebo* and take the gold medal 2–1.

HARRY MALLIN

BOXING

1920 Antwerp
Gold   Middleweight

1924 Paris
Gold   Middleweight

The most successful British boxer in Olympic history with two gold medals to his name, Mallin was born in Shoreditch, east London, in 1892. He was a London policeman and a hugely successful amateur boxer, winning five ABA titles.

His first Olympic title came in Antwerp and after overcoming the American Sam Lagonia – a decision which prompted the US team to consider withdrawing from the competition – he fought through to a final against the knockout specialist Georges Prudhomme, a French-Canadian soldier. It was a tough fight, but Mallin took the judges' verdict and was chaired from the ring. He returned in 1924 to defend his title in Paris and after two straightforward victories in the early rounds he then faced the 23-year-old local hero Roger Brousse in the quarter-finals. It is here that the story takes on almost comic-book proportions.

After three rounds Mallin seemed to have won the bout comfortably, but while the judges were deliberating he approached the Belgian referee and complained that Brousse had been biting him, pointing to several sets of well-defined teeth marks on his chest and shoulder. In these early Games the referee was located outside the ring, making it difficult for him to spot foul play in the clinches. The official was then handed the result and, to the astonishment of the British camp and amid wild euphoria at the Velodrome d'Hiver, announced a 2–1 majority win for Brousse. Mallin, who had never lost a fight in his life, was dumbfounded but left the ring without saying a word.

The British decided not to protest but a Swedish official who saw the fight lodged an official complaint. It then transpired that Brousse's previous opponent had also protested about being bitten during the fight. After hours of deliberation the Jury of Appeal ruled the bites were unintentional, upholding Brousse's view that he had a habit of snapping his jaw when he threw a punch – then disqualified him anyway! When this was announced to the crowd the following day pandemonium broke out in the arena; Brousse was carried shoulder-high around the ring and police were called to repel the hundreds of demonstrators baying for the blood of the jury.

Despite the commotion, the now reinstated Mallin managed to outpoint his Belgian opponent Joseph

Beecken in the semi-final, before meeting team-mate Jack Elliot in the final. The French fans made the bout difficult for the boxers, but impossible for the spectators. They stood in front of the ring, screaming at the judges and at Mallin. The few reports that remain suggest Mallin won a close but uninspired fight, before retreating to the relative safety of the changing area.

The British Olympic Report, usually so matter-of-fact, reported: 'We are unable to give a more detailed description of the fight, owing to the fact that we were seated in the centre of a group of excited and gesticulating Frenchmen, who, not content with making themselves look ridiculous . . . also refused to allow anyone in their proximity to get a view of the fight.' The furore prompted calls for the banning of boxing, the banning of the Olympics and, in one newspaper, war with France!

This was Mallin's last fight; he retired with a record of more than 300 undefeated bouts. Although he returned to the Metropolitan Police, he continued to work in amateur boxing, managing the 1936 and 1952 British Olympic teams and serving as an executive officer for many years with the ABA. He was involved, as a commentator, in the first-ever television broadcast of boxing, for the BBC at Alexandra Palace. He died in Lewisham, south London, in 1969, aged 77.

SHOLTO MARCON

HOCKEY

1920 Antwerp
Gold   Hockey Team

Marcon was a skilful inside-forward and a key component of a formidable front line in English hockey in the early 1920s.

Born in Headington, Oxfordshire, in 1890, Marcon was educated at Lancing School and then Oriel College, Oxford, where he won a hockey blue in his first year. He was made captain of Oxford in 1913, following in the footsteps of his father who had pioneered the sport there. In the same year he made his England debut – he eventually won 23 caps – and was an automatic choice for the Olympics in Antwerp, where England defeated Denmark 5–1 in their opening game before crushing Belgium 12–1. When France scratched owing to illness the gold medal was theirs.

He taught at Cranleigh College and was ordained in 1936, serving as a chaplain in the RAF and then vicar of Tenterden, in Kent, where he died in 1959.

ALBERT MARTIN

YACHTING

1908 London
Gold   12 Metres Class

Martin was a member of the ten-man crew aboard the *Hera* which won the 12 metres class event at the London Games without even appearing at the Olympic Regatta at Cowes. There were just two entries for the event, Thomas Glen-Coats' *Hera* and Charles McIvor's *Mouchette*. With one vessel on the Clyde and the other on Merseyside, the organisers decided to allow the event to take place a fortnight after Cowes – on the Clyde. That was to the advantage of *Hera*, since all the crew, including Martin, were members of the Royal Clyde Yacht Club and knew the course well. Predictably, *Hera* won both races to take the gold medal.

LEONARD MARTIN

YACHTING

1936 Berlin
Gold   6 Metres Class

Three of the five-man crew aboard the gold medal-winning *Lalage* worked together on Britain's 1934 America's Cup effort. Martin, along with Miles Belville and Chris Boardman, crewed on Tommy Sopwith's *Endeavour* and for a while it looked as if the aircraft pioneer had finally provided a winning British boat. *Endeavour* won its first two races only to see Mike Vanderbilt's expensive *Rainbow* fight back to win the series 4–2 and keep the prized trophy in the USA.

Martin, a 35-year-old south London tobacconist, was a member of the Royal Burnham Yacht Club and was invited to join the *Lalage* at the Olympic Regatta in Kiel. The boat pipped the Norwegians by a single point to take the gold, with Sweden in bronze medal position.

STEVE MARTIN

HOCKEY

1988 Seoul
Gold   Hockey Team

One of two Irishmen in the Seoul squad, Martin qualified for his gold medal when he was sent on as a substitute with a minute remaining in the final against West Germany. He had not played in any of the previous games in the tournament, but as a vital squad member the team management decided to let him, and reserve goalkeeper Veryan Pappin, go on with Britain leading the Germans 3–1.

Born in Bangor, County Down, in 1959, Martin was a defender from the Holywood club and played for both Ireland and Britain. He opted to play for Britain at Barcelona, a good move considering the Irish team did not get through the qualifying competition, and is hoping to repeat his gold medal.

Martin works as a hockey development officer at the Ulster Sports Council.

KEN MATTHEWS

ATHLETICS

1964 Tokyo
Gold   20km Walk

One of Britain's most talented walkers, Matthews won major championships at distances between two and 20 miles. He contested five major international walks, winning four of them. The only one he lost was the 1960 Olympic 20km, in Rome, where he badly misjudged the pace, collapsed and dropped out in the burning heat.

Born in Birmingham in 1934, Matthews began his walking career at 18, joined the Sutton Coldfield Walking Club and first sprang to prominence in 1956 when he beat the three men selected for the British Olympic team, destined for Melbourne, in a ten-mile race. He also beat Britain's newly crowned European champion Stan Vickers in a five-mile race in 1958. From the beginning of the 1960s he was virtually unbeatable in domestic competition, winning 17 British titles, including six consecutive RWA ten miles. He won the Lugano Cup in 1961 and 1963, and the 1962 European Championships in Belgrade, but the crowning glory of his great career was the Tokyo Olympics.

His staunchest supporter was his wife Sheila, and his friends at the power station in Sutton Coldfield, where he worked as an electrician, raised the £742 required to send her to Tokyo to join him. Matthews judged the race perfectly to finish a minute and a half in front of East Germany's Dieter Linder in a new Olympic record of 1:29:34. His wife burst through the security cordon around the track to congratulate Matthews and worldwide television covered arguably the longest kiss in Olympic history!

Strangely, Matthews was the only gold medal winner from Tokyo not immediately honoured with the MBE. A campaign to rectify this error was mounted and 14 years after he crossed the line in Tokyo he made his trip to Buckingham Palace to receive the honour from the Queen.

M.K. MATTHEWS

SHOOTING

1908 London
Gold   Small-Bore Rifle Team
Silver   Small-Bore Rifle – Moving Target

Matthews was the star performer of the British team which took the small-bore rifle title. Shooting over 50 and 100 yards he scored 196 points, beating his three team-mates Humby, Pimm and Amoore. Together they scored an invincible 771 points to secure comfortably the gold from Sweden and France.

Matthews, who was a member of north London's Mansfield Rifle Club, took a silver in the small-bore 25-yard moving target competition after a keenly-fought contest with John Fleming. Both marksmen were tied on 24 points and Fleming took the gold after a shoot-off. Matthews also placed fourth in the small-bore rifle prone position event and ninth in the disappearing target competition.

ALEX MAUNDER

SHOOTING

1908 London
Gold   Clay Pigeon Team
Bronze   Clay Pigeon

1912 Stockholm
Silver   Clay Pigeon Team

The key member of Britain's clay pigeon team in London, Maunder was one of two members of the team to go on to defend their title four years later in Stockholm.

The six-man teams had to shoot in three rounds and hit a total of 105 birds. Canada's Walter Ewing had won the individual title and he was the captain of his team. Maunder had finished third in that competition but in the team event he outshot everyone – including Ewing – scoring 83 points to lead the British team to victory by just two points. Intriguingly, it was the same margin by which he beat Ewing's score and without Maunder's showing Britain would almost certainly have been relegated to silver medal position.

Born in Loxbear, Devon, in 1861, Maunder shot for a number of north London rifle clubs and for many years was rated the world's premier clay pigeon marksman. He returned to Olympic competition in 1912, when the British team took silver behind the United States, and was actually selected for the 1924 Paris Games, though he declined to compete.

He died in retirement at Bickleigh, near Tiverton in Devon, in 1929, just a day before his 71st birthday. He suffered a fatal heart attack while playing his nephew in the final of a local billiards competition at the village institute.

RICHARD MEADE

EQUESTRIAN

1968 Mexico City
Gold   Three-Day Event Team

1972 Munich
Gold   Three-Day Event
Gold   Three-Day Event Team

As an Olympic competitor Richard Meade stands head and shoulders above any other British rider. He remains the only Briton to win an individual

Olympic gold medal and his haul of three golds is unmatched.

Born in Chepstow, Monmouthshire, in 1938, Meade was soon immersed in the British equestrian culture. His parents were Joint Masters of Monmouth's Corre Hounds and he was educated at Lancing and Magdalene College, Cambridge, where he took an engineering degree. His Olympic career began in Tokyo in 1964, where he finished a commendable eighth in the individual competition on Barberry. Only a poor display in the show jumping had kept him out of the medals. The experience obviously hardened him for future Games and in Mexico he improved to fourth place in the individual, on Cornishman V. But with Derek Allhusen finishing second and Ben Jones fifth, the British team was assured of the team gold. Meade's finest Olympic achievement was reserved for the 1972 Games in Munich, where he rode Lauriston to victory in the individual competition and led Britain to a team gold. He tried to repeat the feat at Montreal in 1976, on Jacob Jones, but was pipped for the bronze medal by West Germany's Karl Schulz.

At Montreal he matched David Broome's record of competing in four Olympics, only to see Broome break the record by riding in Seoul in 1988. Meade also maintained a brilliant record outside the Olympic arena, winning gold in the victorious British team at the 1967 Europeans and the 1970 World Championships. He also won at the Badminton Horse Trials in 1969 and 1970.

Still very much involved in the sport, Meade joined the 11th Hussars on leaving Cambridge, then worked in the City. He is currently President of the British Equestrian Federation.

TIM MELVILL

POLO

1920 Antwerp
Gold   Polo Team

Melvill's father won a posthumous Victoria Cross for saving the regimental colours at the Isandhlwana Massacre during the Zulu Wars. Melvill himself won the DSO for bravery during the First World War in France.

Melvill was born in South Africa in 1877. His father was killed two years later, but he followed closely in his footsteps, attending Wellington School and the RMC Sandhurst, and joining the South Wales Borderers. But he moved across to the 17th Lancers where he was able to indulge his passion for horses and perfect his polo-playing skills.

He was selected for the British polo team which beat the Spanish 13–11 in the Antwerp final to take the gold, and went on to play for Britain against the USA in the Westchester Cup. A year after the Games he was appointed Assistant Military Attaché in Madrid, but he returned to England to take command of the amalgamated 17/21 Lancers. Coincidentally, in 1927 he handed over command of the regiment to his Antwerp team-mate Vivian Lockett.

On retiring from the army he became the polo correspondent of *The Field* and he died in Norfolk in 1951.

LEON MEREDITH

CYCLING

1908 London
Gold   Three-Lap Pursuit

1912 Stockholm
Silver   Team Road Race

One of the most successful British cyclists of all time, Meredith was unfortunate not to fare better at the London Olympics. He suffered punctures and falls in the 20-kilometre and 100-kilometre finals when highly fancied to win and came away from the Games with just one team medal, albeit a gold.

Born in London in 1882, he was in the happy position of enjoying the patronage of a wealthy uncle who encouraged his cycling career to such a degree that Meredith was able to work at the sport almost full-time. He had a full-time trainer, pacing machine, masseur, the best facilities and was able to travel the world and face the top opposition. In 1902 he won the first of his seven national titles at Crystal Palace, over 50 miles.

Had the British sent a team to the St Louis Olympics in 1904, Meredith would certainly have brought back cycling medals, but he had to wait until 1908 for Olympic competition. By then he had won the seventh of his titles, just a fortnight before the Games, over 25 miles; taken seven world titles at 100 kilometres; and was generally regarded as the best long-distance cyclist in the world. However, after the individual disasters of the Games he had to be content with success in the three-lap pursuit, over 1810 metres, alongside team-mates Clarrie Kingsbury, Ben Jones and Ernie Payne. The British team were far ahead of the rest of the entrants and in the Olympic final they beat the Germans by ten seconds.

Meredith made a second bid for Olympic glory in Stockholm in 1912, but the Swedes held only one

Britain's gold medal-winning three-lap pursuit team: (left to right) Leon Meredith, Ernie Payne, Clarrie Kingsbury and Ben Jones.

The Roehampton team, winners of the 1908 polo tournament held at Hurlingham: (left to right) Charles Miller, Patteson Nickalls, George Miller and Herbert Wilson.

cycling event – a 320-kilometre road race, with an individual and team winner. Though well beyond the distance he was used to, Meredith did well to finish fourth overall and, with fellow Briton Fred Grubb taking the silver, the British team were able to claim a team silver medal. He made a final Olympic bid in 1920 in the 175-kilometre road race, but at 38 years old he was no match for the younger men in the field and finished 18th.

After Stockholm, Meredith used his cycling expertise and national fame to produce and sell a new racing tyre. The company he founded was a major success and made him a wealthy man. Curiously for a cyclist, Meredith indulged in roller skating and was British amateur champion in 1911 and 1912. He even used some of the money from his uncle and his tyre business to build a roller rink in north London. Meredith died of a heart attack while on a winter holiday in Davos, Switzerland, in 1930.

FRED MERRIMAN

TUG OF WAR

1908 London
Gold   Tug of War Team

Britain selected no fewer than three teams to compete in the tug of war competition at the London Games, but the powerful City of London police side were completely dominant. Merriman, born in Campden, Gloucestershire, in 1873, was the heaviest member of the team, at 16st 5lbs. The City went into five months' hard training for the Games, under the supervision of coach and manager Inspector Harry Duke. This training and the sheer size of the City team proved too much for Britain's second and third teams – Metropolitan Police K Division and Liverpool Police – and they won the gold medal comfortably.

There were some eyebrows raised, most notably by the Americans, at the footwear used by the British teams, but the Olympic officials rejected the protests after they were told the teams were wearing standard issue police boots!

Merriman died in his home town in 1940.

CHARLES MILLER

POLO

1908 London
Gold   Polo Team

One of two brothers in the winning 1908 Olympic polo team, Miller took up the game when he graduated and moved to India.

Born in London in 1868, he went to Marlborough School and Trinity College, Cambridge, before he was sent to the Far East to work in the family's merchanting business. On a summer break in England Miller founded the Roehampton Polo Club and when it began to prosper he resigned his position in India and became the club's managing director. Having played in the GB v USA Westchester Cup, he was an experienced campaigner and entered the club as a team for the 1908 Olympic tournament, held at Hurlingham.

There were only two other entrants, Hurlingham and All-Ireland, and with the Irish drawing a bye to the final, the two English clubs played for the other place. Hurlingham, depleted by injury and the absence of their best player, the Duke of Roxburghe, owing to an illness in the family, were beaten 4–1 by Roehampton. Charles Miller played a solid role at the back of the Roehampton side and in the final they completely outclassed the Irish. Leading 7–0 at half-time, they eased up and coasted in at 8–1 for the gold.

Miller served in France as an officer during the First World War, then returned to Roehampton where he worked until a year before his death in London in 1951.

GEORGE MILLER

POLO

1908 London
Gold   Polo Team

Like his younger brother Charles, George Miller was heavily involved in the Roehampton club which won the Olympic title. Born a year earlier, he was also educated at Marlborough and Trinity College, Cambridge, and learned to play polo in India at an early age. He had a rather better national polo record, winning six Champion Cups and two Ranelagh Cups, as well as captaining the British side in the hard-fought Westchester Cup against the Americans.

He was also a more flamboyant player than his brother and finished the 1908 tournament as top scorer with five goals, including four in the first half of the final! In the semi-final Roehampton beat Hurlingham 4–1, on their great rivals' own ground, to qualify for the final against All-Ireland, whom they trounced 8–1 to take the Olympic title. Miller also served in France during the First World War and returned to work at Roehampton, with his other brother Edward. He died on a cruise in the Caribbean in 1935.

JERRY MILLNER

SHOOTING

1908 London
Gold   Free Rifle

Millner was nearly 60 years old when he won the free rifle competition at the London Games, making him the oldest Briton to have won an Olympic gold medal. He was born in Ireland, but the exact date is unknown as registration had not begun. He first came to prominence in shooting circles as a member of the Irish team that toured the United States in the 1870s and was selected for the British team that visited the US a decade later. Millner served with the Territorial Army as a lieutenant in the Finsbury Rifles and then the Carlow Militia, which was disbanded in 1908 with Colonel Millner as the last commanding officer.

At the London Games Millner took part in what was essentially the long-distance shooting event, hitting a six by ten target located 1000 yards away, with a three-foot bull. He scored 98 points out of a possible 100 to secure the gold by five points from the USA's Captain Kellogg Casey and Britain's Maurice Blood.

A year before the Games he joined the National Rifle Association's ruling council and served until the outbreak of the First World War. In retirement in Ireland he devoted much of his time to breeding sporting dogs and wrote a book on the subject. He died in Dublin in 1931, aged 82.

EDWIN MILLS

TUG OF WAR

1908 London
Gold   Tug of War Team

1912 Stockholm
Silver   Tug of War Team

1920 Antwerp
Gold   Tug of War Team

Mills was one of only three men to pull for Britain in the medal-winning tug of war teams across three Olympic Games. Police officer Mills, born in Stretton Bushville, Warwickshire, in 1878, was past his 42nd birthday when he won his last gold in Antwerp, in what was to be the last Olympic tug of war competition.

Weighing 15st 9lb, Mills was in the British team that won its first Olympic title at the London Games, easily beating Liverpool 2–0 in the final. He was also in the team defeated by Sweden in 1912 and returned to the Olympic fray after the First World War to win in 1920, holding off the challenge of Holland, Belgium and the USA.

Mills died in 1946 in Ashby-de-la-Zouche, Leicestershire.

HARRY MITCHELL

BOXING

1924 Paris
Gold   Light-Heavyweight

When Mitchell set off with the British team for the Paris Olympics he had already clinched his third successive ABA light-heavyweight title. Born in Tiverton, Devon, in 1898, he boxed for the Polytechnic Club and worked his way through Britain's amateur ranks. At the Velodrome d'Hiver he found the competition reasonably straightforward until he faced the awkward Italian Carlo Saraudi in the semi-final. Saraudi's spoiling tactics and persistent holding could have proved difficult for Mitchell, but he managed to build a good enough lead in the final round to get the judges' verdict. The final pitted him against Denmark's Thyge Petersen, but again Mitchell had little difficulty in outboxing him and taking the gold.

Jerry Millner took the free rifle title in 1908 to become the oldest Briton to win an Olympic gold medal.

Adrian Moorhouse competing in the USA in the run-up to the Seoul Games,
where he became Olympic 100 metres breaststroke champion.

BELLA MOORE

SWIMMING

1912 Stockholm
Gold   4 × 100 Metres Freestyle Relay

Bella Moore remains the youngest British woman ever to win an Olympic gold medal at a Summer Games. She was just 17 when she earned selection for the first-ever women's swimming team in Stockholm.

Born in Tynemouth, Northumberland, in 1894, she swam for Glasgow's Premier Club and held a variety of Scottish titles and records, although she never won a British championship. In Stockholm she won the first Olympic women's swimming race – the first 100-metre heat – thereby setting the first-ever Olympic record of 1:29.8. It was immediately beaten and Moore went out of the competition in the semi-finals. But she returned to help the British relay team to victory by more than 12 seconds over the Germans, in a world record time of 5:52.8.

She died in 1975.

F.W. MOORE

SHOOTING

1908 London
Gold   Clay Pigeon Team

Moore captained Britain's successful clay pigeon team at the London Games, though he was not among the top scorers. He had finished equal seventh in the individual event and in the three-round team event he scored 60 points from a possible 105. But the six-man team score of 407 was enough to pip the Canadians by just two points and take the gold.

ADRIAN MOORHOUSE

SWIMMING

1988 Seoul
Gold   100 Metres Breaststroke

One of the highlights for the millions of TV viewers who stayed up through the night to watch the 1988 Olympics unfold was the success of Adrian Moorhouse. Despite producing the best times in the years leading up to the Games he had failed to land one of the world's top honours.

Born in 1964 in Bradford, Yorkshire, he won his first major title at just 18, when he took the gold at the Commonwealth Games, and a year later he won the European Championships 200 metres breaststroke. In the Los Angeles Olympics the following year, he finished fourth in the 100 metres and won the 200 metres B final. He won the 100 at both the 1985 and 1987 Europeans and after adding a second Commonwealth gold in 1986 he was among the favourites to win the 100-metre event in Seoul. He did it the hard way. Lying in sixth place at halfway, after the Soviet Union's Dimitri Volkov had set a blistering pace from the start, Moorhouse slowly began to edge back. At the line it was desperately close and only when Moorhouse's name was flashed up on the scoreboard did he know he had snatched the gold from Hungary's fast-finishing Karoly Guttler.

Amid scenes of great family celebrations, Moorhouse's father, sitting in the stand, told a TV reporter, with masterful understatement: 'He left it late, did that boy.' His winning margin was just a 100th of a second and his time 1:02.04. He was eliminated in the heats of the 200 metres event – not surprising in the wake of his earlier success – but returned home to a hero's welcome.

In 1989 he finally landed the world record that had eluded him for so long. He shaved 0.16 off American Steve Lundquist's five-year-old 100 metres record at the European Championships in Bonn, in 1:01.49, before going on to win his fourth successive title. He took his third Commonwealth title in 1990 and equalled his own world record in the same year at Crystal Palace.

STEWART MORRIS

YACHTING

1948 London
Gold   Swallow Class

One of the century's most distinguished sailors, Morris learned to sail on his father's punt on the Norfolk Broads. Born in 1909, Morris spent his childhood summers playing on the narrow rivers on a variety of craft, usually with close friends John Winter and the late Sir Peter Scott. Morris won his first regatta at the age of ten at Oulton Broad.

Educated at Charterhouse and Trinity College, he raced for the Cambridge University Cruising Club and in 1934 helped found the Oxford and Cambridge Sailing Club. His glittering sailing career included a record 12 victories in the Prince of Wales Cup for the International 14 Class, spanning the years 1932 to 1965. This, he once revealed, was due partly to his own dedication and skills, but also to his habit of meticulously writing up race reports after every competition, which he built into a reference work for all waters.

He was awarded the OBE in 1945 for wartime service in the RNVR, particularly during the Normandy landings, leaving as Acting Temporary Commander after serving on the destroyer HMS *Ambuscade* and the carrier *Indomitable*. He was an exceptional tactical seaborne fighter, likening it to three-dimensional dinghy sailing. After selection as an alternate for the Berlin Olympics, Morris joined David Bond for the 1948 Games, held in Torquay, and, in the keelboat *Swift*, came within 15 seconds of losing the gold medal to a Portuguese crew. Morris collected a variety of other titles, including the 1938 Europeans, 1949 and 1951 Firefly Nationals and four Swallow Nationals. He could still be spotted sailing his Olympic winning craft in Chichester Harbour well into the late 1970s.

The family's successful hop business meant he could afford time not just to compete but to help administer the sport he loved, serving on the Royal Yachting Association's council until 1969, and he was instrumental in setting up many of the sport's racing rules. He succeeded the Duke of Edinburgh as President of the RYA from 1980 to 1983. In 1950 he was involved in the opening of reservoirs for sailing and belonged to no fewer than 16 yacht clubs. He died at a nursing home near Chichester in 1991.

ROBERT MORRISON

ROWING

1924 Paris
Gold   Coxless Fours

A member of the great Eton and Trinity four that stayed together for almost six years, Morrison reaped a rich harvest of rowing medals and trophies. Born in Richmond, Surrey, in 1902, Morrison won his blue in the Cambridge crew at the 1923 Boat Race. He won a staggering eight events at Henley, although his most successful year was 1925, just after the Paris Games.

In France the Trinity crew of Macnabb, Morrison, Sanders and Eley found the going easy. They had stayed together through Eton and now at Cambridge, and in the final their experience told. They beat off the Canadian challenge quite comprehensively to take the gold. The following year Morrison won three Henley events, the Goblets, Stewards and Visitors, before retiring from competitive rowing. He became an engineer and eventually retired to Cambridge, where he died in 1980.

LUCY MORTON

SWIMMING

1924 Paris
Gold   200 Metres Breaststroke

Britain's world record-holder in the event, Irene Gilbert, was widely tipped for the gold, while 26-year-old second-string swimmer Lucy Morton was coming to the end of her marvellous career. Incredibly, Gilbert finished only fifth in the final because of illness and Morton produced an astonishing burst of speed to take the gold in what would be her last major race.

Born in Blackpool in 1898, she won her first senior title in 1912 – the 100 yards Northern Counties breaststroke. A year later she posted two world records: the 150 yards backstroke and the 200 yards breaststroke. She could also swim distance and in 1914 she won the women's mile in the River Mersey.

In 1916 she bettered her two world records, while she also came second in the Kew to Putney race in the River Thames and was the first woman home in the cross-Morecambe Bay swim. Disappointment followed when it was discovered there were to be no backstroke or breaststroke events for women at the 1920 Antwerp Olympics, but she gained some consolation when the Amateur Swimming Association added her favourite distances to their calendar – and she won them both.

Her career seemed to be winding down when the Olympic Committee introduced a breaststroke event to the Paris programme and she made the team. At the Games she came through the heats and, after trailing America's Agnes Geraghty for more than 150 metres, put on a great finish to snatch the gold in 3:33.2 – some 13 seconds outside Gilbert's world record.

She married in 1927 and soon after became a well-known swimming teacher and coach in Blackpool, helping three local swimmers to international honours. She finally retired in 1972. She died in her native town in 1980, aged 82, and a few years later was inducted into the International Swimming Hall of Fame, in Fort Lauderdale, as an Honour Swimmer.

ROBERT MURRAY

SHOOTING

1912 Stockholm
Gold   Small-Bore Rifle Team – 50 Metres

Edinburgh-born Murray was a member of the four-man British team that took the gold in the 50-metre small-bore team event in Stockholm. He joined forces with Pimm, Lessimore and Pepé to build an impressive total of 762 points and win by 14 points from the Swedes and the Americans. Thirty-eight-year-old Murray also placed fifth in the individual small-bore event featuring a 25-metre disappearing target and sixth in the individual prone position.

He founded the nation's first small-bore rifle club, Urmston Miniature Rifle Club, and served as the club chairman for many years.

PHILIP NEAME

SHOOTING

1924 Paris
Gold   Running Deer Double Shot Team

Neame holds the distinction of being the only man to be awarded the Victoria Cross, a knighthood and an Olympic gold medal. This extraordinary achievement in no way flatters a fine sportsman and war hero.

Born in Faversham, Kent, in 1888, he was educated at Cheltenham College and then the RMA Woolwich, after which he was commissioned into the Royal Engineers. During the First World War he served in France and won the VC at Neuve Chapelle in 1915. Two years later he was awarded the DSO and after the war rose through the ranks to reach lieutenant general in 1940. He received his knighthood for services to both war efforts in 1946.

Neame was a natural sportsman: he was a keen hockey and polo player, skier and mountaineer, as well as a crack shot. At the 1924 Olympics in Paris he was part of the four-man British team which took the gold by a single point from Norway. The Running Deer competitions were held at a range in the beautiful surroundings of Versailles, and Neame was the only member of the team who did not take part in the individual events.

He served with distinction during the Second World War and escaped from an Italian PoW camp, where he wrote his autobiography. In it he makes little reference to the Olympics, save to mention he thought he was representing the British Empire rather than just Great Britain.

A member of various army shooting teams, he was a familiar face at Bisley and maintained his interest in shooting in retirement. He died in his native Kent in 1978, aged 89.

GEORGE NEVINSON

SWIMMING

1908 London
Gold   Water Polo Team

English international defender Nevinson formed an almost impenetrable back line with the Scottish giant George Cornet. Together they reduced Belgium to few scoring opportunities at the open-air pool at London's White City stadium. Britain had eased into the final after they drew a bye in the first round and Austria scratched from the semi-final. Belgium were no match for the slick passing and non-stop swimming of the British side and went down 9–2. Nevinson, born in Wigan in 1882, swam for Salford SC and would have been selected for the Olympic team to defend their title in Sweden but for injury.

A joiner with the Lancaster Council, he died in 1963.

QUEENIE NEWALL

ARCHERY

1908 London
Gold   National Round

Sybil 'Queenie' Newall had a similarly privileged social background to Britain's other gold medal-winning archer of the London Games, Willy Dod. Her family were prominent in high society, owning a large estate at Hare Hill in Lancashire, where the family tradition dated back to the fourteenth century.

Newall joined the fashionable Cheltenham Archers in 1905 and what began as a pleasurable hobby turned into a passion when she won dozens of competitions around the country. Curiously, the woman generally regarded as Britain's finest archer, Alice Leigh, decided to miss the Olympics and concentrate on the British Championships. It is reasonable to suggest that Leigh would certainly have won the event as her record would show 22 national titles between 1882 and 1922. However, Newall won the two-day Olympic competition by 43 points from Lottie Dod, who was the sister of Willy and an ex-Wimbledon tennis champion. Newall, at 53, became the oldest woman to win an Olympic gold medal – a record that still stands.

She was beaten in the national championships just a week after the Olympics by Leigh, though Newall did take the title in 1911 and 1912. She continued to take part in competitions after the war and her last recorded score was with the Cheltenham Archers in 1928, when she was 74. She died less than a year later in Cheltenham.

J. NICHOLAS

ASSOCIATION FOOTBALL

1900 Paris
Gold   Soccer Team

Upton Park Football Club had played three games on their September tour of 1900, in Dorchester, Yeovil and Weymouth. The fourth fixture was in Paris at the Olympic soccer tournament. On the day of the game the regular centre-forward Harrower was replaced by Nicholas. The new leader of the attack justified his inclusion, scoring a goal in both halves as Great Britain's representatives defeated the Parisian XI 4–0 to win the Olympic title.

GUY NICKALLS

ROWING

1908 London
Gold   Eights

The nineteenth century rowing legend Guy Nickalls was called out of retirement to ensure a British victory in the eights at the London Games. So anxious were the selectors about the challenge of Belgium's Club Nautique de Gand that they put together a team of the most experienced and decorated rowers available. Nickalls certainly fitted the bill. He had amassed an incredible 23 victories at 16 Henleys, dating back to 1887, and dominated the rowing scene with his brother Vivian.

Born in Sutton, Surrey, in 1866, Nickalls went to Eton and Magdalen College, Oxford, and rowed in five Boat Races. Such was the domination of the Nickalls brothers that their father donated a special Challenge Cup in 1895 to commemorate their Goblets successes. Guy's last Henley victory came in 1907 in the Stewards Cup, after which he retired from competitive rowing. But when he got the call from Leander to take part in the Olympics, he did not think twice. In the event, the threat of the Belgians was greater than their performance, and the Leander crew beat them comfortably by two lengths to take the gold.

It was his last race and at 41 he became the oldest gold medallist in Olympic rowing history. He maintained an interest in the sport as the rowing correspondent of the *Morning Post*. When the First World War broke out he was approaching his 50th birthday, yet he enlisted in the Royal Engineers and supervised bayonet training in France.

A City stockbroker by profession, he went back to the financial world after the war and was able to see his son Guy, known as Gully Nickalls, win two Olympic silver medals in the 1920 and 1928 British eights, before he died after a car crash in Leeds, in 1935, on his way to a fishing holiday in Scotland.

PATTESON NICKALLS

POLO

1908 London
Gold   Polo Team

Nickalls was the only blue on the Roehampton team for the 1908 Olympic tournament, having played three times for Oxford before the turn of the century. Born in Widdlington, Essex, in 1876, he went to Rugby before going up to New College, Oxford, where he began to attract national attention as a fine polo player. He fought in the Boer War in the Durham Light Infantry and was involved in the Relief of Ladysmith. After the war he became a member of the stock exchange and was able to use the money he made to spend time on his polo and other sporting pursuits.

He was a member of the growing Roehampton Club and was selected to represent them in the 1908 Olympic tournament, which comprised just three entries – Roehampton, Hurlingham and All-Ireland. The Irish won a bye to the final, so Roehampton had to beat Hurlingham, which they did 4–1, before taking the gold by completely outclassing the Irish 8–1 in the final. Nickalls scored three goals in the tournament, including Roehampton's eighth in the final.

He served his old regiment in the First World War and won a DSO for bravery in 1918 before returning to the City, where he spent the rest of his working life. He died in Rugby, Warwickshire, in 1946.

DANNY NIGHTINGALE

MODERN PENTATHLON

1976 Montreal
Gold   Modern Pentathlon Team

The youngest member of Britain's gold medal trio, Nightingale had just turned 22 when he left for Montreal. Born in Redruth, Cornwall, in 1954, he was studying engineering at the University of Sussex, but despite his tender years he was British champion in Olympic year and for the following two years.

In Montreal the team had battled to fifth place

after the first four events, but the final cross-country was their speciality. The team ran brilliantly to overhaul the four teams in front of them and take the gold medal. Nightingale finished tenth in the individual event and returned to Olympic competition in Moscow four years later, this time as team captain. He finished 15th individually and the team, which included Peter Whiteside and Nigel Clark, finished eighth.

One record Nightingale still holds is as the only Western pentathlete to win the Spartakiad, in the Soviet Union, which he claimed in 1979.

Married with four children, he worked for many years as an executive for the Modern Pentathlon Association, helping to develop the sport in Britain, and is now teaching physical education, humanities and history at a school near his home in North Yorkshire.

ALAN NOBLE

HOCKEY

1908 London
Gold   Hockey Team

England won the first-ever Olympic hockey competition in what was tantamount to a home nations championship. Only the four home countries took part and England crushed Ireland 8–1 in the final.

Noble, who played for Huyton, Formby, Bebington and Alderley Edge, played left-half in a tournament in which England scored 24 goals and conceded just three. He played three other matches in 1908 and made no further impact on the international hockey scene.

EVAN NOEL

RACKETS

1908 London
Gold   Singles
Bronze   Doubles

One of the very few Olympians to attain a gold medal without actually having to compete for it, Noel battled through to the final of the 1908 rackets tournament only to find his opponent could not play. The final was supposed to be a duel between Noel, the 1907 amateur rackets champion, and fellow Briton Henry Leaf. But Leaf had injured his

Lucy Morton ended her career on a high note when she won the 200 metres breaststroke in Paris in 1924.

Heavyweight wrestler Con O'Kelly took gold in the 1908 freestyle competition.

Albert Oldman, who won the heavyweight boxing title in 1908.

playing hand in defeating J.J. Astor in the semi-finals and doctors advised him not to continue. Consequently, Noel was awarded a walkover, the match and the gold medal without having to swing a racket.

Born in Stanmore, Middlesex, in 1879, Noel attended Winchester School and Trinity College, Cambridge, where he studied law and captained the cricket team. In 1901 he was admitted into the Inner Temple, but two years later he retreated from the legal business and took up the post of Sports Editor at *The Times*, a job he enjoyed until doctors warned that his failing health was caused by the long hours and advised him to quit. This he did, in 1909, and in 1914 he was appointed the secretary and manager of Queen's Club, where he worked until his death in 1928.

A keen historian of the court game scene, his daughter Susan became a leading tennis and squash player, three times British champion and the first foreigner to win a US squash title. She wrote extensively about the game until her death in October 1991.

CON O'KELLY

WRESTLING

1908 London
Gold   Heavyweight Freestyle

Although he was born and raised in Ireland, O'Kelly learned the rudiments of the sport while serving as a fireman in Hull. A tall, powerful man, he had left Ireland in 1903 to find work in England and discovered something of a wrestling tradition in the local fire brigade. His size and strength made him an almost instant success and within four years he had risen from local fire service events to the British Championship. At 6ft 3in and weighing almost 16 stone, O'Kelly certainly measured up to the sport – he had a 50½-inch chest and a 22½-inch neck!

In 1908 a fire-fighting accident prevented him from defending his national title, but he was fit enough to be selected for the London Games and eased through to a final clash with the 33-year-old reigning American champion Jacob Gundersen. His veteran opponent was a Norwegian who had lived in New York for nine years and, although he was giving away 11 years to O'Kelly, he made it very tough for the Briton. In the first bout of the best-of-three series, O'Kelly managed to pin his opponent with just two minutes left on the clock. The second bout was over in a matter of minutes as the older Gundersen visibly tired, and the gold was O'Kelly's.

He too emigrated to the United States in 1922, but his family did not settle and soon returned to his native Ireland, where he spent the rest of his life farming. His son Cornelius Junior carried on the family's Olympic tradition by representing Britain in the 1924 Games as a heavyweight boxer.

Born in Glounthaune, County Cork, in 1886, O'Kelly died in Stockport in 1947.

ALBERT OLDMAN

BOXING

1908 London
Gold   Heavyweight

The heavyweight competition at the London Games was less than Olympian in standard and Oldman was hardly forced to break sweat to win the gold medal. Born in Mile End, east London, in 1883, Oldman served in the Horse Guards before joining the City of London police.

At the Olympics, the heavyweight competition was an all-British affair, with Oldman winning a place in the semi-finals by knocking out Manchester's Isaac Myrams in less than a minute of the first round. Injuries meant Oldman then had a bye in the semis and moved straight through to a final against Reading's Sid Evans, who was the reigning ABA champion. Evans should have been favourite, but he had hurt his shoulder in an earlier round and was having difficulty throwing hard punches. The aggressive Oldman knocked him out inside two minutes of the first round and took the gold medal without fighting more than a full round of boxing in the entire competition.

Two years after the Games he left England and joined the police in Ceylon.

JOHN OSBORN

YACHTING

1976 Montreal
Gold   Tornado Class

Reigning world champions John Osborn and brother-in-law Reg White were firm favourites to take the gold in the Tornado class at the Olympic Regatta in Kingston. The pair had won five major international competitions in the 1976 season and were deemed to be unbeatable in what was the first time the class — the speedy two-man catamaran — was included in the Olympic programme.

With gold medals a little thin on the ground for Britain elsewhere in the Games, it was heartening news when the pair performed brilliantly. Such was their domination that they won four of their first six races. They had the gold medal in the bag before the last race and were able to spectate on the final day. Both men were awarded OBEs in the New Year's Honours List after the Games. Osborn, born in 1945, now lives in Barrie, Ontario.

STEVE OVETT

ATHLETICS

1980 Moscow
Gold   800 Metres
Bronze 1500 Metres

The roar of the crowd has receded into memory, and Steve Ovett does not regret its passing. Reality is the estate on the Scottish borders, and there among the lakes and forests he finds the peace which he prizes most dearly. For three years, Ovett and his wife Rachel have found their fulfilment in the task of restoring the vast and beautiful house once owned by the Marquess of Queensberry. Together, they have brought the place alive, and Ovett views the achievement with the pride he once reserved for titles and records.

When he was at the peak of his powers, from the late 1970s to the mid-1980s, Ovett seemed to deliver those titles and records almost to order. From the English Schools 400 metres title in 1970 to the Commonwealth 5000 metres gold medal in 1986, he won virtually everything his sport had to offer. In the course of that extraordinary career, he set two world records at the mile and three at 1500 metres.

Yet he did more than even the statistics suggest. His longstanding rivalry with Sebastian Coe, his equally gifted contemporary, helped establish track and field as one of the most popular and vibrant sports in Britain. Ovett played a major part in creating the golden age of British athletics.

That English Schools success is recalled most warmly: 'I remember the whole family coming up to Solihull,' he says. 'All of them bundled into one car, and they'd all come to watch me. I was 14, and I was desperate to win it for them.'

He freely acknowledges his debt to his parents, Mick and Gay: 'They were supportive without being overpowering, which is very difficult,' he says. 'They weren't particularly well off, but they bought my equipment, clothes and things right

through to quite a late stage in my career, when there was virtually no money in the sport. They were tremendous.'

As he grew older and stronger, the basic speed of a 400 metres runner was supplemented by the strength required for 800 metres. His ascent was swift and inevitable, and by 1974, at the age of 18, he moved into world class with a silver medal at the European Championships in Rome.

By now, he had come under the influence of Harry Wilson, a shrewd and gifted coach, and together they worked towards the 1976 Olympics. But Montreal was not a happy experience, as he recalls: 'For the first time in a major championships, they ran the first lap in lanes. Muggins here had lane eight in the final, so I ran 400 metres without seeing anyone at all. Well, by the time we broke, there was a Cuban guy called Alberto Juantorena who was 20 yards in front. He won by a mile, and I didn't even get the chance to say goodbye to him.'

His performances in the seasons following Montreal suggested that he was ready to achieve something momentous in the Games of Moscow. In September 1977, he won the World Cup 1500 metres in Dusseldorf in 3:34.5, a race which Coe regards as the finest exhibition of 1500 metres running he has ever seen. 'It was one of those occasions when you're never breathing heavily at any stage, when you know you could have taken seconds off the world record,' says Ovett.

The European 1500 metres title was won in the following year in Prague, and on 1 July 1980 he made his Olympic intentions clear with a world mile record of 3:48.8 in Oslo. He returned to the Norwegian capital two weeks later, on the very eve of the Games, to equal the world 1500 metres record while easing up. With Coe revealing similarly daunting form, the whole world awaited their showdown in Moscow. And not only awaited, but took sides with a kind of partisan fervour that British athletics had never previously known.

Ovett had refused to speak to the press for several seasons, following a post-race argument at Crystal Palace. Coe, on the other hand, was eloquent and eminently approachable. Most of the media were rooting for the younger, smoother man; the public, you sensed, had a soft spot for the irascible rebel. 'Looking back, it was an awesome task for both of us,' says Ovett. 'It wasn't simply a case of winning, but when and how you were going to win. The pressure Seb and I suffered was quite exceptional. And I was always aware that Seb was a far better athlete than I was. That's not false modesty, that's the truth. He was a far greater natural talent. So I just trained as hard as I could and thought: "Well, that's all we can do, Steve. Now just get out there and run."'

The conventional wisdom was that Coe, as world record-holder, would win the 800 metres, while Ovett would take the 1500, a distance at which he

Steve Ovett wins gold ahead of Seb Coe in the final of the 800 metres at the 1980 Moscow Games.

had been unbeaten since May 1977. But, having reached the final with economy of effort, Ovett was cautiously ambitious: 'I knew I wasn't as fast as Seb, but I also knew that somebody would have to run really well to stop me,' he says.

The 800 metres final was what Ovett calls 'A physical race'. As he says: 'There were some guys in there who were bouncing off me. I didn't run into them deliberately, they came across me and they found I was stronger than they thought. But I made the right moves at the right time. I was conscious that I mustn't make mistakes.' By contrast, Coe was making every mistake in the book, drifting off the pace, then becoming boxed as he worked his way back.

Coming off the final bend, Ovett was in a perfect position to deliver his kick, and his change of pace was brutally effective. 'I remember thinking: "I can't hear any noise, there's no footsteps, where are they? Better hold something back." But they never came. And that was it: "Steve Ovett: Olympic champion", I thought. "Thank God it's over."'

Ovett's gleeful relief contrasted sharply with his rival's dejected air at the medal ceremony. For the first time, Coe, the silver medallist, attracted a degree of criticism for his attitude. Ovett understood: 'Perhaps his reaction could have been a bit better,' he says, 'but I think he was true to himself, and that's what matters. He wasn't play-acting. He felt just as he looked on the rostrum.'

Declining once more to attend the official press conference, Ovett went off to celebrate with his mother and father and several bottles of Russian champagne. 'I ran into a few of the Irish fans at my parents' hotel, and they insisted on pouring champagne down my throat for God knows how long,' he says. 'I woke up feeling terrible, wanting to go home, and realising I had to go through it all over again.'

Looking back, Ovett believes that his mental preparation for the 1500 metres left everything to be desired. 'I'm not taking anything from Seb or any of the lads who ran in the final, because I tried my damnedest,' he says. 'But if the 1500 had been first, I'd probably have won that. And then lost the 800.'

In fact, the 1500 final represented Coe's revenge, ending Ovett's long unbeaten record at the distance and reducing the overwhelming favourite to bronze medal position. But they had each taken an Olympic title, the nation was satisfied and Ovett could return with a clear conscience to his celebrating Irish friends.

But soon he was back to doing what he did best, and within a month, as if to prove a point, he had lowered the world 1500 metres record in Koblenz.

Although his career continued to be littered with records, Ovett was never again to experience Olympic success. He worked himself into superb condition for the Los Angeles Games of 1984, but he was struck by a virus a few days before the start

of competition: 'My body wouldn't function,' he says, 'but my mind couldn't accept it. I just pushed myself too hard, and I passed out at the end of the 800 semi-final.'

He forced himself to defend his Olympic title, but there was nothing to offer and he finished last in the final. Amazingly, he actually qualified for the 1500 metres final, but he was carried from the track after collapsing in the closing stages. His courage at those Games won him even more admirers than ever before. 'I was amazed by the number of letters I got,' he says. 'It was the first time I've ever felt that a lot of people out there really did like me.'

The last significant flourish of his career came with the one title which had eluded him, and he takes a special pleasure in his Commonwealth 5000 metres gold medal.

Now, in his splendid Scottish retreat, he spends his days at a more leisurely pace with Rachel and his two young daughters, and only rarely does he look back to the way things were. 'I was very lucky,' he says. 'I was given a talent, not much of one, but a talent. Also an ability to train hard, and a sense of humour, which was vital. Against all the odds, I've been able to remain myself, just as Seb has. I think we're still friends, which is amazing when you consider what we've been through. You could say that I'm content.

'I think the Olympic title means more to other people than it does to me. They know how to bracket you when you've got a title. If I'd lost, I suppose they'd have called me "Steve Ovett, the failure". On balance, I prefer Olympic champion. But I never worry about it. If people want to look back in a hundred years at someone who could run around a track in three and a half minutes, and if they think that's wonderful, then that's fine. I've enjoyed it, it was great fun . . . but there really are more important things in life, aren't there?'

ANN PACKER

ATHLETICS

1964 Tokyo
Gold   800 Metres
Silver 400 Metres

The emotions flickered across her face like the pages of a fairy tale. There was triumph, of course, along with pain, exhaustion, delight and relief. But, above all, there was an almost tangible sense of amazement when Ann Packer crossed the finishing line.

This was not part of her plans, not the race which had brought her to Tokyo. Yet it carried a golden reward, just like any other event. And on that autumn afternoon in 1964, Ann Packer devoured her improbable Olympic title.

In retrospect, Tokyo may be seen as the last of the innocent Olympics. Free from terrorist threats, drug scandals or political boycotts, it offered a fitting stage for a fairy tale. As leading lady, Ms Packer was a piece of inspired casting.

Her talent was beyond question. From the earliest days of her Berkshire childhood, when she discovered that she could run faster than all the other children at primary school, she was destined for an exalted sporting career. For a time she was side-tracked by an ambition to play hockey for England at Wembley, but the phase passed when she joined Reading AC and started to put her ability to appropriate use.

In 1959, at the age of 17, she was English Schools 100 yards champion. In the following year, she became WAAA long jump champion and made her international debut at that event. In 1962 she reached the final of the European Championships 200 metres and the Commonwealth Games 80 metres hurdles. Eventually, in 1963, she discovered where her greatest gifts lay, when she took up 400 metres running and began to record a string of formidable times.

By then, she had become engaged to Robbie Brightwell, Britain's finest 400 metres runner and himself a solid prospect for Olympic gold in Tokyo. They found teaching posts in nearby schools and they began to train together with Tokyo as their target. Packer grew faster and stronger, and her successes in internationals against Hungary and the Soviet Union established her as favourite for the Olympic 400 metres. But the Games were only six months away when she made her first, faltering attempts at the two-lap event. She regarded it as an optional extra to the 400 metres, something to occupy her time when the serious business was done.

She loved Tokyo, loved the team spirit in the British camp — for which her fiancé, as captain, was largely responsible — loved the superb Japanese organisation and loved the riotous celebrations which had attended her room-mate Mary Rand's long jump gold medal. Her affection for the place grew even stronger when she set personal bests in the heat and semi-final of the 400 metres.

Came the final, and she ran a European record of 52.2 seconds, only to find Australia's Betty Cuthbert returning from semi-retirement to record 52.0 for the gold medal. 'I suppose a lot of people would be very happy with a silver medal,' she says. 'But I had hoped for the gold and I was favourite for the gold. I just wasn't good enough on the day, and I shall always be disappointed about it.'

Robbie Brightwell was even more disappointed with his own performance. He too had started as favourite for the 400 metres, but he was run out of

the medals and reduced to fourth place. Suddenly, Tokyo seemed a much less agreeable city.

Packer was left with her consolation event, upon which she embarked with no great relish. 'I found it very difficult to pick myself up next day for the heat of the 800,' she says. 'We lined up for the race in lanes. Now, in the two races I'd run at home, just before we left, we ran off an arc and just sort of jostled for position over the first few metres when the gun went. But in Tokyo we ran the first bend in lanes, and I didn't even know when I was supposed to cut in. So it was: run the first bend hard, then left-turn, then find a space on the kerb. Nobody would be in an Olympic final today after so little preparation. When it came to the tactics of the event, I was clueless. I ran some awful times, around 2 minutes 12 seconds, but I was in the final. I knew I could finish among the first few in the world. I'd been given a second chance.'

In fact, she refused to give herself a real chance of success. 'I'd been doing a lot of fast, high-quality speed work in preparation for the 400,' she says. 'I hadn't put in much mileage at all. But in theory I knew that if I was still with the field at 400 metres, and certainly at 600, my basic speed was good enough to take them on over the last 150. But athletics isn't theoretical; it's getting out there and doing it when it counts. I could see that, logically, a gold medal could be a possibility. But I didn't expect it.'

But she put the theory into glorious practice. She remembers every metre of the race; tracking the field, hanging on to the pace, then making the long run for home off the final bend when she passed runner after runner and came through in a new Olympic and European record of 2:01.1, ahead of Maryvonne Dupureur of France and Marise Chamberlain of New Zealand. She stumbled on past the line and fell into the arms of her fiancé: 'Robbie had just run the semi-final of the 4 × 400 metres relay and the team had managed to stay on the track to watch my race,' she says. 'It was really lovely to share that moment with my friends.'

The relay team went on to win silver medals, but Ann Packer had run her last race. 'Robbie and I had decided to retire after Tokyo,' she says. 'I wouldn't do the same thing today, because I could have carried on and made a good living out of my gift. But things were different then. We had planned a December wedding and we wanted to start a family right away and I didn't want to combine having a family with training. It was a wonderful time for us, but we're both quite private people and it was nice to slip back out of the spotlight. I've never regretted my decision.'

The Brightwells now have three sons, of whom they are immensely proud. 'We exposed them to sport, but we didn't push them,' says Ann. The oldest, Gary, might have been a talented athlete but chose to run simply for pleasure, while Ian and

Ann Packer, gold medallist in the 800 metres in 1964, with fiancé Robbie Brightwell, silver medallist in the 4 x 400 metres relay.

David have made an impact in professional football with Manchester City.

Ann Packer now leads the quiet and pleasant life of a Cheshire housewife; gardening, entertaining, eternally pleased to have slipped out of that spotlight. But she can look back down the years and recognise the extraordinary gift she once possessed. 'Once you recognise that you have a talent,' she says, 'you have to be able to follow it through. The world's full of people with talent, but following it through is something quite different. There was nothing very special about me, except that I really wanted to do it. At that time in my life, I wanted it more than anything else.'

EDGAR PAGE

HOCKEY

1908 London
Gold   Hockey Team

A keen all-round sportsman, Page played cricket, football and hockey to a high standard. Born in Wolverhampton in 1884, he went to Repton School and qualified as a chartered accountant. In three matches of the London Games, the England team scored 24 goals and conceded just three, beating Ireland 8–1 in a completely one-sided final.

Page played centre-half for the Olympic side and made a total of 15 appearances for England between 1907 and 1920, playing mainly with the Wolverhampton and Northampton clubs. He played cricket for minor league Staffordshire and soccer for the Old Reptonians. During the First World War he won a Military Cross, and he died in his native Wolverhampton in 1956.

CHARLES PALMER

SHOOTING

1908 London
Gold   Clay Pigeon Team

1912 Stockholm
Silver   Clay Pigeon Team

The only man to compete in three British Olympic clay pigeon shooting teams, Palmer won his gold at the London Games. He was part of the six-man team that beat Canada, over three rounds at rain-sodden

Bisley, by just two points. Palmer, born in 1869 in Old Warden, Bedfordshire, then went on to help the British team to silver behind the United States in Stockholm. His farewell Olympic appearance came in the 1920 clay pigeon team, in Antwerp, where Britain finished outside the medals in fourth place.

VERYAN PAPPIN

HOCKEY

1984 Los Angeles
Bronze   Hockey Team

1988 Seoul
Gold   Hockey Team

Pappin made the journey to Seoul as reserve to the record-breaking British goalkeeper Ian Taylor and there seemed little prospect of his playing unless something unfortunate happened to the first-choice man. However, with a minute left on the clock in the Olympic final and Britain leading the West Germans 3–1, the British managers decided to put on the only two squad members who had not played just to ensure they received a medal. It was a magnanimous gesture in such a pressure situation, but the Germans did not threaten again and all 16 squad members were able to celebrate with a gold medal. Pappin, born in Henley-on-Thames in 1958, was able to add the gold to the bronze he picked up in Los Angeles four years earlier in similar circumstances.

The first-choice keeper for Scotland, his chances were limited until Taylor decided to step out of the international arena. For many years a PE officer in the RAF he left the force in 1990 and was unable to find a suitable job in civvy street. Despite being appointed Under-21 coach by the Hockey Association, he decided to teach PE to the United Arab Emirates Air Force and left Britain in 1991.

ADRIAN PARKER

MODERN PENTATHLON

1976 Montreal
Gold   Modern Pentathlon Team

Despite the experience of Jim Fox and the youth of Danny Nightingale, Adrian Parker was the key to Britain's success in the Montreal team event. He also figured in one of the most controversial incidents in Olympic history.

Born in Croydon in 1951, Parker had been the British champion in the year before the Games and was rated as one of the world's best runners in the event. He did not even let the bizarre incident involving a Soviet fencer upset him. It was while Boris Onischenko was fencing against Parker that the British team first noticed something strange about the Soviet athlete's epee. Parker lost his bout when Onischenko's automatic light registered a hit when Parker said he had not been touched. After the same thing happened to Jim Fox the officials took the weapon away for examination, discovered it had been tampered with and disqualified Onischenko and the Soviet team.

Britain was lying in fifth place after four events and hopes were high that with a good run a bronze or silver medal was possible. Parker, the first runner of the day, then produced a sensational run in the 4000-metre cross-country, coming home in 12 minutes and nine seconds – the fastest time ever recorded in Olympic competition. With Fox and Nightingale also running well, Britain managed to leapfrog over the four teams in front of them and take the gold from Czechoslovakia by just 108 points.

After Montreal Parker retired from competition and runs the family's music business in London.

BRIDGET PARKER

EQUESTRIAN

1972 Munich
Gold   Three-Day Event Team

Bridget Parker joined the British team for Munich as one of two reserve riders for the eventing team. The first event of the competition, the dressage, was due to start at 8am. Bridget received a telephone call at 6am telling her that she would be competing because team member Debbie West's horse Baccarat had gone lame. The team selectors judged Bridget and horse Cornish Gold to be stronger than the other reserve Lorna Clarke, so in she went. Within minutes she was walking the course and making preparations to start the competition.

With Meade winning the individual and Gordon-Watson finishing fourth, Bridget performed heroics to finish tenth and, as the third scoring member, to secure the team gold. The trio performed such a marvellous cross-country round that they were 80 penalties clear going into the show jumping and only a disaster could have robbed them of the gold.

In 1974 she took a silver in the World Championships and has since remained a key figure in the

sport. In 1990 she broke her back in a riding accident, but she is still a selector on the pony three-day event team, as well as a technical delegate and steward.

Born in 1939, she married an army officer in 1959 and overseas postings often hindered her early career. When her husband left the army in 1968 and settled in Somerset she was able to concentrate on serious competition. She is now training her daughter who is in Britain's junior three-day event team.

RODNEY PATTISSON

YACHTING

1968 Mexico City
Gold   Flying Dutchman Class

1972 Munich
Gold   Flying Dutchman Class

1976 Montreal
Silver   Flying Dutchman Class

The outstanding yachtsman in British Olympic history, Pattisson won three medals, each with a different crew. His incredible level of fitness and painstaking attention to detail lifted him above other competitors – even at Olympic level – and moved the sport into a new era.

Born in Campbelltown, Scotland, in 1943, he won his first major title in 1960 in the World Cadet Championships. In the 1960s he had difficulty finding a like-minded crewman and decided to advertise in newspapers and yachting magazines. The plan attracted plenty of responses but nobody suitable, and it was providence that eventually threw up the figure of Iain MacDonald-Smith, who was a friend of Pattisson's brother. The pair met in 1967 and in their first year they placed second in the British and European Championships. In Olympic year they served notice of their intentions with success at the British and European events and the trials for the Games.

In Mexico they provided a demonstration of sailing excellence: after being disqualified in the first race, they reeled off five successive wins to secure the gold. The duo won two world titles before splitting and Pattisson eventually recruited Chris Davies as his partner to defend the title in Munich. They won four of the first six races and did not even need to turn out on the final day, such was their dominance. An attempt for a Flying Dutchman hat-trick in Montreal foundered with Julian Brooke-

Rodney Pattisson, the most successful yachtsman
in British Olympic history.

Vane Pennell partnered J.J. Astor to victory in the
doubles final of the 1908 rackets competition.

Houghton, but they still managed a silver medal. With no boats going to Moscow, Pattisson made a final attempt to make the team for Los Angeles, but just missed out.

Such was his versatility that he co-skippered Peter De Savary's *Victory* in the 1983 America's Cup. After Mexico he resigned his commission in the Royal Navy to concentrate on yachting and began working with a boat building firm in Dorset. He still lives in the county and is currently involved in the trimaran importing business. But he still competes and in 1991 got back together with Davies for a local yacht club event – and won.

ERNEST PAYNE

CYCLING

1908 London
Gold   Three-Lap Pursuit

The only Olympic champion to swap sports and play for soccer giants Manchester United, Ernie Payne lived up to his nickname – 'The Worcester Wonder'. Born in Worcester in December 1884, Payne's interest in cycling coincided with a grass-track racing revival. Nearby Boughton had a grass track and Payne borrowed his brother Walter's bike at a local meeting. The founder of Worcester St John's Cycling Club, T.W. Badgery, recalled: 'It was seen at once that he was going to be a champion.'

During his first season as a cyclist he won 13 of his 14 races, placing second in the other. By the end of 1903 he had earned his Worcester Wonder nickname, courtesy of *The Cyclist* magazine, and was building an extraordinary record in handicap races. In 1903 he won the 100 guinea Bath City Challenge Cup (a five-mile scratch race for reputedly the largest cup in England), a mile handicap and a half-mile scratch – all in the same afternoon. He was carried off the track shoulder-high by local fans.

The stocky racer, trained by his brother, won 20 races in 1903 and in the following years made a huge impression at the NCU Championships. Between 1905 and 1907 he was champion of England in the mile and for two years quarter-mile title holder. Curiously, his greatest achievement is not even mentioned in the club minutes of St John's CC. He joined the riders Ben Jones, Clarrie Kingsbury and Leon Meredith in the British team pursuit, clinching the gold for Britain with some superb riding over the last two laps. The team came home in 2:18.6 – ten seconds ahead of the second-placed Germans.

He retired from competitive cycling in 1910 and

resumed his soccer career – something he had enjoyed before his cycling days – first with local Worcester Early Closers, then signing for Worcester City, who won the Birmingham League in 1912. His performances as a goalscoring forward earned him a transfer to Manchester United, where he made 11 first-team appearances, usually standing in for the legendary Welsh international Billy Meredith. During the First World War he was a motorcycle despatch rider with the Guards Division and he retained his interest with St John's until his death in the city in 1961.

BILL PEACOCK

SWIMMING

1920 Antwerp
Gold   Water Polo Team

Peacock scored the opening goal in Britain's 3–2 win over the host nation Belgium in one of the stormiest events of the Games. It was a tough and fiercely competitive game and when the referee blew the final whistle a crowd of home fans began to throw missiles at the British players. They then stormed the pool and armed police had to lead the winning side to the dressing rooms before returning to disperse the crowd.

Twenty-year-old east Londoner Peacock had been a reserve on the 1912 Olympic team and was again selected as a reserve for the 1924 Paris Games, where Britain ended their dominant reign, going out in the first round. He died in Huntingdonshire in 1948.

VANE PENNELL

RACKETS

1908 London
Gold   Doubles

A former public school rackets champion, Pennell developed into one of the country's top real tennis players. However, he took part in the Games primarily for fun and was rarely persuaded to turn out at major championships.

Born in London in 1876, Pennell was educated at Charterhouse and Trinity College, Cambridge, but could not make the university rackets team. In 1901 he became the British rackets doubles champion, alongside his friend Dames Longworth, but he did not play again until 1908, when he won the title for a second time, again with Longworth. Heartened by this result he agreed to join the Olympic competition and teamed up with J.J. Astor, winning the final against fellow Britons Edward Bury and Cecil Browning in five tough sets, 6–15, 15–7, 16–15, 15–6, 15–7.

He also entered the singles but was beaten in the early rounds by the eventual winner Evan Noel, a situation that was repeated in the real tennis competition. He was the British real tennis champion in 1904 and appeared in the final seven times during his 21-year career, even though he entered the competition only nine times.

He served overseas with the Royal Army Service Corps during the First World War and after the hostilities returned to sport, playing ice hockey for Britain and writing the first book on Auction Bridge. He died in Bournemouth in 1938.

JOSEPH PEPÉ

SHOOTING

1912 Stockholm
Gold   Small-Bore Rifle Team – 50 Metres
Silver   Small-Bore Rifle Team – 25 Metres

Pepé represented Britain in the two small-bore team events at the Stockholm Games. The organisers decided to divide the event into two separate distances – 25 and 50 metres – and Britain sent two teams. However, such was Pepé's ability that he, and team-mate William Pimm, were selected for both teams. In the 25-metre event Britain finished behind Sweden in silver medal position, but they gained revenge over the longer distance, finishing 14 points ahead of the host nation.

Manchester-born Pepé, who was a member of the Wimbledon Park Rifle Club and was only 27, just missed out on a full set of Olympic medals when he was squeezed out of the bronze in the individual small-bore event after a shoot-off.

HERBERT PERRY

SHOOTING

1924 Paris
Gold   Running Deer Double Shot Team

At just 30, Perry was an unusually young member of a British Olympic shooting team – but in the end probably the most vital. He was the last man in the competition to shoot and Norway were leading by some 67 points. Perry started slowly but then got his distance and made 68 points to give Britain the gold by just a single point.

Born in South Africa in 1894, he was educated at Felsted School in Essex, and joined the Special Reserve. In 1916 he married and was commissioned into the Royal Artillery as a lieutenant. Owing to wounds suffered during service in France, he was eventually invalided out in 1920, with the rank of captain. A fine army marksman, he first realised he had a natural eye while in training at the barracks at Woolwich. In Paris he also entered the individual Running Deer competition but could only finish in 13th place.

He worked for the Ministry of Pensions for much of his life and his family like to relate a Second World War story that involves Perry and his shooting prowess. One day during the height of invasion talk he spotted a man he thought was snooping around his drive and shouted from a window for him to identify himself. The intruder started to run away, so Perry picked up a revolver and fired a shot that ricocheted past the man, stopping him in his tracks. The terrified man walked gingerly back, only to reveal he was a Post Office engineer checking cables!

A keen sports marksman and flyfisher, Perry died from cancer at his home in Bridport, Dorset, in 1966.

MARY PETERS

ATHLETICS

1972 Munich
Gold   Pentathlon

Arthur Peters was a practical man. On his daughter's 16th birthday, he bought her two tons of sand and helped her build a long jump pit. On her next birthday, he bought her more sand and several bags of cement, and together they built a shot-put circle. His daughter greeted these gifts with mixed

1972 pentathlon champion Mary Peters, with West German silver medallist Heide Rosendahl (left) and Burglinde Pollak of East Germany (right) who took bronze.

feelings. 'Deep down, I wanted a pretty dress and a pair of high-heeled shoes,' says Mary Peters. 'But, looking back, I'm glad of the presents I got. In the long run, they were just the right things.'

For Mary P, as she is known to Belfast and to the wider world outside the north of Ireland, had discovered the pentathlon. And such an event demanded facilities which were not readily available in the Ulster of the mid-1950s. But even in those early years, Mary believed that each problem came complete with a solution. It was just a matter of searching.

There are those whose athletic talent is so vivid, so glaring that an Olympic title seems no more than an inevitable reward for their extraordinary gift. There are many others, like Mary Peters, for whom success evolves from struggle, toil and patient improvement, allied to that dash of inspiration which is the hallmark of the champion. Mary's entire career was drenched in sweat, which made her ultimate success the more worthy and the more welcome.

She completed her first pentathlon in the summer of 1955; a 15-year-old schoolgirl from Portadown matched against the Northern Irish Olympians Thelma Hopkins and Maeve Kyle. Her progress was such that by 1958 she was selected for the four-woman Northern Ireland track and field team to compete at the Commonwealth Games in Cardiff. There was no pentathlon and Mary was picked for the shot and high jump. The team was provided with green blazers but, in those absurdly restrictive days, the athletes were required to buy their own grey skirts for the journey. Mary, a first-year domestic science student, had to raid her Post Office account for the skirt, and she was so thrilled at the elegant, grey-pleated number that she emerged from the store and rang the Irish team manager to report her acquisition. Sadly, she left the carrier bag containing the skirt in the telephone box, and when she rushed back, it had disappeared. She wept, then she decided to empty her savings account by purchasing a replacement.

Athletically, the games were not an overwhelming success for Mary P. She went out of the high jump at five feet and finished last but one in the shot. But the experience was beyond price, and when she returned to Belfast her career found an even more significant development.

In common with other Ulster athletes, she received a letter from a coach named Buster McShane, announcing that he was starting weightlifting classes at his gymnasium and inviting them to take part. Three years later, he took over her athletics coaching as well as her weight training. Buster was indispensable: 'He was always there when I needed him,' says Mary. 'When things didn't go well, he was there to touch your arm and say: "Come on, there's another day tomorrow." I could never have done what I did without him.'

Her first Olympics arrived with the Tokyo Games of 1964. She managed fourth place in the pentathlon, to general surprise, but now the real work began. She set herself to win the shot at the European Championships and Commonwealth Games of 1966, and she put on three stones of solid muscle with these objects in mind. She failed at both, and she was miserable at the size of her body and the scope of her failure. She virtually skipped the season of 1967 and began to train with extraordinary intensity for the Mexico Olympics of 1968. It was a grave disappointment. She strained an ankle a few days before the event, told nobody of her problems and finished ninth.

She started to sense that, athletically, her time was running short. But the authorities obliged her by including the pentathlon in the Commonwealth Games for the first time and she duly won in some style at Edinburgh in 1970; the first gold medal of her career.

In Mary's mind, everything was merely a prelude to Munich 1972. At 33, it was her last real chance of taking an Olympic gold medal. 'I wanted to do it for myself, and I wanted to do it for the province I love,' said the woman who was born in Lancashire but had become as much a part of Belfast as the Falls or the Shankhill.

Like everything else in her career, the Olympic pentathlon would be riddled with problems which required solution. Her principal opponents were clearly the West German Heide Rosendahl and the world record-holder Burglinde Pollak of East Germany. But Mary took the start she had sought in the hurdles when she returned 13.3, a fifth of a second faster than her best time. After the hurdles, all competitors were supposed to stay together to warm up for the shot. The two West German competitors were absent. They had been allowed to warm up privately. Mary's tolerance snapped. She created a splendidly indignant scene, bawling at officials until the privileged ones were returned.

She pushed out the shot to 16.20 metres, the best she had achieved in a pentathlon, taking a slim lead over Pollak and Rosendahl. Somehow, she had discovered a mood of confident determination she had never before experienced. She was ready for the high jump.

Her progress was smooth until she reached 1.71 metres, at which height she failed twice. She looked up to the stands and saw Buster. He wore a yellow anorak so that Mary could pick him out. He was standing on his seat, pumping his arms to indicate that she should run harder at the bar. She was infected by his confidence. She sailed over at the final attempt, cleared the next height first time and cleared 1.76 metres at her third trial. She went over 1.78 metres first time, equalling her finest performance and now she was alone in the competition. The opposition had been destroyed.

Some 80,000 spectators were chanting her name

and she was reacting like a prima donna; taking bows, blowing kisses, relishing the moment. Mary P from Belfast was stepping drastically out of character, and loving every moment. She finally ended her efforts by clearing 1.82 metres, way beyond her personal best. At the day's end, Mary had amassed 2969 points, Pollak 2872 and Rosendahl was fifth on 2668. But the West German girl's strongest events were still to come.

Mary performed to expectations in the long jump with 5.98 metres, but her confidence was brutally shaken by Rosendahl's 6.83 metres, the merest whisker off her own world record. With one event remaining, she clung to a precarious lead.

In the end, it all came down to a 200 metres sprint. And it had to be the fastest sprint that Mary P had ever run. All the leaders assembled for the final heat. Mary's task was simple; she had to finish as near to Pollak and Rosendahl as humanly possible, Running out of lane three, she threw herself into the bend and maintained her drive as the strength drained from her body. She came through the line, stared at the scoreboard, and prayed. Up came the times: Rosendahl 22.96 seconds, her fastest ever. Pollak 23.93. Peters, in fourth place, 24.08. Mary had run beyond her known limits. She had broken the world record. And she had won the gold medal by ten points, or one tenth of a second.

She received her medal from Lord Burghley, then she set about some serious celebrating. As the champagne flowed and dawn came up over Munich, she received a call from Malcolm Brodie, the distinguished sports editor of the *Belfast Telegraph*, who told her they were setting up a fund to commemorate her victory. How would she like the money spent? 'Malcolm,' she said, 'I'd like a new track for the young people of Belfast.'

The track was opened in 1976, an even greater achievement than the gold medal performance which made it possible. After the ecstatic welcome home to Belfast, Mary had set herself to raise the funds for the track. The intensity of her efforts was sharpened by deep personal tragedy. On the Easter after the victory in Munich, Buster McShane was killed in a road accident. She decided to compete in one more major championship to honour his memory, and she won her last gold medal at the 1974 Commonwealth Games in New Zealand. After Munich, she was afraid that her own people in Ulster might change their attitude towards her. The fear was unfounded: 'They're the kindest, warmest people you could imagine,' she said. 'And they took me to their hearts.'

She rewarded them with her time and her efforts, chairing the committee of the Ulster Games Foundation, which brings international athletics to the track which Mary built, and acting as an energetic member of the Sports Councils of Britain and Northern Ireland. She was a team manager with the British athletics team for five successful years and she now devotes herself to promoting the sport and to running her own successful health club.

How, she was asked, would she like to be remembered in years to come? 'I think,' she said, 'I think I'd like people to say: "She did more than win an Olympic gold medal. She put something back."'

MARK PHILLIPS

EQUESTRIAN

1972 Munich
Gold   Three-Day Event Team

1988 Seoul
Silver   Three-Day Event Team

Seemingly better known for his marriage to and subsequent separation from HRH The Princess Royal, Captain Phillips enjoyed an excellent competitive career as a horseman. Born in Cirencester, Gloucestershire, in 1948, Captain Phillips, of the 1st Queen's Dragoon Guards, was educated at Marlborough and the RMC Sandhurst. His first taste of the Olympics was as a reserve for the Mexico Games in 1968. His first major international success came as a member of the British three-day event team that won the 1970 World Championships in Chicago. He followed that in 1971 with another gold in the Europeans and in 1972 took Olympic gold as the non-scoring member of the eventing team which boasted the talents of Richard Meade, Mary Gordon-Watson and Bridget Parker. The following year he married Princess Anne and together they ran Gatcombe Park, which became one of the country's premier riding venues.

In 1988 he again joined the Olympic trail and collected a silver medal as the non-scoring member of the team after his horse pulled a hamstring, forcing him out of the cross-country stage of the competition.

J.F. PIKE

SHOOTING

1908 London
Gold   Clay Pigeon Team

One of the top scorers in the clay pigeon team competition during the London Games, Pike helped Britain to the gold over their arch rivals Canada.

Only team-mate Alex Maunder and Canada's individual Olympic champion Walter Ewing scored more points than Pike during the team event. The contest took place at Uxendon Shooting Club and his second-round effort of 22 shots from a possible 25, the best in the competition, kept Britain on the road to the gold. After three rounds Britain just managed to edge Canada by two points and Pike's effort was vital. In the individual event, however, he could not repeat his team form and came home in 12th place.

WILLIAM PIMM

SHOOTING

1908 London
Gold   Small-Bore Rifle Team

1912 Stockholm
Gold   Small-Bore Rifle Team – 50 Metres
Silver   Small-Bore Rifle Team – 25 Metres

A member of Britain's two gold medal-winning small-bore teams in London and Stockholm, Pimm's best individual Olympic placing was a disappointing sixth. Born in London in 1864, Pimm was a member of the Wandsworth Rifle Club and the only marksman to win two golds for Britain until Malcolm Cooper repeated the feat 76 years later.

At the London Games he was part of a crack four-man team that overwhelmed Sweden comfortably to win the gold. Individually, he placed sixth in both the moving target and prone competitions.

Four years later he returned to win his second gold in the 50-metre team competition and a silver in the 25-metre event. Individually he fared little better in Stockholm, finishing seventh in the 25-metre disappearing target event.

J.M. POSTANS

SHOOTING

1908 London
Gold   Clay Pigeon Team

Postans performed poorly in the first two rounds of the clay pigeon team event at the London Games. He hit just 30 birds from a possible 55 and Britain were under considerable pressure from Canada, who were led by the individual Olympic clay pigeon champion Walter Ewing. But Postans pulled himself together in the final round and finished the fourth top scorer overall in the British six-man team, helping to pip the Canadians for the gold by just two points.

JONATHAN POTTER

HOCKEY

1984 Los Angeles
Bronze   Hockey Team

1988 Seoul
Gold   Hockey Team

A talented centre-half and an influential member of Britain's hockey side, Potter was just 20 when he took part in the Los Angeles Olympics. He was the youngest member of the team and gained invaluable experience in helping the side bring back a surprise bronze medal.

Born in London in 1963, Potter was still at Southampton University, studying geography, when he went to the Los Angeles Games. After graduating, he joined the prominent Hounslow team and soon became the linchpin of his club side and then the national side, winning silver medals in the 1986 World Cup and 1987 European Cup.

He played in every match during the Seoul Games and scored against India. Britain were rocking in the early group matches, but came back strongly to reach the semi-finals, knocking out favourites Australia before beating the West Germans 3–1 in the final.

Now captain of Hounslow, who have won the national title and cup, as well as the European clubs' cup, Potter made his 100th British appearance in Berlin in September 1991. He works as product manager at KP Foods.

ALFRED POWLESLAND

CRICKET

1900 Paris
Gold   Cricket Team

Powlesland was a good amateur all-rounder and his skill was reflected in the Olympic final. He took a total of five wickets in the match and scored 14 with the bat to help Britain to victory.

Born in Newton Abbot, Devon, in 1875, Powlesland was an opening bowler for the Exeter side and local papers relate his appearance in a county show Single v Married match in Olympic year. Between the wars he was well known as the local newsagent and tobacconist in the village of Chudleigh, where he died in 1941, aged 65.

REGGIE PRIDMORE

HOCKEY

1908 London
Gold   Hockey Team

A county cricketer as well as an Olympic hockey player, Pridmore was a naturally talented sportsman whose life was tragically cut short by the First World War.

Born in Birmingham in 1886, he excelled at school at both cricket and hockey. He played inside-forward for Coventry Hockey Club and played for England 19 times. His international career began in some style in 1908 and during the London Games he was England's top scorer with ten of their 24 goals, including four in the 8–1 drubbing of Ireland in the final.

In cricket he played 14 times for Warwickshire before the war intervened and he took a commission in the Royal Horse & Field Artillery. He won a Military Cross for his bravery on the Somme before he was killed in action at the Piave River, in Italy, in 1918.

NOEL PURCELL

SWIMMING

1920 Antwerp
Gold   Water Polo Team

An Irish rugby international, Purcell played for the British water polo team in 1920. A furore had been created when the selectors picked an all-English side for the Games, so a final trial was held to justify the selection. A team of Irish, Welsh and Scottish internationals duly beat them comprehensively 6–0. A dramatic rethink then took place and one of the changes was the drafting-in of 28-year-old Irish international Purcell.

Purcell, educated at Trinity College, Dublin, had been playing for Ireland since 1910 and had won a number of Irish swimming titles, as well as being a top roller skater. But Irish sports fans knew him better as a rugby player with Lansdowne RFC where his performances earned him selection for the Barbarians and the Irish side.

In Antwerp he played in all three of Britain's matches, including the stormy final victory over host nation Belgium, after which the team was led from the pool by armed guards to protect them from the hostile crowd. In the 1924 Paris Games Ireland competed as a nation for the first time and Purcell captained the water polo side, but despite earning selection for the 1928 Games he decided to retire and concentrate on his legal practice.

He became a rugby referee and then a selector, and retired to Dun Laoghaire where he died in 1962.

CLYDE PURNELL

ASSOCIATION FOOTBALL

1908 London
Gold   Soccer Team

A goalscoring inside-left, Purnell scored four in Britain's opening victory over Sweden and helped the side to the Olympic title without losing a match. Britain moved on to the final where they comfortably defeated Denmark by two goals to nil.

Born on the Isle of Wight in 1877, Purnell won four England amateur caps and his greatest success outside the Olympics came the year after the Games when he scored for Clapton in their epic 6–0 FA Amateur Cup win over Eston United at Ilford. He died in Kent in 1934.

BILL QUASH

ASSOCIATION FOOTBALL

1900 Paris
Gold   Soccer Team

Barking-born Quash played left-half in the Upton Park side which won the first Olympic football gold in the Paris Games of 1900. Thirty-one-year-old Quash was one of many sporting all-rounders in the team and he also played cricket, for Barking.

Ironically, Quash and his team-mates may not have been aware of the significance of their achievement. The second modern Olympiad took a back seat to the World Exhibition held in Paris the same year. Events were spread over five months; organisation, and consequently attendances, were poor. Only three teams entered the football tournament and only two matches were played. A Parisian XI defeated the Belgian representatives 7–4, but were beaten 4–0 by Upton Park, who took the title.

However, the east London side may have seen the match in Paris as just another fixture on their 16-day tour of the West Country, Channel Islands and France. Bill Quash could well have been one of the athletes unaware that the tournament they had taken part in was the Olympic Games.

PAUL RADMILOVIC

SWIMMING

1908 London
Gold   Water Polo Team
Gold   4 × 200 Metres Freestyle Relay

1912 Stockholm
Gold   Water Polo Team

1920 Antwerp
Gold   Water Polo Team

One of the nation's greatest-ever swimmers, Radmilovic took part in five Olympic Games and was the first Briton to be inducted into the International Swimming Hall of Fame. Curiously, it was after his gold medal-winning days that he recorded his best-ever swimming performance, taking all but one of the 1925 national swimming titles, in an amazing sweep from 100 yards to five miles. He was still swimming a quarter of a mile every day until his death in 1968 at the age of 82.

Though born in Cardiff, he spent most of his life in Weston-super-Mare, where he swam for the local club. His first major international event was the 'renegade' Olympics in Athens in 1906, where he made two finals. But by 1908 he had assumed the mantle of the world's top water polo player and was in the British team that beat Belgium 9–2 to take the gold. He also won gold in the 4 × 200 metres relay, swimming the second leg, alongside Derbyshire, Foster and Taylor.

He captained the water polo side that successfully defended the Olympic title in 1912 and 1920 and it was at the Antwerp Games that he had his greatest moment, scoring the winning goal in a combative 3–2 final win over the host nation Belgium. The side lost in the opening round of the 1924 Games but Radmilovic, aged 42, was again in the 1928 team that narrowly missed a medal in Amsterdam.

He was an excellent long-distance swimmer and won national titles at the event 18 years apart – in 1907 and 1925 – bettering his earlier time by four minutes. 'Raddy', as he was known, was also an outstanding soccer player and a scratch golfer. He ran the Imperial Hotel, in Weston-super-Mare, until his death.

GODFREY RAMPLING

ATHLETICS

1932 Los Angeles
Silver   4 × 400 Metres Relay

1936 Berlin
Gold   4 × 400 Metres Relay

See Godfrey Brown, page 32.

MARY RAND

ATHLETICS

1964 Tokyo
Gold   Long Jump
Silver   Pentathlon
Bronze   4 × 100 Metres Relay

The golden girl of British athletics in the 1960s, Mary Rand brought home a full set of Olympic medals from Tokyo to reflect her status on the world scene. She became the first British woman to win an Olympic athletics title and represented the country at no fewer than ten events, held two world records and increased the British long jump record ten times.

Born Mary Bignall, in Wells, Somerset, in 1940, she finished second in the English Schools long jump in 1955 and won a sports scholarship to Millfield, where she developed into a brilliant all-round athlete. She won her first international vest against Poland in 1957, winning the high jump, an event in which she placed fifth in the following year's Commonwealth Games in Cardiff. She also took second place in the long jump. In 1959 she became the first British woman to clear 20 feet in the long jump and hopes were high that she would win a medal at the Rome Olympics. But she finished a disappointing ninth after misjudging her run-ups and, although she came fourth in the 80 metres hurdles, she knew there was better to come.

After the Games she married Olympic sculler Sidney Rand and, just four months after the birth of their daughter, Mary was competing in the European Championships in Belgrade, where she took two bronze medals, in the long jump and sprint relay. In Tokyo she made no mistake in the long jump, gradually improving to smash the world record with her fifth jump, a mighty 22ft 2¼in. She was the first woman to exceed 22 feet. She then added a silver in the pentathlon and a bronze in the relay before coming home to rapturous welcome, this being the first Games beamed live by satellite to TV screens in Britain.

Although she won a Commonwealth long jump title in 1966, injury stopped her from anything more active than a BBC commentator's role in Mexico in 1968.

Her marriage to Rand ended in divorce and in 1969 she married the US decathlete Bill Toomey, whom she met in Mexico. They lived for many years in California, but their marriage also ended in divorce. She now runs a fitness centre in California.

ALFRED RAWLINSON

POLO

1900 Paris
Gold   Polo Team

One of the early pioneers of flying in Britain, Rawlinson was also a war hero, inventor and peer . . . as well as an Olympic gold medal winner. Born into a privileged background in London in 1867, the son of Major-General Sir Henry Rawlinson, he went to Eton and joined the 17th Lancers. It was here that his polo-playing talents were honed and he played in the Foxhunters team at the 1900 Paris Games, helping the side to a 3–1 victory over another Anglo-American team, Wanderers, in the final.

Having left the Lancers for a time, he rejoined when the First World War broke out and after receiving a commission in the RNVR he was appointed second in command of London's aerial defences. In 1916 he was awarded the CMG and the following year he rejoined the army as a lieutenant colonel with the Royal Garrison Artillery. In 1919 he was awarded the CBE for his war services, and the DSO after leading a special mission to Ezerum. But in the following year he was captured by the Turks. On returning to Britain he became heavily involved in motoring and aviation and invented a car engine as well as flying dozens of experimental planes.

In 1925 he succeeded to the family baronetcy and died nine years later in south London.

RONALD RAWSON

BOXING

1920 Antwerp
Gold   Heavyweight

A successful boxer at school, Rawson did not enter any open competitions until after the First World War. Within ten months he had won the ABA heavyweight title and an Olympic gold medal.

Born in Kensington, west London, in 1882, Rawson went to Westminster School where he excelled at all sports, especially cricket, before going up to Trinity College, Cambridge, where he began to box. He twice won titles for the university against Oxford before the war interrupted his boxing career. He served as a captain in the Royal Engineers and won two bars to the Military Cross — a rare distinction.

At the end of hostilities he joined the Polytechnic Boxing Club and began open competition, first winning a novices' event, then the ABA title, before leaving for Antwerp and the Olympics. He was a smart boxer, with a sledgehammer punch, and during his entire career only one man went the full three rounds with him — Britain's Harold Franks, the 1920 ABA light-heavyweight champion, who then lost on points.

In Antwerp, Rawson knocked out every opponent, including the Dane Soren Petersen, whom he met in the final. He retired from competition in 1921 after

Mary Rand, the first British woman to win an Olympic athletics title, came home from the 1964 Tokyo Games with a full set of medals.

Ronald Rawson, who took the heavyweight boxing title at the 1920 Antwerp Olympics.

Steven Redgrave, whose gold medal-winning partnership with Andy Holmes in the 1988 coxless pairs was one of the highlights of the Seoul Games.

winning a second ABA title and having been in top-class amateur boxing for just over a year. He had won all 28 fights, 27 by knockout.

He died in Kensington in 1952, aged 69.

STEVEN REDGRAVE

ROWING

1984 Los Angeles
Gold   Coxed Fours

1988 Seoul
Gold   Coxless Pairs
Bronze   Coxed Pairs

The dominant force in modern British rowing and regarded as one of the finest oarsmen the world has ever seen, Redgrave leaped onto the international scene in 1983 when he won the Diamond Sculls at Henley at just 21. The following year he was a household name in Britain as part of the coxed fours at the Los Angeles Olympics.

Despite the Eastern Bloc boycott, the competition was still strong and the British crew had to sprint past the Americans to snatch the gold in the closing part of the race. His next major target was Seoul, but between Olympics he amassed an enviable string of successes, including another Diamond Sculls, a gold in the 1986 World Championships coxless pairs, three Commonwealth Games golds and a second world title in 1987. This last title, in the coxless pairs, was with Andy Holmes, who was also a member of the gold medal-winning Los Angeles crew.

In Seoul it was virtually certain that the duo would win a medal of some kind in the coxless pairs or coxed pairs. They were widely regarded as the strongest sweep-oared crew in the world after their World Championship triumph. The run-up to the Games was hardly smooth, but they arrived early in Korea for special acclimatisation training and produced a near-perfect performance in the coxless pairs, leading all the way, to take the gold. A second gold was perhaps asking too much, given that the final was the following day, but with cox Pat Sweeney they did well to take a bronze.

A member of the Marlow Leander Club, Redgrave was aiming for a third consecutive gold in Barcelona. Married to Ann, a member of Britain's 1984 Olympic rowing team, he has also taken a keen interest in bobsleighing and was a member of the British championship crew.

BERNARD REDWOOD

MOTOR BOATING

1908 London
Gold   8 Metres Class
Gold   Under 60-Foot Class

The atrocious weather conditions for the motor boating events meant that Redwood and fellow crew member John Field-Richards spent most of their time bailing out their vessel – a rather strange way to win Olympic gold. Redwood was a well-known figure on the British motor boating scene and a member of the Royal Motor Yacht Club. He was once awarded the medal of the Royal Society of Arts for a paper on motor boats.

As a crew member aboard Tom Thornycroft's *Gyrinus II*, Redwood won two golds when the only other vessel in their class failed to finish thanks to the poor weather. Their finishing time over the 40 nautical mile course is given as 2:28.26 in the 8 metres class and 2:28.58 in the under 60-foot class.

Born in Finchley, north London, in 1874, the son of Sir Boverton Redwood, he attended Bath College and Peterhouse College, Cambridge, where he was a keen cyclist. He died in 1911, at the age of 36, after contracting pneumonia.

PERCY REES

HOCKEY

1908 London
Gold   Hockey Team

Right-winger Rees was an ever-present member of the England side throughout the 1908 season, and he played in all the matches during the Olympic tournament. Born in south London in 1883, Rees won a total of 14 England caps and was goal provider for the sharp-shooting forwards Pridmore and Shoveller. England had a comfortable passage to the final, scoring 24 times and conceding only three, and they crushed the Irish side by 8–1 to take the title.

Rees died in Surrey in 1970, aged 86.

JOHN RHODES

YACHTING

1908 London
Gold   8 Metres Class

There were strong family ties in the crew of the winning boat in the 8 metres class at the London Games. Blair Cochrane owned the gold medal-winning *Cobweb* and Rhodes and crew mate Henry Sutton were two of his brothers-in-law.

Rhodes, born in Twyford, Berkshire, in 1870, fought in the Boer War and at Gallipoli in the First World War. A keen yachtsman, he lived on the Isle of Wight and was Commodore of Bembridge Sailing Club and a member of the Royal Victoria Yacht Club, which played host to the Olympic Regatta. At the Games *Cobweb* won its first two races and was able to coast in third on the final day to secure the gold ahead of Sweden and a second British boat.

Rhodes died at his home in Ryde in 1947.

J.T. RIMMER

ATHLETICS

1900 Paris
Gold   4000 Metres Steeplechase
Gold   5000 Metres Team Race

Doctors once banned the skeletal 'JT' Rimmer from taking part in a Scottish road race because they feared he would die on the course! The physicians had to be persuaded that it was Rimmer's natural gaunt appearance and that he was a double Olympic champion. Despite fearing he would collapse after a few hundred yards, they eventually agreed to let him compete and the amazing athlete then won the 20-mile race by a clear half-mile. The astounded doctors examined him after the event and found him to be barely taxed by the experience!

The great John Thomas Rimmer was born in Birkdale, Lancashire, in 1878, and began running as a teenager, winning his first open race at 19 – the mile at the Litherland Sports. He then put together a long string of titles, ranging from 880 yards to 20 miles, in a glittering career spanning more than 15 years. He sprang to the attention of the Olympic selectors after running second in the 1899 AAA ten miles, then clinched his place in Paris by taking first place in the 1900 AAA four miles. The wiry Rimmer trained hard for the Games, specifically

for the 4000 metres steeplechase, and came home in 12:58.4, ahead of team-mate Charles Bennett. He added a second gold in the 5000 metres team race, alongside Bennett, Sidney Robinson, Alf Tysoe and Australia's Stan Rowley.

A short time after the Games he joined the Liverpool Police and in one amazing force event raced seven different athletes over a mile, one after the other, and beat them all! He joined Sefton Harriers in 1903 and continued his road racing career, winning countless scratch handicaps and team races. In 1909 he won the Liverpool cross-country title and remained a keen runner up to the First World War, after which he gave up competitive athletics. He stayed on in the sport as a much-respected and well-liked official, continuing after retirement from the police. He died in Liverpool in 1962, aged 83.

MAJOR RITCHIE

LAWN TENNIS

1908 London
Gold   Men's Singles
Silver Men's Doubles

A great ambassador for tennis, Ritchie travelled all over the world, playing and promoting the game. A steady rather than explosive player, his game was built on an almost impenetrable defence and a devious lob.

Born in Westminster in 1870, he learned to play on the family's court at home in Putney but it was at gymnastics that he excelled at school. He did not start playing tennis seriously until his early twenties and his first major title, the French covered court singles, did not come along until 1899. He then built on that success, primarily on the Continent, but with some home victories.

At the 1908 Olympics he met the young German Otto Froitzheim in the final and, despite giving away 15 years, managed to beat him in straight sets. Curiously, the German decided to play Ritchie at his own game and tried to beat him from the baseline. It did not work. Ritchie also took a silver in the doubles, alongside James Parke, after losing to George Hillyard and Reg Doherty in the final. But he missed out on a full set of medals when he and Lionel Escombe lost in a bronze medal play-off in the indoor doubles competition.

In 1908 Ritchie claimed his first Wimbledon title, taking the doubles with New Zealander Tony Wilding in a tough five-setter against fellow Olympians Arthur Gore and Roper Barrett. The following year he lost to Gore in the singles final, but returned in 1910 to win the doubles title again. His last final appearance came in a doubles defeat in 1911, by which time he was 41 and retirement was beckoning.

He died in Ashford, Middlesex, in 1955, but his son Richard carried on the family tennis tradition, serving as secretary to the Queen's Club for 30 years.

CHARLES RIVETT-CARNAC

YACHTING

1908 London
Gold   7 Metres Class

Rivett-Carnac was a fabulously wealthy financier whose fortune was based on generations of prosperity in the Far East. He was also, at 61 years old, the oldest British yachtsman to win an Olympic gold medal – even though he had no opposition.

Born in India in 1853, he was educated in England and worked in the civil service in India before joining the colonial government in Burma as Accountant General. He then became financial adviser to the King of Siam before moving back to England in 1905 after the death of his first wife.

He remarried a few years later and his second wife Frances was on the crew of his yacht *Heroine* in the Olympic Regatta at Cowes, making them the first husband and wife team to win Olympic gold medals. It was an easy passage as their only opposition pulled out at the last minute, enabling them to win the title on a sail over.

Rivett-Carnac, whose family were so well known in India that Kipling mentions them in *The Tomb of his Ancestors*, died in retirement in Jersey in 1935, aged 82.

FRANCES RIVETT-CARNAC

YACHTING

1908 London
Gold   7 Metres Class

Frances Rivett-Carnac had only just become the second wife of the wealthy financier before the London Games. Their success, unopposed though it was, made them the first married couple to win Olympic gold medals.

Mrs Rivett-Carnac, a clergyman's daughter, sailed as a member of the crew aboard her husband's yacht *Heroine* in the regatta at Cowes. There was to be only one other entry but a last-minute withdrawal left them without a race and they were awarded the gold on a sail over. She lived for many years in the Channel Islands until the death of her husband in 1935. She then returned to England and died in Hampstead in 1962, aged 87.

BILL ROBERTS

ATHLETICS

1936 Berlin
Gold   4 × 400 Metres Relay

See Godfrey Brown, page 32.

ARTHUR ROBERTSON

ATHLETICS

1908 London
Gold   Three Miles Team Race
Silver   3200 Metres Steeplechase

Robertson may well have made the London Olympics as a cyclist had a succession of accidents and injuries not persuaded him to swap the cycle track for the running track. In the mid-1890s he was ranked in the top echelon of cyclists in Britain and his brother Dabbs took part in the 1908 Games in the cycling competition.

The son of a Glasgow doctor, Robertson was born in 1879, at Harthill near Sheffield, and although he was regarded as a major sporting talent at King's School, Peterborough, he did not begin to take athletics seriously until he was in his mid-twenties. His first major race was the 1906 AAA mile, in which he placed fifth, but it was over the longer distances that he enjoyed success, particularly over cross-country courses. In 1908, running for Birchfield Harriers, he won both the English title in Newbury, and the international title in Paris, while also taking second place in the AAA four miles.

These performances earned him selection for the Olympics, where he was pipped to the gold in the 3200 steeplechase by team-mate Arthur Russell and ran in the successful team race, coming home second alongside Joe Deakin and Bill Coales. It was to be a successful year for Robertson, as in September he ran in Sweden, on a banked cycle track in Stockholm, where he set a new world 5000 metres record of 15:01.2, beating the former holder and local hero Johan Svanberg into the bargain. The following day he failed by just 83 yards to beat the great Walter George's one-hour record.

The year after the Games he came runner-up in the AAA mile and four miles before retiring, at 30, to go back to cycling. For many years he ran a family sports shop in Peterborough, where he died in 1957.

ARTHUR ROBERTSON

SWIMMING

1900 Paris
Gold   Water Polo Team

Britain invented the game of water polo, so it was perhaps fitting that the first Olympic title should come to the home of the sport. Britain was represented by Manchester's Osborne Swimming Club and they won both their matches, against the French side Libellule de Paris and Belgium's Swimming et Water Polo Club, to take the gold, scoring 17 goals and conceding just three. Twenty-year-old Robertson played in both games.

ERIC ROBINSON

SWIMMING

1900 Paris
Gold   Water Polo Team

A member of the Manchester Osborne Club which represented Britain at the Paris Olympics, 22-year-old Robinson played in both matches during the Games. The team first beat the host nation's premier club Libellule de Paris 10–1, then ensured the gold medal for Britain by defeating Belgium's Swimming et Water Polo Club 7–2 in the final.

JOHN ROBINSON

HOCKEY

1908 London
Gold   Hockey Team

Robinson came from a family with a fine pedigree in top-class hockey, with two brothers captaining Cambridge. After Radley School, he went to Merton College, Oxford, winning his blue in his freshman year and playing for the first XI in all four years, often against his twin brother Laurence who was on the Cambridge team.

Robinson, born in Burton-on-Trent, Staffordshire, in 1885, played for England nine times between 1907 and 1911 and was a natural selection at right-half for the Olympics. The English side met with few problems in the tournament, scoring 24 goals, conceding only three and winning the final against Ireland by 8–1.

On leaving Oxford Robinson began teaching. When the First World War began he was commissioned in the North Staffordshire Regiment and was wounded in action in Mesopotamia. He died after being shipped back to a military hospital in Roehampton, London, in 1916.

SIDNEY ROBINSON

ATHLETICS

1900 Paris
Gold   5000 Metres Team Race
Silver   2500 Metres Steeplechase
Bronze   4000 Metres Steeplechase

Robinson succeeded in winning a full set of Olympic medals at the Paris Games. However, he perhaps cherished the silver and bronze medals more than the gold, which was won as part of the 5000 metres team, comprising Charles Bennett, J.T. Rimmer and Alf Tysoe. Bennett and Rimmer came home first and second, with Robinson finishing sixth and Tysoe seventh. By virtue of first and second places, Britain took the gold ahead of France.

But his performances in the steeplechases were excellent, with a bronze in the 4000 metres, behind team-mates Rimmer and Bennett, in a clean sweep of medals for Britain; then a silver in the 2500 metres, four seconds behind Canada's George Orton. Robinson, who ran for the Northampton Cycling & Athletic Club, collected an impressive haul of AAA titles, including four steeplechases and two ten miles. Prior to the Paris Games he also twice won the national cross-country title.

LAURENCE ROOK

EQUESTRIAN

1956 Melbourne
Gold   Three-Day Event Team

As a child, Rook had always wanted to join the navy, but he was turned down because his eyesight was not good enough. Born in Ednalton, Nottinghamshire, in 1921, he left Brackley College to join the Maritime Artillery, manning anti-aircraft guns on merchant ships and indulging his love of the sea. When that disbanded, a friend convinced him to transfer to the 1st Household Cavalry in Egypt.

During the war he won the Military Cross for single-handedly capturing a German observation post and marching his captive back to British lines through a German minefield. An unflappable character, Rook was known as 'The Leader' in the army and when he finally left during the mid-1950s he settled in Sussex, then Gloucestershire, where he farmed. A keen huntsman, marksman and yachtsman, Rook was an excellent horseman and took up show jumping after the war.

He was selected for the British eventing team at the Helsinki Olympics in 1952, and a gold medal was in prospect when his horse Starlight put a foot in a hidden drainage ditch and threw him. Rook managed to complete the course, despite suffering concussion, but was unaware that he had strayed the wrong side of a flag and was disqualified. The accident cost him and the team the chance of a gold, but he went on to capture two individual European titles and was again selected for the 1956 Olympic team.

Held in Stockholm because of Australian quarantine rules, Rook finished sixth in the individual competition, on Wild Venture, but with Frank Weldon winning a bronze and Bertie Hill performing well, Britain clinched the team gold. He gave up competitive riding soon after and became heavily involved in national and international horse trials, travelling the world as a delegate and judge. His duties included officiating at two Olympic Games.

Major Rook died in Guy's Hospital, London, in 1989, and will be remembered as one of the equestrian world's most remarkable characters.

ARTHUR RUSSELL

ATHLETICS

1908 London
Gold   3200 Metres Steeplechase

Russell came to the attention of athletics fans as a schoolboy and his rapid rise made him something of a boy wonder in the Midlands. Born in Walsall in 1886, he was competing in open races before he was 14 – and winning them. He was taken under the wing of Joe Taylor, who ran cross-country in the Midlands, and Birchfield Harrier Tommy Birch, and together they coached him well.

His first big success was second place in the Coventry Philanthropic Mile – when just 15 – and he came second in his first AAA steeplechase in 1903 when still only 17. He gathered a phenomenal number of regional titles while still a teenager and he returned to the AAA Championships to win the steeplechase title for three successive years — 1904, 1905 and 1906. He then missed 1907, and was surprisingly beaten in the 1908 AAA event by Sparkhill Harrier Reg Noakes. But when Noakes dropped out of the Olympics Russell became Britain's number one hope for the 3200 metres event. He eased through the heat and then in the final ran away from team-mate Arthur Robertson to win the gold by a couple of yards in 10:47.8.

Sidney Robinson, who won individual silver and bronze in two steeplechase events at the 1900 Paris Games, as well as gold in the 5000 metres team race.

Arthur Russell comes home ahead of team-mate Arthur Robertson to win the 1908 3200 metres steeplechase.

HARRY RYAN

CYCLING

1920 Antwerp
Gold   2000 Metres Tandem
Bronze   1000 Metres Sprint

A speedy cyclist with an impressive career record, Ryan won his gold medal with a tandem partner with whom he had ridden for barely half a season.

Born in Euston in 1893, Ryan began competitive cycling just before the outbreak of the First World War and was at the top of his sport for more than a decade. He had already won four national titles before the Antwerp Games and was made one of the favourites to take a medal in the sprints. He also decided to enter the tandem event and got together with Polytechnic club-mate Tommy Lance early in 1920. In June the pair, with Ryan steering, set a new British quarter-mile record and went into the Games confident of bringing home a medal.

In the sprints Ryan claimed a bronze, behind fellow Briton Tommy Johnson and winner Maurice Peeters from Holland. But in the tandem event they easily disposed of the Dutch pair in the semi-finals and were too strong for the German pair in the final, putting in a staggering last 200-metre finishing spurt, timed at an amazing 11.6 seconds, to leave them trailing in their wake.

After the Games Ryan carried on his winning ways, taking the 1921 and 1922 national tandem titles, this time with Catford's Tom Harvey. On retiring from competitive cycling, he became a prominent administrator in the sport and returned full time to the family business, the London hardware company Buck & Ryan, until his death in Ealing, Middlesex, in 1961.

TERENCE SANDERS

ROWING

1924 Paris
Gold   Coxless Fours

Sanders came through the junior ranks at Eton and then Trinity College, Cambridge, alongside James Macnabb, Maxwell Eley and Robert Morrison, and together they formed the crew of the gold medal-winning boat.

Born in Ireland in 1901, Sanders won his first Henley title in 1922, the first of three Stewards Cup victories, before rowing in the Boat Race the following year. The four knew each other well and maintained their unbeaten record in Paris, even though their boat and oars had been 'mislaid' by French officials for three days. In the final they destroyed a useful Canadian crew by almost ten seconds to take the gold.

The quartet broke up after the Games but Sanders took part in one more Henley success, as a member of the Leander eight that took the Grand in 1929. By this time he had started lecturing in engineering at Cambridge. He joined the civil service in 1941, rising to Director of Technical Development in the Defence Department in 1946.

He was chairman of an engineering firm in later life as well as High Sheriff of Surrey. He died in the county in 1985, aged 84.

RONALD SANDERSON

ROWING

1908 London
Gold   Eights

Son of a Cambridge rowing blue, Sanderson was in the university boat that ended Oxford's nine-year winning streak in 1899. Born in Uckfield, Sussex, in 1876, Sanderson was also in the Cambridge boat that won the race in the following year. A keen football and cricket player, he received a commission in the Royal Field Artillery on leaving Cambridge in 1900 and rowed for the regimental team.

At the Olympics, Sanderson, who was educated at Harrow and Trinity College, took his usual number six position in an experienced crew of hardened rowing campaigners. The British selectors were concerned that the Belgians would upset their plans to win every Olympic rowing event at the London Games. Their anxieties proved ill-founded as the Leander eight easily beat Belgium's Club Nautique de Gand by two lengths, coming home in seven minutes and 52 seconds.

A keen huntsman and polo player, Captain Sanderson was killed in action with the RFA in France in 1918.

TESSA SANDERSON

ATHLETICS

1984 Los Angeles
Gold   Javelin

The javelin duels between Tessa Sanderson and great rival Fatima Whitbread were among the highlights of a golden age of British athletics in the 1980s. Between them they won dozens of international events, including Commonwealth, European, World and Olympic titles. But it was Sanderson who won the biggest confrontation in Los Angeles when Whitbread could only muster a bronze.

Born in St Elizabeth, Jamaica, in 1956, she was brought up by her grandmother when her parents came to England in search of work. She joined them as a nine-year-old but the bleak West Midlands were a distinct contrast to the island home she had just left and it took some time for her to settle. Sanderson's potential as a javelin thrower was first noticed at school and she joined the local Wolverhampton & Bilston AC. In 1975 she won the first of eight national javelin titles and made the Olympic team for Montreal a year later after three times improving the British javelin record.

At the 1976 Olympics she finished a creditable tenth and continued to make good progress before winning her first major title at the Edmonton Commonwealth Games in 1978. She was among the favourites to win the gold at the Moscow Games in 1980, but incredibly froze in the qualifiers and failed to make the final. Her best throw of the season was more than a metre better than the eventual winning distance. Four years later she made amends with a throw of 69.56 metres to beat world record-holder Tina Lillak and Whitbread.

Though often hampered by injury, she managed to win the Commonwealth title again in 1986, yet failed to make the Olympic final in Seoul. She managed a place on the British team for the 1990 European Championships in Split, but could only make 12th place in the final. In the same year, she won her third Commonwealth title in Auckland, New Zealand.

She began a new career as a sports presenter on television and works as a fitness consultant.

JOHN SEWELL

TUG OF WAR

1912 Stockholm
Silver   Tug of War Team

1920 Antwerp
Gold   Tug of War Team

City of London police tug of war teams were a dominating force in the sport across three Olympics, successfully representing Britain twice and placing second once. It was in the silver medal-winning team of the 1912 Games, in Stockholm, that policeman Sewell made his Olympic debut. The City police were the defending champions but lost to the host nation in the final.

Scotsman Sewell, born in Halfmorton in 1882, returned to the team in Antwerp and they successfully held off Belgium, Holland and the United States to take the gold in what was to be the last-ever Olympic tug of war competition.

Sewell, who was also a top-class Cumberland & Westmoreland wrestler and was British heavyweight champion for four successive years from 1907, died in Cambridge in 1947.

IVAN SHARPE

ASSOCIATION FOOTBALL

1912 Stockholm
Gold   Soccer Team

Sharpe was a fast and clever outside-left who enjoyed an outstanding amateur career with Watford, Glossop, Leeds United and Derby County. He won 12 England amateur caps and was rewarded for his work in the number 11 shirt with a call-up to the Stockholm Olympics. He played in all three matches during the Games, in which Britain maintained an unbeaten record and won the final against Denmark 4–2, after the Danes had a player carried off with the score 2–1 in Britain's favour.

Sharpe, at 31, came back to the Olympics in Antwerp in 1920, but Britain surrendered the title in the first round after an embarrassing defeat at the hands of Norway. When he retired from playing he became a sports journalist, rising to editor of the *Athletic News*, and became Chairman of the Football Writers' Association. He died in Southport in 1968, aged 78.

Tessa Sanderson, Olympic javelin champion in 1984, celebrates her victory with team-mate and rival Fatima Whitbread (second left).

Olympic fencing champion Gillian Sheen, who won the individual foil in Melbourne in 1956.

GILLIAN SHEEN

FENCING

1956 Melbourne
Gold   Individual Foil

Gillian Sheen, a 28-year-old London dentist, was regarded as one of the unlikeliest of Britain's gold medal winners. The nation hardly boasted a history of fencing success and few newspapers were speculating on the possibility of a gold emerging from the sport when the team set off for Australia. Nevertheless, Britain had won Olympic medals: two silvers in the men's team epee, in 1908 and 1912, and three silvers in the women's foil. Gladys Davis in 1924, Muriel Freeman in 1928 and Judy Guinness in 1932 were forerunners of Sheen's event.

Born in 1928 in Willesden, Gillian took up the sport at school in Kent. She won the national schools title in 1947 and her first senior title two years later. She left school and went to London University where she kept up the sport, winning the British Universities title five times, taking a team third place in the World Championships in Monaco in 1950 and a gold in the World Universities Championships in 1951. She made her Olympic debut in Helsinki in 1952, but went out in the second round. What little publicity there was about her in the run-up to Melbourne suggested that the new electric foils, being used for the first time at an Olympics, were too heavy for the slim Londoner, but she should certainly have been marked out as a medal possibility.

Determined not to let the disappointment of Helsinki happen again, Sheen, despite working long hours as a dentist at London's University College Hospital, trained even harder for the Melbourne Games. 'Once there, my concentration was intense,' she recalls, 'and this combined with so many other circumstances gave me my best performance at the right time. So many things can affect one's performance; training, climate, team support, spectators, accommodation, they all seem unimportant in themselves, but when so little separates winning from losing, they make a huge difference.'

She scraped into the final by beating world champion Lydia Domolki of Hungary in a barrage to decide fourth spot in her semi-final group. In the final, held at St Kilda town hall, Sheen lost her first bout to Romania's Olga Orban, but then won her next six, finishing equal first with the girl who had defeated her. In the barrage to decide on gold and silver, Sheen produced her best-ever performance to win 4–2.

She continued to fence and won the British Empire title in 1958. She also competed in the World Championships in Philadelphia, which led her to a post-graduate course in children's dentistry in Rochester, New York, where she met her future husband. In 1960 she clinched her tenth British foil title and was persuaded to defend her Olympic title in Rome, where she was eliminated in the second round.

She retired from competitive fencing in 1963, the same year in which she married, and set up home in New York State, bringing up four children and running a dentistry practice.

JOHN SHEPHERD

TUG OF WAR

1908 London
Gold   Tug of War Team

1912 Stockholm
Silver   Tug of War Team

1920 Antwerp
Gold   Tug of War Team

One of only three City of London policemen to represent Britain in three Olympic tug of war competitions, Shepherd won two golds and a silver medal. Born in Bicknor, Gloucestershire, in 1884, he was among the heaviest of the 1908 team, weighing in at well over 16 stone, and the highly trained City side eased through the competition, beating Britain's second and third teams – Metropolitan Police K Division and Liverpool Police – to win the title.

After losing out to the Swedes in the 1912 final, Shepherd's police career was interrupted by service in the Military Police during the First World War, after which he returned to the City and the tug of war team for the 1920 Games in Antwerp. The team held off the challenge of Holland, Belgium and the USA to win the title in what was to be the last-ever Olympic tug of war competition.

Shepherd, who was the British Cumberland & Westmoreland heavyweight wrestling champion in 1922 and 1923, died in Aston, Herefordshire, in 1954.

IMRAN SHERWANI

HOCKEY

1988 Seoul
Gold   Hockey Team

The hero of the hour in the 1988 Olympic final, Sherwani scored two of Britain's three goals against West Germany. It was certainly more than adequate compensation for missing the team's previous Olympic adventure because of injury and he decided to retire from international hockey immediately after Seoul.

Born in Stoke-on-Trent in 1962, Sherwani won silver medals in the 1986 World Cup and 1987 European Cup and notched up 49 England caps and 45 British caps. He played in all seven games in Seoul and made a telling contribution with his tricky play on the left wing. It was his second goal – Britain's third – that wrapped up the game against the Germans when it was looking as though they might stage a comeback.

He still plays for local side Stourport and runs the family newsagents in Stoke, where he has just installed a small sports section.

STANLEY SHOVELLER

HOCKEY

1908 London
Gold   Hockey Team

1920 Antwerp
Gold   Hockey Team

Shoveller was one of the greatest-ever hockey players produced in Britain and the first man to win two Olympic gold medals in the sport. In truth, it would have been difficult to beat his record because he played in the first two Olympic hockey tournaments – the sport was not contested in 1912. However, in a long career he scored 76 goals in 35 England games.

Born in Kingston Hill, Surrey, in 1881, Shoveller and contemporary Gerald Logan, who also played in the 1908 Olympic final, went to Kingston Grammar School, where they established the game. Like Logan, he went on to play for Hampstead, Surrey and then England, making his debut in 1902. He scored ten goals as centre-forward in the 1908

Games, where England cantered to victory, scoring 24 times, conceding three goals, and trouncing Ireland 8–1 in the final.

From 1910 until his retirement from international hockey in 1921, Shoveller captained the national side and could have broken all appearance records had it not been for the First World War, in which he won the Military Cross while serving as a captain in the Rifle Brigade.

In his last Olympic Games, Shoveller captained the side to the gold, scoring a memorable eight goals in England's 12–1 defeat of Belgium, and celebrating his 39th birthday during the tournament. He died in Broadstone, Devon, in 1959.

CHARLES SMITH

SWIMMING

1908 London
Gold   Water Polo Team

1912 Stockholm
Gold   Water Polo Team

1920 Antwerp
Gold   Water Polo Team

The big goalkeeper captained the British side to victory at the London Games and remained the man between England's posts for an astonishing 25 years. Smith was born in Pemberton, Lancashire, in 1879 and was with the Salford Swimming Club until after the London Games. He conceded just two goals in the final against Belgium, which Britain won 9–2 to take the gold.

At an agile 6ft 2in and weighing 17 stone, Smith was a top sprint swimmer and diver. He switched to Southport SC after 1908 and went on to play in both Britain's successful Olympic title defences in 1912 and 1920. In Antwerp, where Britain edged the host nation Belgium 3–2 with a goal three minutes from the end, Smith was 41 years old, making him the oldest gold medal-winning water polo player in Olympic history.

He returned with the British team at the 1924 Paris Games, but the side surprisingly went out in the first round to Hungary. He made his last appearance for England in 1926 and died in Southport in 1951.

FAULDER SMITH

HOCKEY

1920 Antwerp
Gold   Hockey Team

Right-winger Smith enjoyed a marvellous England career spanning ten years and including a total of 26 caps. He was born in Carlisle in 1886 and went to Marlborough College and then Trinity Hall, Cambridge, where he won his hockey blue. He played for a variety of clubs, including Beckenham, Blackheath and Lowestoft, before making his England debut in 1911. He would certainly have won considerably more caps but for the First World War, in which he served as an officer in the army.

He was selected for the Olympic side as a right-winger and played in both England's matches, the 5–1 thrashing of Denmark and the 12–1 mauling of Belgium. Both these sides had beaten France, who were England's opponents in the final, but the French called off because of sickness and England were awarded a walkover and the gold.

By this time Smith had joined his father in the family businesses, a textile manufacturers and an insurance brokers, where he worked until retirement. He died in London in 1937.

HERBERT SMITH

ASSOCIATION FOOTBALL

1908 London
Gold   Soccer Team

Born in 1879 in Oxfordshire, Herbert Smith was educated at Oxford County School and Beccles School, and started his club career with home town side Witney Town. A powerful left-back, he went on to play for many other teams, amongst them Oxford City, Stoke, Derby County and Reading. While at Reading he captained the professional side.

Unusually, Smith won his four full England caps *before* his debut for the amateur side in 1907. In 1908 he played in the British side which, with three straight victories, won the Olympic title. His international career lasted until 1910, by which stage he had made 17 appearances for the amateur side.

A leading figure in Oxfordshire football throughout his life, Smith joined the county's FA council in 1910 and became president in 1919. He held this post until his death, at the age of 71, in 1951.

JOHN SOMERS-SMITH

ROWING

1908 London

Gold   Coxless Fours

Somers-Smith inherited his talents from a great sporting family: his father was twice the AAA half-mile champion and his brother rowed for Oxford. He was born in Walton-on-Thames, Surrey, in 1887, and attended Eton and Magdalen College, Oxford. Curiously he never won a rowing blue and his first major success on the water came at the London Olympics, where he rowed for his college.

Magdalen beat Canada in the semi-finals and went through to meet the Leander Club in an all-British affair at Henley. At 10st 13lb he was the lightest member of the crew and he stroked them to victory by some two lengths. The official report mentions him by name as the star of the event, rowing beautifully and not losing an inch of water. After the Games he went on to further success at Henley, twice winning the Grand, in 1910 and 1911.

He won a Military Cross in 1916, but was killed in action in France a few months later. His brother also died at the Front. Strangely, the fortunes of the winning Magdalen crew at the 1908 Games varied dramatically – two killed in the First World War the other two going on to be knighted.

DICK SOUTHWOOD

ROWING

1936 Berlin
Gold   Double Sculls

Southwood's contribution to the most dramatic Olympic victory at the Berlin regatta is often underplayed. The usual reason is that his partner in the double sculls was the legendary British rower Jack Beresford, who had already won two golds, two silvers and a vast collection of assorted rowing titles before arriving in Germany.

Ironically, it was Beresford who first spotted Southwood's potential at Auriol Rowing Club. Born in Fulham, south-west London, in 1906, Southwood joined Beresford at the London Rowing Club and

Dick Southwood (left) and the legendary Jack Beresford, winners of the double sculls at the 1936 Berlin Games.

Eighteen-year-old Terry Spinks lands a punch on his way to becoming
Olympic flyweight champion in 1956.

made the final of the 1932 Olympic single sculls, in Los Angeles, only to suffer acute cramp and finish last. In the years before Berlin, Southwood and Beresford trained hard for the Games, but were dismissed as too old by the German favourites. After losing in the heats, the duo made their way to the final by the back-door route and then scored a sensational win, drawing level with the Germans at 1800 metres, rowing neck and neck for the next 100, and then pulling away to win by two and a half lengths.

The pair rowed in the inaugural double sculls at Henley in 1939 where they dead-heated with an Italian pair. It would be Southwood and Beresford's last competitive race. Southwood went on to run a successful jewellery business and when he died in Suffolk in 1986 he left a fortune to a London hospice for the terminally ill.

F.G. SPACKMAN

ASSOCIATION FOOTBALL

1900 Paris
Gold   Soccer Team

The World Exhibition, held in Paris in 1900, had an adverse effect on the second Olympic Games, which took place during the same period. The Games became little more than a sideshow to the exhibition and attendances suffered accordingly. However, the visit of the Essex football side, Upton Park, who played a Parisian XI for the Olympic title, attracted a reasonable crowd.

F.G. Spackman played at inside-right for Upton Park in this game and, although he did not score in the 4–0 victory, was rated one of the side's best performers.

ANNIE SPEIRS

SWIMMING

1912 Stockholm
Gold   4 × 100 Metres Freestyle Relay

Annie Speirs never won a national swimming title and the high point of her career was the relay victory in Stockholm. She also performed a minor miracle to reach the final of the 100 metres freestyle, in which she finished fifth and last – but only a stroke away from Britain's number one,

Jennie Fletcher. It was Fletcher who had kept Speirs out of the national scene for so long, winning every 100-yard title for six successive years. But reaching the final clearly gave Speirs a lift and she performed well in the relay.

Born in Liverpool in 1889, she swam for the city's ladies' swimming club and was successful in northern counties events. In the relay she joined Fletcher, Bella Moore and Welsh champion Irene Steer, and they beat the Germans into second place by 12 seconds, in a world record time of 5:52.8. It was apt timing for Speirs as she had celebrated her 23rd birthday the day before the relay final. She died in Liverpool in 1926.

TERRY SPINKS

BOXING

1956 Melbourne
Gold   Flyweight

He was built like a jockey and had the looks of a choirboy, and there was considerable opposition in some boxing circles to sending the 18-year-old Terry Spinks to Melbourne. Born in West Ham, east London, in 1938, Spinks' boyhood ambition was to become a jockey and as a stable lad he earned his fighting spurs in stable competitions before winning the English Schoolboys title. He created something of a stir in coming from nowhere to upset the odds and win the 1956 ABA flyweight title, the contest being effectively a trial for Olympic selection. Some selectors poured scorn on the idea of taking such a young man to the Games, but popular opinion was behind the exciting young fighter and he made the trip.

He repaid the faith of Britain's boxing fans in full with his performances at the West Melbourne Stadium, fighting through the semis, where he disposed of the much-fancied Frenchman Rene Libeer, to the final, where the favourite Mircea Dobrescu, the hard-hitting Romanian, lay in wait. In one of the best performances of the competition, Spinks was quick enough to elude the punches of the Romanian and boxed brilliantly to win on points and take the gold.

He celebrated his 19th birthday a few months after the Games and then decided to turn professional, fighting his way through the crowded pro ranks to a British featherweight title fight with Bobby Neill in September 1960. It was his 37th fight as a professional and he took the title when the referee stopped the contest in the seventh round. A few months later he successfully defended against Neill, knocking him out in the 14th round, before losing the title to Welshman Howard Winstone, a future world champion, in May 1961. Spinks retired soon after, with a professional record of 47 wins, one draw and seven defeats. He now runs a public house in Kent.

HARRY STAMPER

ASSOCIATION FOOTBALL

1912 Stockholm
Gold   Soccer Team

Stamper was among the reserves who travelled in the party for the Stockholm Games. With no substitutes allowed, his only hope of playing lay with injuries to others. When first-choice centre-half Ted Hanney was hurt in the opening game the selectors drafted in Stamper for the semi-final against Finland. Britain won the game, but the team was changed again for the final and the 30-year-old Geordie was left out. Britain went on to win the final against Denmark 4–2 and retain the Olympic soccer title.

HENRY STAPLEY

ASSOCIATION FOOTBALL

1908 London
Gold   Soccer Team

Henry 'Harry' Stapley was one of the stars of the 1908 Olympic soccer tournament. Top scorer in Britain's gold medal-winning side with six goals, Stapley's finest moment came in the second round when he tormented Dutch keeper Reinier Beeuwke and scored all the goals in a resounding 4–0 victory. Such free-scoring habits characterised a distinguished career with Woodford Town, West Ham, Glossop and England.

A teacher by profession, the 25-year-old Stapley took up a post at Woodford College in 1904, subsequently captaining the local football club. A year or so later he joined West Ham United and went on to score 41 goals in two and a half seasons. Stapley came from something of a footballing family; his brother Will was an accomplished centre-half who, like Harry, enjoyed international recognition at amateur level. In 1908 the brothers pooled their talents, joining struggling Derbyshire side Glossop.

Stapley more than repaid the faith of Glossop's patron, Sir Samuel Hill-Wood, who brought the striker to Derbyshire. Harry was top scorer over four consecutive seasons, scoring 67 times in 135 appearances. Hill-Wood also proved something of a patron to Harry Stapley. Initially the former teacher combined his sporting and academic skills as football and cricket coach to Hill-Wood's three sons. Later in life Stapley served as Sir Samuel's private secretary, following the latter's election to Parliament (as MP for High Peak). Hill-Wood also nominated Harry to the boards of directors of several local companies.

Born on 29 April 1883, in Kent, Harry Stapley died exactly 54 years later in Glossop.

IRENE STEER

SWIMMING

1912 Stockholm
Gold   4 × 100 Metres Freestyle Relay

So tiny was Welsh swimmer Irene Steer that when local sports writers first saw her compete they likened her to a water beetle skimming across the water! She was a natural swimmer with an almost perfect stroke, so much so that when she first ventured to London to find a coach, there was no one who could improve it.

Born in Cardiff in 1889, she started swimming seriously as a ten-year-old after a friend took her on a trip to the local baths. Her swimming successes grew rapidly, but her size did not. At her peak she was less than five feet tall, weighed no more than eight stone and had size three feet. Her head was so small that she could comfortably wear a baby's bonnet.

She dominated the freestyle sprint at the Welsh Championships, winning the 100 yards for seven successive years, until her retirement in 1913 – the year in which she won the British 100 yards title and tied the world record. She was unfortunate to swim in the same era as the great Daisy Curwen, who held the world 100 yards record and dominated the short-distance races. Curwen was rushed to hospital after qualifying for the 1912 Olympic 100 metres freestyle final and underwent an emergency appendectomy.

Earlier in the competition, disaster had also befallen Steer, when a rival swimmer drifted into her lane and knocked her out of her stroke. She failed to make the final. But she bounced back in the relay, anchoring the team of Bella Moore, Jennie Fletcher and Annie Speirs to victory by the huge margin of nearly 12 seconds over the Germans in a new world record of 5:52.8.

Although she retired from swimming in the following year she remained a sports fanatic, passionate about soccer, rugby, tennis and swimming, while raising a family of four. Her only son died tragically from diphtheria, aged five, but her three daughters all excelled at sport, one playing lacrosse for Wales, another tennis at Wimbledon. Her father was a director of Cardiff City football club and it was there that she met her husband, Dr Bill Nicholson, who later became chairman of the club. She devoted her life to the family and to sport and died in her native city in 1947.

DOUGLAS STEWART

EQUESTRIAN

1952 Helsinki
Gold   Prix Des Nations Team

Douglas Stewart was among Britain's bravest wartime commanders and one of the nation's finest horsemen. He remains the only man to have competed at Olympic eventing and show jumping competitions.

Born in 1913 in Herefordshire, the son of Brigadier-General Ian Stewart, Dougie was educated at Rugby and Sandhurst before joining the famous Scottish cavalry regiment, the Royal Scots Greys, as a subaltern in 1933. In 1938 he went with the Greys to Palestine in a peace-keeping force which was to be the last mounted cavalry regiment of the line. Three years later it was mechanised. During the war, Stewart became recognised as one of Britain's finest armoured fighting soldiers. He fought with the regiment at Alamein, Salerno, in the Normandy landings, and right through north-west Europe to the Baltic, where the Greys met the Russians. He earned lasting fame at the Battle of Nofilia where he fought a tank duel with a German officer. He received the Military Cross for his bravery in the Western Desert and a Bar at Salerno. He was decorated again after the Normandy landings and the north-west Europe campaign, during which he realised a lifelong ambition by commanding the regiment.

Having earned a reputation as a fine horseman he was selected for the British eventing team at the London Olympics in 1948. But his borrowed horse Dark Seal went lame before the cross-country phase and he was forced to withdraw. In Helsinki in 1952, riding Aherlow, he joined his close friend Harry Llewellyn and Wilf White in the victorious

British show jumping team. Two years later he was captain of the British team which won the Aga Khan Cup in Dublin. He then retired from competition.

Lt. Colonel Stewart retired from the army in 1954 to take up farming, first in England, then Scotland. After learning to fly he was involved in yet another famous story, when he scared off the Great Train Robbers from their farmhouse hideout while trying to land in a field!

A keen huntsman and marksman, he pursued his hobbies in the Highlands and continued farming, often allowing top riders the use of his pastures to rest their competition horses. In the mid-1980s he suffered a bad accident on his farm when a tractor reversed over him. His health began to decline and he died in July 1991 in Kilkirk.

HARRY STIFF

TUG OF WAR

1920 Antwerp
Gold   Tug of War Team

Britain won the last-ever Olympic tug of war competition in Antwerp and, as usual, the team was provided by the City of London police. Stiff, born in Sudbury, Suffolk, in 1881, was a member of the police side which was probably the only team to train seriously for competitions, which they won all over Europe. In Antwerp they overcame the Dutch, Belgian and American teams to take the title. Stiff died in Finchingfield, Essex, in 1939.

ARNOLD STRODE-JACKSON

ATHLETICS

1912 Stockholm
Gold   1500 Metres

Jackson was one of the most extraordinary athletes to compete at an Olympic Games. An outstanding natural athlete, he excelled at every sport he contested, including cricket, football, boxing, hockey, golf and rowing. Born in April 1891, he competed in all these – as well as athletics – while at Malvern College and later Brasenose College, Oxford.

It was difficult for him to choose a sport in which

to specialise, but he was persuaded to opt for the track by his uncle, Clement Jackson, who had held the 110 metres hurdles world record in 1865. With training that even in those days looked casual, Strode-Jackson won two mile races for Oxford and was selected as one of the nine 1500 metres athletes in the British team for the Stockholm Games. Despite a complete lack of preparation for the event, his natural athleticism and startling finishing burst saw him home. He kicked from seventh to first in the home straight, beating off the much-fancied Americans, including then world record-holder Abe Kiviat, in a British and Olympic record 3:56.8.

Strode-Jackson cared little about domestic competition; he never ran in the AAA Championships and took part in only occasional Oxford races. In April 1914 he took part in his last event, the Penn Relays in the United States, anchoring the Oxford quartet to victory in the 4 × 1 mile.

At the outbreak of war Jackson became a brevet-major in the regular army, then joined the King's Royal Rifle Corps, where he achieved a quadruple DSO – a distinction shared by only six other officers throughout the war. While serving on the Western Front he was badly wounded three times and when demobbed, as an Acting Brigadier, he was unable to resume his track career. He served on the British delegation to the Paris Peace Conference and was awarded the CBE. In 1921 he married an American girl, left the army and emigrated to the United States, where he lived in Madison, Connecticut, and ran the family business. He became an American citizen in 1945 but spent his last years in England, where he died, in his beloved Oxford, in 1972.

WILLIAM STYLES

SHOOTING

1908 London
Gold   Small-Bore Rifle – Disappearing Target

1912 Stockholm
Silver   Small-Bore Rifle Team – 25 Metres

Styles won an extraordinary event in which nine marksmen, eight of them British, all scored a perfect 45 points for the 25-metre disappearing target event. Styles, of Wandsworth Rifle Club, took the gold, despite the driving rain, after judges ordered a tie shoot, with team-mates Hawkins and Amoore taking silver and bronze.

He finished a disappointing 13th when he returned to Olympic competition to defend his title in

Stockholm, but earned some consolation with a silver in the 25-metre team competition.

HENRY SUTTON

YACHTING

1908 London
Gold   8 Metres Class

Henry Sutton had an impressive yachting pedigree; his father Sir Richard had led Britain's bid for the America's Cup in 1885. Unfortunately, Sir Richard's boat *Genesta* was beaten 2–0 by the USA's *Puritan*, but the setback did not put him off sailing. Henry was Sir Richard's fourth son, born in 1868, and he was educated at Radley and joined the Royal Yacht Squadron, his father's outfit. He also served as Commodore of the Royal Victoria Yacht Club, which played host to the 1908 Olympic Regatta in Cowes. Sutton joined two of his brothers-in-law on board the *Cobweb*, owner Blair Cochrane and fellow crewman John Rhodes. The boat won its first two races and then cruised home third in the final race to take the gold.

Sutton died in Berkshire in 1936.

SIDNEY SWANN

ROWING

1912 Stockholm
Gold   Eights

1920 Antwerp
Silver   Eights

Swann was yet another Cambridge oarsman who came from a multi-talented sporting family. His father rowed in the Boat Race and his brother won a blue for athletics. He was born in the Isle of Man in 1890, and educated at Rugby and Trinity Hall, Cambridge. It was for the college that he first tasted rowing success at Henley, stroking the winning crews in the Visitors and Wyfold trophies in 1910. He rowed in the Boat Race for three years and was in Leander's winning eight at Henley in 1913, the year in which he also won the first of two Goblets with his brother Arthur.

At the 1912 Olympics, he was in the winning Leander crew which defeated fellow Britons New College, Oxford, in the final. He followed family

Arnold Strode-Jackson hits the tape to take the 1500 metres title at the Stockholm Games in 1912.

Henry Taylor, Britain's finest swimmer of all time, is chaired around the stadium after his efforts ensured gold for the 4 x 200 metres freestyle relay team in 1908.

tradition by entering the Church, but stayed close to rowing and, after the First World War, reappeared in the Games to take a silver in Leander's eight in Antwerp. Only he and Ewart Horsfall remained from the winning Stockholm crew.

He worked in Africa for many years and in 1941 was appointed chaplain to King George V. He died in Minehead, Somerset, in 1976, aged 85.

JOHN SYMES

CRICKET

1900 Paris
Gold   Cricket Team

Symes probably attracted the attention of the Devon County Wanderers organisers while batting against a Blundell's School Old Boys XI in Olympic year. A number of the British side came from the Blundell's stable and Symes scored 48 for North Devon in the match, earning himself a place at number three on the Olympic team. In Paris he made a modest 15 in the first innings, but was out for just a single in the second.

Born in 1879, Symes attended Marlborough College and became a solicitor. During the First World War he served with the 6th Devon Regiment and reached the rank of captain by the end of hostilities. He was awarded the OBE in 1919 for services to the war effort. He died in his native Crediton, Devon, in 1942.

GERALD TAIT

YACHTING

1908 London
Gold   12 Metres Class

Tait was a member of the ten-man Royal Clyde Yacht Club crew aboard the gold medal-winning *Hera*. The vessel was owned by Thomas Glen-Coats, a prominent figure in the Glasgow club, and they were able to compete in the Games on home territory. There were just two craft in the competition and the organisers decided to stage it on the Clyde, with the other boat, the Liverpool-based *Mouchette*, preferring to travel to Scotland rather than to the regatta in Cowes.

Tait, born in Campbelltown in 1866, was a longstanding member of the club and was invited by Glen-Coats to take part. The *Hera*, using its knowledge of the river, won both its races by more than a minute to take the gold.

A solicitor by profession, Tait died in Glasgow in 1938.

HENRY TAYLOR

SWIMMING

1908 London
Gold   400 Metres Freestyle
Gold   1500 Metres Freestyle
Gold   4 × 200 Metres Freestyle Relay

1912 Stockholm
Bronze   4 × 200 Metres Freestyle Relay

1920 Antwerp
Bronze   4 × 200 Metres Freestyle Relay

One of Britain's Olympic giants, Henry Taylor was undoubtedly the nation's finest swimmer and one of the greatest the world has ever seen. An orphan, he was brought up by his brother and learned to swim in the canals and streams around the cotton mills where he worked. The only time he used the local baths was on 'dirty water' day when admission was cheaper.

Born in Oldham, Lancashire, in 1885, he swam for the local Chadderton club and first came to prominence as a 14-year-old, winning the Schoolboys Championship Shield in 1898. His first national achievement was as a 19-year-old when he placed second in the 220 yards in 1904. He placed third in three events at the 1905 national championships and the following year, at the 'renegade' Olympics in Athens, he won gold, silver and bronze medals.

He then wreaked havoc on the national championships, winning four titles — from 440 yards to the mile — and claiming the inaugural world record of 11:25.4 in the 880 yards. His world record-breaking continued at the 1908 Olympics, where he won three gold medals, and he was chaired around the stadium by the swimming team after an incredible performance in which he hauled the 4 × 200 metres relay team from nowhere to first place.

Taylor, just 5ft 5in, had switched clubs to Hyde Seal before the London Games and eventually won 15 national titles, including three long-distance events, the last being his farewell victory in 1920 when he was 35. An England water polo player, he won medals in the 1912 and 1920 Olympic relay teams.

In 1922 he should have won the Morecambe Bay swim, but the boatman carrying the judges could not keep up with him and although he made the crossing first he was not awarded the prize because the judges had not seen him do it! When his swimming career ended he bought a pub, mortgaging all his medals and trophies to make the down payment. But the business failed.

He worked for many years as an attendant at Chadderton Baths, the town in which he remains a legend. A picture of him still hangs outside and his trophies are displayed inside. He died in Chadderton in 1951 and was inducted in the International Swimming Hall of Fame, in the United States, in 1969.

IAN TAYLOR

HOCKEY

1984 Los Angeles
Bronze   Hockey Team

1988 Seoul
Gold   Hockey Team

One of the best players to pull on an England jersey and arguably the greatest goalkeeper in the history of world hockey, Taylor was the foundation of Britain's hockey renaissance and produced some breathtaking saves in the most important games to keep the side on the rails.

Born in Bromsgrove, Worcestershire, in 1954, Taylor made his international debut in 1977, going on to play 80 times for Britain and 91 for England. He collected a hatful of medals as Britain's hockey took off, including a bronze in the Los Angeles Olympics in 1984, a silver in the 1986 World Cup and a silver and bronze in European Cups. But his finest hour came in Seoul when his heroics kept Britain on course for the gold medal in a classic semi-final win against Australia and then in a thrilling 3–1 final victory over West Germany. He left the field a minute before the end of the game to allow reserve goalkeeper Veryan Pappin to play and qualify for his gold medal.

Taylor, who played for East Grinstead, retired from international hockey soon after Seoul and now works as a promotions manager of a synthetic sporting surfaces company, specialising in man-made hockey pitches and tennis courts.

HARRY THOMAS

BOXING

1908 London
Gold   Bantamweight

One of the few early British Olympic boxers to turn professional after the Games, Thomas was the only reigning ABA champion to take a gold medal despite Britain winning all five Olympic divisions. Born in Birmingham in 1889, Thomas boxed locally and won the Midlands bantamweight title before his victory in the ABA championships.

At the London Games Thomas beat Scottish champion Frank McGurk and then got a bye in the semis. His final opponent was fellow Briton John Condon, who would win the 1909 ABA title and had beaten the only foreign entrant in the division, Frenchman Paul Mazior, and then Londoner Bill Webb. The lack of a semi-final bout clearly gave Thomas an advantage and looking the fitter of the two he fought off a brave Condon in a close and gruelling contest to win on points.

The following year he turned professional and although he did not fight for the British title he left the country with an unbeaten record when he emigrated to the United States in 1911. He continued to fight in the USA, as well as Australia, before retiring from competition in 1916. As an American citizen he fought in the US Navy during the First World War and made occasional visits to England. He died in America in 1961.

DALEY THOMPSON

ATHLETICS

1980 Moscow
Gold   Decathlon

1984 Los Angeles
Gold   Decathlon

Arguably the greatest all-round athlete the world has ever seen, Thompson is still aiming for a hat-trick of Olympic decathlon titles at Barcelona. Sports commentators, writers and fans have over the years learned to write off the man at their peril, though another medal in his fifth Olympiad, at 33, would be miraculous even by his standards.

Before Thompson took part in the 1980 Games, a postcard arrived at the California home of America's double Olympic decathlon champion Bob Mathias.

Harry Thomas, bantamweight champion in 1908.
Britain won all five divisions in the boxing
competition at the London Games.

In Los Angeles in 1984 Daley Thompson confirmed
his status as the world's greatest decathlete by
winning the Olympic title for the second time.

It read simply: 'I'm going for three!' The card was typical Daley Thompson, the enigmatic character who could be funny and charming, aloof and cold, unpleasant and arrogant, occasionally all at the same time – but he was always his own man.

Born in north London in 1958, the son of a Nigerian father and Scottish mother, his sporting powers surfaced at boarding school in Sussex. He won his first decathlon in 1975 soon after joining the Essex Beagles club and was the youngest entrant in the competition at the Montreal Olympics the following year, where he finished a creditable 18th, but was already being tipped by the champion Bruce Jenner as the man for the future. He took the first of his three Commonwealth titles in 1978 and at the start of the 1980 season posted the first of his four decathlon world records in Austria.

It was here that he beat West Germany's Guido Kratschmer, who was to be his great rival for the Moscow Games. But when the Germans joined the Western boycott Thompson broke training to compete against Kratschmer and took the world record in the process. By comparison the Olympics were comfortable, with only rain on the second day stopping Thompson rewriting the record books again.

After a 1981 lull, he bounced back in 1982 with two world records, the second in winning the European title in Athens, before another Commonwealth gold in Australia. In the year before the Los Angeles Olympics he became the first-ever decathlon world champion in Helsinki. For the Los Angeles Games his great rival was again expected to be a West German, this time the giant Jurgen Hingsen, who then held the world record.

Thompson started with an astonishing 10.44 100 metres and was never headed in the competition, equalling Hingsen's world record. When the points were recalculated in the following year his record returned and he still holds the mark of 8847 points.

After winning his third Commonwealth title in 1986 in Edinburgh, Thompson lost his world crown in Rome, and along with it his aura of invincibility. He went for this third Olympic title in Seoul but, dogged by injury, was pipped for the bronze by his friend, Canada's Dave Steen, on the last event.

It says much about Thompson that he considers himself fit enough to train for Barcelona and it is just possible that his Californian postcard message might actually come true.

DON THOMPSON

ATHLETICS

1960 Rome
Gold   50km Walk

In the eyes of the great British public, race walkers are an eccentric breed; all stiff legs, pumping arms and mobile bottoms. It must be said that, through a long and distinguished career, Donald James Thompson has done nothing to dispel that reputation for eccentricity.

More than three decades after the Games of Rome, 1960, the images of his victory remain fresh in the mind; the Foreign Legion cap, the clip-on sunglasses and the dramatic pause as he entered the Olympic Stadium. But most memorable of all were the curious preparations carried out in a suburban bathroom.

Don Thompson was concerned to ensure that he did not become 'one of those British athletes who are good on home territory but can't take a bit of heat'. So he decided to turn his bathroom into a steam heat chamber, to simulate the conditions which awaited him in Rome. 'I got this oil stove and put it in the bath,' he says. 'Then I got a kettle which had been boiled on the gas ring downstairs, and I put that on top of the stove. The place was hot and steamy, and I closed the door and window and let the whole thing simmer for about 20 minutes. Then, when the temperature had reached around 110°F, I waded in wearing an old tracksuit and did exercises on the spot for half an hour, by which time I was feeling pretty dizzy.'

Several years passed before the former fire insurance clerk came to realise the dangers. 'It was a paraffin heater and there was no ventilation,' he says. 'So, of course, all the carbon monoxide fumes weren't getting away. The dizziness was a form of carbon monoxide poisoning, which was affecting me three times a week over a period of five months.'

Stripped of its comic overtones, that story offers a telling illustration of the fanatical dedication which underpinned Don Thompson's talent. He had experimented with race walking at the age of 18, following a tendon injury which restricted his running. He promised himself that he would return to running when the injury mended. Twenty years were to pass before that promise was honoured.

Coached and encouraged by Harold Whitlock, the 1936 Olympic 50km champion, Thompson was 21 when he entered his first Middlesex County 20-mile walk in 1954. He remembers: 'A few people thought it was too far for me, and when I was leading after 15 miles, a chap came out, offered me a tracksuit and said: "Come in, Don.

You've done pretty well. Now let the real men show you how it's done." But I waved him away, won by a couple of minutes and beat the record.'

Whitlock was staggered: 'This youngster has confounded all our notions about waiting for physical maturity before attempting feats of stamina,' he said. 'What will be the limit of his ultimate performance?' But Thompson's talent seemed to recognise no obvious limits. In that same year, he made his first attempt on the London–Brighton race and finished second. It was the prelude to eight successive victories in that exhausting trek down the A23.

His improvement was such that he was rated among the favourites for the Melbourne Olympics 50km title. But he failed to take sufficient liquid during the race, dehydration claimed him three miles from home and, in his own words: 'The road suddenly came up and hit me.'

That unhappy experience prompted the bathroom experiment. He was determined that never again would heat and humidity disrupt his ambitions. He flew out to Rome just three days before his event, and the British team doctors pronounced him completely acclimatised.

The field contained all the post-war 50km Olympic champions: John Ljunggren of Sweden (1948), Guiseppe Dordoni of Italy (1952) and Norman Read of New Zealand (1956). But it was the 41-year-old Swede who posed the most potent threat.

Thompson had taken sensible precautions against the 87°F heat with his cap and glasses. 'The glasses had a tremendous psychological effect,' he says. 'They cut out the glare, and somehow the heat didn't seem so bad.' By halfway he had secured a lead of one minute and was looking enviably strong. But Ljunggren chipped away at his advantage and by 30 kilometres, Thompson had been caught.

He noticed, however, that the Swedish athlete was taking a little longer at each feeding station. 'At the last one, at 45km, he was very tired and he virtually stopped,' he recalls. 'I gained a few seconds, then I pulled out a few more, and I came into the stadium about 20 seconds in front.' The Roman crowd awarded him an enormous ovation as he seemed to pause and sniff the air. Four years earlier, during a race in Milan, they had noted that mannerism and had named him Il Topolino, the little mouse.

The little mouse accepted their cheers as he toured the track. 'With 300 metres to go, I realised this was the big one, and I almost tied up,' he says. 'It was the sudden thought that I was actually going to win. I wasn't elated at the finish, I was just feeling sort of smug and happy.'

Suddenly, Thompson was a national celebrity, and public attention reflected his new status. 'I got lots of invitations to go to dinner dances,' he says, 'but I turned most of them down. I wanted to carry on in athletics, and I knew that if I started on that circuit, my athletics would suffer. I just couldn't afford too many late nights.'

The athletics career proceeded to plan. He returned to Italy two months later for a 100km walk, completing the first 50km at a pace which was 24 minutes faster than his Olympic winning time. The second half of the race was also faster than Rome, but Thompson will accept no credit for the feat. 'I just can't move that fast,' he says. 'I'm sure it was a short course.'

The Olympic title was defended in Tokyo four years later, but he finished back in tenth place. He continued to compete for Britain until 1966, and he chose the London–Brighton, which by now he had won nine times, as his final race.

In 1969, he gave up the insurance business and started a teacher-training course. On completion, he began to teach in a primary school in Battersea, south London. Then, as he puts it: 'I made the mistake of transferring to the secondary sector, and got eaten alive. When I walked into the classroom, the kids would start swinging from the chandeliers.' In 1983, at the age of 50, he was offered, and accepted, early retirement.

With his wife and two teenage children Thompson moved to Hythe in Kent, where he works as a self-employed gardener. But he has been unable to cut himself off from the sport he loves. On six days a week, he rises at dawn for a training stint; eight miles most days, between 20 and 30 on Saturdays. He also runs marathons, which he completes in around three and a half hours. But some of his most remarkable achievements have been reserved for recent years. In 1990, at the age of 57, he emerged from retirement and finished second in the National Road Walking 100-mile championship. In the following year, he completed two 100-mile races in France, finishing the second in seventh place, the first British athlete home.

The essential modesty has remained charmingly constant through the years. 'I'd like to be remembered as a fairly good athlete who didn't cause too much aggro on his way through life,' he says. 'When you're competing, you must have a killer instinct. When you're not, you ought to be pleasant.'

His immediate ambition is simply stated: 'I'll carry on competing until I can think of a good reason for stopping. But I can't see that happening, ever. In fact, that's what I'd like people to say of me: He died with his Reeboks on.'

Don Thompson, who overcame the heat of Rome to win the 50km walk at the 1960 Olympics.

GORDON THOMSON

ROWING

1908 London
Gold   Coxless Pairs
Silver   Coxless Fours

A fine all-round sportsman, Thomson played top-class rugby and won trophies at swimming as well as being an Olympic oarsman. Born in south London in 1884, he tried his hand at a career in business after leaving Hampstead's University College School and eventually went up to Trinity Hall, Cambridge, in 1906. A keen oarsman with the Thames Rowing Club, Thomson's first major success came with Leander at the 1908 Olympics. He entered two events: the pairs alongside John Fenning and the coxless fours.

In the fours the Leander crew were beaten in the final by Magdalen College, Oxford, but Thomson and Fenning comfortably took the pairs gold from another Leander pair by two and a half lengths. The following year he rowed in the Boat Race and in 1910 won the Goblets at Henley.

During the First World War he served with the RAF and won the DSC for his low-level photographic reconnaissance work over enemy lines at Gallipoli. He was also awarded the DFC. He played rugby for the UCS Old Boys, Surrey and London Scottish, and ran a merchanting business in Westminster. He died in Kent in 1953.

ERNIE THORNE

TUG OF WAR

1920 Antwerp
Gold   Tug of War Team

After the Antwerp Olympics the IOC decided that tug of war was not attracting enough competitors and axed it from future Games. Only five nations took part in the 1920 Games and Britain, represented as usual by the highly-trained City of London police, were too strong for Holland, Belgium, America and France.

Thorne, born in south London in 1887, was a member of the police team that took the gold and went on to win many national police titles. He died in Taplow, Buckinghamshire, in 1968, aged 81.

TOM THORNYCROFT

MOTOR BOATING

1908 London
Gold   8 Metres Class
Gold   Under 60-Foot Class

A talented and much-respected sculptor, Thornycroft designed his own boat for the London Olympics and it was built in the family boatyard. He was born in Basingstoke, Hampshire, in 1881, and attended St Paul's School before joining the family boat engineering and building firm. His father Sir John Thornycroft had established the company and, like his parents and grandparents, Tom became a sculptor and designer.

His boat *Gyrinus II* had little opposition in its two classes – just one other vessel which failed to finish the course – but with his two-man crew of Bernard Redwood and John Field-Richards he was able to deal with the appalling weather conditions.

As a yacht designer his influence was felt in the development of the Swallow class boats and he continued to compete in yachting and motor boating events, his greatest success coming in 1931 when he won the Prince of Wales Cup as helmsman. He was also a keen motorcycle racer and took fifth place in the Isle of Man Tourist Trophy in 1908.

He had resigned from the board of the family business in 1934 over differences in future planning and worked independently until the war. In 1952, Thornycroft, then 70, was selected as alternate for the British yachting team, but he was not called upon to compete and reacquaint himself with the Games.

He died in his native Basingstoke in 1955, aged 73.

TOM THOULD

SWIMMING

1908 London
Gold   Water Polo Team

1912 Stockholm
Gold   Water Polo Team

Thould played for many years alongside the great Paul Radmilovic in both the British water polo team and their club side Weston-super-Mare. Together they formed the core of the club side that three times won the national title and Thould played in the Olympic title-winning team at the London Games.

Born in Somerset in 1886, he represented the county as a swimmer and worked most of his life as a clerk for the local gas company. He was 22 years old when he made his Olympic debut, playing alongside Radmilovic in the 9–2 defeat of Belgium to take the gold medal. It was Britain's only game, as they had earned a bye in the first round and Austria had scratched from the semi-final.

He died in Weston-super-Mare, where he had lived most of his life, in 1971, aged 85.

MONTAGUE TOLLER

CRICKET

1900 Paris
Gold   Cricket Team

The most naturally talented cricketer in the British Olympic side, Toller had already played six times for Somerset before the Games. A fast bowler of some note, he had a quiet first innings, scoring two and not featuring in the British bowling attack. But the second innings was a different story. After missing the batting, when Britain declared, Toller wreaked havoc among the French batsmen, taking an extraordinary seven wickets for just nine runs. The French limped to a total of 26 all out and the Olympic title was Britain's.

Toller was born in Barnstaple in 1871 and attended Blundell's School, where he was a first-team rugby and cricket player. He played occasionally for the Devon county side and died in Titchfield, Hampshire, in 1948.

NOEL TURNBULL

LAWN TENNIS

1920 Antwerp
Gold   Men's Doubles

Despite playing a number of Davis Cup games for Britain, Turnbull's greatest tennis achievement was his Olympic success in Antwerp. He and his partner Max Woosnam were not expected to win the tournament and their victory was greeted with great enthusiasm by Britain's tennis fraternity.

Born in Highgate, north London, in 1890, Turnbull was educated at Charterhouse and then joined the family shipping company. His career was soon interrupted by the outbreak of the First World War and he was commissioned into the RASC. He won a Military Cross and was mentioned in despatches during the Battle of the Somme. After the war he resumed his tennis career and made a Davis Cup debut in 1919 before selection for the Olympics.

In Antwerp he finished fourth in the singles, but with Woosnam fought through to a final with Japan's Ichiya Kumagae and Seiichiro Kashio, where they won in four sets. Although he played in the 1921 Davis Cup he then decided to take a few years out of tennis to concentrate on his career and play golf. He returned in the mid-1920s, winning two Portuguese Championships and making the 1926 Davis Cup team.

On retiring from competitive tennis he returned to the shipping business, and died in Whitby, Yorkshire, in 1970, aged 80.

R.R. TURNER

ASSOCIATION FOOTBALL

1900 Paris
Gold   Soccer Team

Turner played most of his football in north London, as a forward with Crouch End Vampires. However, the outside-right joined the east London side Upton Park on their September tour of 1900. During this tour Upton Park beat a French side 4–0 in Paris. Reports of the time refer to a match 'at the Paris Exhibition last week'. However, the game was not just part of the World Exhibition but the Olympic Games' first soccer final. Turner, perhaps unknowingly, had won a gold medal.

ALF TYSOE

ATHLETICS

1900 Paris
Gold   800 Metres
Gold   5000 Metres Team Race

Tysoe was already a major running star in the north when he came down for his first AAA Championships in 1897. He made an impressive start and took both the mile and ten miles, demonstrating

Noel Turnbull (left) and Max Woosnam,
men's doubles champions in 1920.

Emil Voigt, Olympic five-mile champion
in 1908.

Alf Tysoe, winner of two gold medals at the 1900 Paris
Games – in the 800 metres and the 5000 metres team race.

what a vast talent he possessed.

Born in Skerton, near Lancaster, in 1874, Tysoe was a farm hand who trained in the fields and began winning middle-distance events on the northern counties circuit. But after his AAA performance he was a man of international class and he decided to drop down to half-mile runs, winning the AAA 880 yards in 1899 and 1900, the latter in a world best time for the year of 1:57.8.

This earned him selection for the Paris Games, to be held just a week later. There he followed a sluggish pace on the first lap and then roared around the second in 56.2 to win easily from America's John Cregan, in 2:01.2. Although he finished seventh in the 5000 metres team race he won a second gold as the fourth scoring Briton. The last race of his career came at the end of the 1900 season and was a curious challenge match in which he beat the newly-crowned Olympic 1500 metres champion, Charles Bennett, over 1320 yards.

He died tragically, aged just 27, in the following year at his father's home in Blackpool after contracting pleurisy.

BRYN VAILE

YACHTING

1988 Seoul
Gold   Star Class

Few people expected a medal to come from the Star class pairing of Bryn Vaile and Mike McIntyre at the 1988 Games. Yachting experts had pinned their hopes on other classes and the duo were able to prepare for Seoul without too much pressure. But all that changed in South Korea when they became the first Britons to win a race at the regatta in Pusan.

It was day two of the event and the press were alerted to a possible shock when Vaile and McIntyre claimed a famous victory and started a thrilling run to the gold. A fourth place on day three was followed by a freak accident on shore and a head injury to Vaile, and there were doubts as to whether he would be able to continue. But with stitches inserted in the wound he carried on, finishing 14th in the fifth race and sixth in the penultimate. That left the pair needing to win on the final day and for the Americans to finish sixth or worse.

The British pair performed superbly, winning by 11 seconds. When they came ashore they found that the Americans had given up after their mast had broken. It was the unlikeliest British medal success of the Games and one of the most celebrated.

Vaile, born in Enfield, Middlesex, in 1956, sailed for the Royal Lymington Yacht Club and had only started competing with McIntyre a few years before the Games.

EMIL VOIGT

ATHLETICS

1908 London
Gold   Five Miles

Emil Voigt turned the Olympic five-mile event into something of a Manchester derby. The race had been a nip-and-tuck battle between him and fellow Mancunian Eddie Owen, but Voigt's fitness allowed him to sprint away in the final lap to win by some 50 yards.

Born in Manchester in 1882, of German parents, the 5ft 5in Voigt had substantial success in northern counties miles and half-miles after joining Manchester AC and took his first AAA title – the four miles – just ten days before the Games. This victory earned him selection for the five-mile event, the last time it was run at the Games, where it was thought the Swedish world 5000 metres record-holder Johan Svanberg would prevail. South Africa's Charles Hefferon, who would win a silver in the marathon, was also a danger, as well as Britain's Archie Robertson. But the little Manchester man, at 26, was too quick for the rest of the field and easily won the gold.

After retaining his four-mile AAA title in 1909 and then winning the one-mile championships the following year, Voigt retired and emigrated to Australia, where he began his own broadcasting business, pioneering radio commentaries of sports events. He became a well-known figure in radio circles and was President of the Australian Federation of Broadcasting Stations for 12 years.

He moved back and forth between Australia and New Zealand and when he was in his mid-eighties he sent a letter to Manchester AC's Fallowfield Stadium to say he would be making a final visit to his old home town. The club presented him with a special scroll and remember him as a man of remarkable health; he demonstrated his special fitness routines and exercises, and talked over old times.

He returned to New Zealand, where he died in 1973, aged 90.

HARRY WALDEN

ASSOCIATION FOOTBALL

1912 Stockholm
Gold   Soccer Team

Harry Walden was a music hall comic, but the opposing defences in the 1912 Olympic tournament could not share his sense of humour. He scored 11 times in Britain's three matches, including six in the opening game against Hungary. Britain ran out winners of the tournament by beating Denmark 4–2 in the final and Walden was again on the scoresheet.

The Manchester-born forward began playing competitive football in the army and represented them in inter-service games. It was here that he was spotted by the England selectors and by Bradford City, who signed him.

At the Olympics Walden was the outstanding marksman and it was probably his own decision that he never played for the international amateur side outside the 1912 Games. After the war Walden left the army, played for a variety of non-League sides and began touring northern clubs as a comic, eventually graduating to music hall around the country. He died in Leeds in 1955.

MICHAEL WARRINER

ROWING

1928 Amsterdam
Gold   Coxless Fours

Three times a Boat Race winner, Warriner was in the British four in Amsterdam that surprisingly brought back the gold. The Germans were clear favourites and in the semi-final were leading the British crew with just 50 metres to go, when one of their oarsmen blacked out and collapsed. The British were able to glide past and take their place in the final, where they outsprinted the Americans over the last 20 metres after trailing for most of the race.

Born in Chipping Norton, Oxfordshire, in 1908, Warriner attended Harrow and Trinity Hall, Cambridge, winning his blue and the Visitors trophy at Henley in 1928 – as well as an Olympic gold medal. The following year he won the Stewards Cup and the Ladies Plate before leaving Cambridge and joining the Sudan Government Service. He returned to England in 1934 and began working in the engineering business, which he returned to after war war service in India, Greece and the Middle East. Lt. Colonel Warriner was awarded the MBE for his war efforts in 1945. He died in Warwickshire in 1986.

FRANK WELDON

EQUESTRIAN

1956 Melbourne
Gold   Three-Day Event Team
Bronze   Three-Day Event

The only British Olympic gold medal winner to escape from Colditz, Lt. Colonel Weldon established an unprecedented run of success at major championships. What made his competitive success all the more remarkable was that he trained his own horse Kilbarry himself – quite a feat considering the horse was a steeplechaser.

Weldon was born in India in 1913, and was educated at Wellington and Sandhurst, where he was a first XV rugby player. He joined the army to pursue his interest in horses but soon afterwards the active cavalry was replaced by cars. During the war he was captured and spent four years as a PoW, the last three at Colditz Castle, where he was continually caught attempting to escape. After the war he returned to England to command the King's Troop of the Royal Artillery.

His competitive winning streak began at the European Championships in 1953, where he took gold in the team event, following suit in the next two years. He won the individual title in 1955 on his horse Kilbarry, who was still doing full daily duty as an officer's charger in the cavalry regiment. In fact, Weldon rode the Irish-bred grey gelding in the Queen's Coronation procession.

Weldon and Kilbarry then joined Britain's Olympic event team in Stockholm (equestrian events were held in Sweden because of Australian quarantine rules) alongside Laurence Rook and Bertie Hill. As captain of the team, he took the bronze in the individual contest, becoming the first British rider to win an individual equestrian medal, and helped lift the team into gold medal position.

In 1959 he placed second in the individual European Championships and made another Olympic bid in 1960, finishing fourth in the team and 25th in the individual. He continued to serve the sport after retiring from the army and was Director of the Badminton Horse Trials between 1966 and 1988, a council member of the British Horse Society and for many years equestrian correspondent of the *Sunday Telegraph*.

ALLAN WELLS

ATHLETICS

1980 Moscow
Gold   100 Metres
Silver   200 Metres

Four years after abandoning the long jump and the idea of following his boyhood idol Lynn Davies into the Olympics, Wells found himself on the medal rostrum in Moscow receiving gold for being the world's fastest man. He was already 24 when he decided that long jumping was not going to win him any major honours and turned to serious sprinting. He joined a hard-working and secretive group of athletes in Edinburgh under the aegis of the wily old coach Wilson Young, a former professional sprinter. Wells, a blacksmith's son, was born in the Scottish capital in 1952. He enjoyed the punishing training, and the atmosphere motivated him to work and perform. The results were tangible and almost immediate; he ran Britain's fastest legal 100 metres of 1976 in 10.55, in his first year of competition.

The progress continued and in the winter of '77–78 Wells tried out some of his own training ideas, while wife Margot, herself an international athlete, helped push him still harder. In the summer of 1978 the new, powerful Allan Wells exploded on to the British track scene, equalling Peter Radford's 29-year-old British 100 metres record of 10.29 – then lowering it a week later to 10.15. At the Commonwealth Games the same year in Edmonton, he took two golds and a silver. Allan Wells had arrived.

In 1979 Wells twice bettered the British 200 metres record and won the Europa Cup 200 in Turin. He had made this progress without using starting blocks, which he detested, but when the IAAF changed their rules he was told he would have to use them in Moscow. Much fuss was made about the rule, but Wells made light of the situation, setting a new British mark of 10.11 in the 100 heats, then winning a photo-finish final with Cuba's Silvio Leonard, in 10.25, to become the oldest winner of the Olympic sprint title.

Wells recalled the race thus: 'It felt like I was in a tube, with that one lane stretching out in front of me and you are sort of outside yourself. You've done it a hundred times before, you've run it a hundred times before, you've slept it a hundred times before, but now it's real and you can feel the ground, but it's like you're looking through your own eyes at yourself.

'I saw the Cuban Leonard, he was right up there and I thought to myself, "Well, I'm going to get a medal anyway, I'll bloody well make a dive for the line and give it everything", but I wasn't sure and neither was Leonard.'

After an interminable wait the announcement came that gave Wells and Leonard the same time – but Wells the gold. He looked likely to win the 200 and emulate his hero Valeri Borzov, but Italy's Pietro Mennea caught him on the line to pip him for the gold. The Americans, who had boycotted the Games, poured scorn on Wells as the Olympic champion but he silenced all critics by beating US star Stanley Floyd in a post-Games meeting in Cologne.

The following year he took the Golden Sprints title in Berlin, confirming his status as the world's greatest sprinter by destroying a world-class 200-metre field after taking second in the 100. At 30, Wells took the Commonwealth 100 metres, tied the 200 and added a bronze in the relay, before his star finally began to fade. He managed a creditable fourth in the inaugural World Championships in Helsinki in 1983, but went out in the semis at the Los Angeles Olympics. His last great run came in 1986, when he beat Ben Johnson in Edinburgh.

Awarded the MBE in 1982, Wells lives in Guildford with Margot and their two daughters, where he works as a technician at the University of Surrey. He also coaches and advises in other sports, notably tennis, and has recently been involved in the Olympic bobsleigh team.

HENRY WELLS

ROWING

1912 Stockholm
Gold   Eights

A talented cricketer at school, Wells became one of the finest coxes of the early Olympic era. Born in London in 1891, he went to Winchester School before going up to study law at Magdalen College, Oxford, which had a fine rowing tradition. He coxed the Oxford crew to a new record time in his first Boat Race in 1911, and remained in the job for three more years. At the 1912 Olympics he coxed the Leander crew to victory in an all-British final against Oxford's New College.

In 1914 he was called to the Bar, but his legal career was interrupted by the First World War, in which he served with the 6th London Brigade and was awarded the MBE. He continued in law after the war and in 1934 was made a county court judge, finally stepping down in 1958. He died in 1967, at his retirement home in Newton Abbot, Devon.

REG WHITE

YACHTING

1976 Montreal
Gold   Tornado Class

Reg White and his brother-in-law John Osborn guided Britain to the first-ever gold medal in the Tornado class at the Olympic Regatta in Kingston. It was a demonstration of sailing excellence: the pair won four of the six races and were able to sit out the last day with the gold medal already assured.

Born in 1935 in Brightlingsea, on the Thames estuary, White was the son of an oyster merchant, and his fascination with boats began almost immediately; he started designing and building as a young man. In 1961 he won an award for a catamaran he had designed with a friend and three years later claimed the world title in the Hornet class. He continued building and established his own company, designing and building the boat in which he and Osborn won the Olympic title.

White spent nine months training for the Games, often running, sailing and slogging through gym work for nine hours a day. At 39 he realised it could be his last chance to win an Olympic gold medal and he was not going to waste it. A friend took over his business to allow him to concentrate on the Olympics.

He was also world champion in the Tornado class in 1976 and 1980 and was awarded the MBE for services to the sport in 1977. His son Rob has followed in father's footsteps, finishing sixth in the Tornado class in Los Angeles and eighth in Seoul, while his other son David is a world record-breaking windsurfer. He still lives and works in Brightlingsea, designing and building boats, and spends a lot of time encouraging young talent into the sport.

WILF WHITE

EQUESTRIAN

1952 Helsinki
Gold   Prix Des Nations Team

1956 Melbourne
Bronze   Prix Des Nations Team

Wilf White's outstanding show jumping successes were created with one amazing horse – Nizefella.

Together they became known as the 'fullbacks' of British show jumping, but even so they were unlucky not to be even more successful.

White, born in Nantwich, Cheshire, in 1904, was one of the nation's few pre-war show jumpers and he bought Nizefella as a four-year-old in 1946. They scored their first victory the following year in a small competition in Shrewsbury. They made their first appearance in a British team in Nice in 1949; made a triumphant tour of North America; and over the next ten years were part of 12 winning show jumping teams.

At the 1952 Olympics in Helsinki, White was among five riders tied in gold medal place and forced into a do-or-die jump-off. Controversy surrounded the event because, despite losing a stirrup iron, White appeared to go clear, only for one of the two water judges to raise a flag. Even today eyewitnesses doubt there was an infringement, but it cost White an individual gold. In the jump-off against the clock, the big horse could not cope with the speed required and White recorded 12 faults and finished last of the five, well out of the medal frame. The gold went to France's Pierre Jonqueres d'Oriola. However, with Douglas Stewart and Harry Llewellyn performing well the three scores added up to a team gold, just ahead of the Chile and US teams.

Four years later White made a second Olympic bid, this time finishing joint fourth in the individual competition, but the British team, which included Pat Smythe and Peter Robeson, was good enough to clinch the bronze.

A Cheshire farmer, White was for many years a member of the executive committee of the British Show Jumping Association and in 1958 was awarded the OBE for services to the sport.

HAROLD WHITLOCK

ATHLETICS

1936 Berlin
Gold   50km Walk

Harold Whitlock was the last man to leave Berlin's Olympic Stadium as the walkers set off on the 50km course around the city – but he was the first man back. 'Some people thought we were going for a five-mile race,' he once recalled. 'I really enjoyed picking them off one by one.'

Whitlock took the gold despite acute sickness at the 38km mark after accepting a cup of tea from someone by the roadside. Born in Hendon, Middle-

Scottish sprinter Allan Wells, who took the title of world's fastest man at the Moscow Olympics in 1980.

Harold Whitlock in the home straight at the end of the 1936 50km walk. He had been the last man to leave Berlin's Olympic Stadium – but was the first one back!

sex, in 1903, he took up walking while an apprentice as a racing car mechanic because he was bored with soccer. He took to the sport quickly and joined the Metropolitan Walking Club, where he began a tremendous series of victories at home and abroad. He won every national 50km title between 1933 and 1939, except one: in 1934 he dropped out in agony with a few miles left after the new shoes he had worn ripped the skin from all his toes. The following year he became the first man to walk the 52-mile London to Brighton course in under eight hours and spent almost a year preparing for Berlin.

He was working as a mechanic for Bentley's Sir Henry Birkin and they allowed him time to train when he was not preparing cars for major races at Brooklands and abroad. Although he forgot his passport, Whitlock had a marvellous Games and, despite the sickness, his victory was never in doubt – he came home a minute and a half in front of Switzerland's Arthur Schwab. When he returned home the mayor offered him a motorcade around the town, but forgot it was early closing for the shops and few people saw their Olympic champion pass by!

In 1938 he added the European title to his list of achievements but the war stopped him defending his Olympic title and he worked on aircraft engines during the hostilities. His brother Rex took part in the 1948 Olympics 50km event and Harold was persuaded to come out of retirement for a last crack at the race in 1952, where he finished an impressive 11th, at the age of 48.

He continued his racing car work and became a respected judge, administrator and coach. He had the odd fortune of being Chief Judge in the 1960 Rome Olympics, where his protégé Don Thompson competed and won.

In 1966 he was awarded the MBE for his services to the sport and he died in retirement in Norfolk in 1985, aged 82.

ALLEN WHITTY

SHOOTING

1924 Paris
Gold   Running Deer Double Shot Team

A lifelong army man, Whitty was rated the finest rifle coach the services ever produced and was still shooting into his eighties. He won scores of medals and trophies for his marksmanship but his finest hour was certainly the gold medal at the Paris Olympics in 1924.

Born in Martley-Hillside, Worcestershire, in 1867, he enlisted in his county regiment in 1884 and was soon posted to India, where he taught musketry. Promotion was fast and he became a colour sergeant at 23 and regimental sergeant major six years later. In 1900, during the Boer War, he received his commission with the regiment's 3rd Battalion, reckoned to be the best shooting battalion in the army.

He served in France during the First World War, and was involved in the retreat from Mons, for which he was awarded the DSO. He was promoted to major, then lieutenant colonel, and was mentioned in despatches three times before hostilities ended. He became a senior recruiting officer after the war and finally retired from the army in 1932, with 48 years' service under his belt.

He represented England on many occasions as a marksman, captained the army team and also the 3rd Battalion team that won the Queen Victoria Trophy five times. With exceptions for war, he attended Bisley every year from 1896 to 1948 – the year before he died, in Aldermaston, Berkshire, at the age of 82.

In Paris, he joined the Running Deer team that pipped Norway by a single point to take the gold.

DAVID WILKIE

SWIMMING

1972 Munich
Silver   200 Metres Breaststroke

1976 Montreal
Gold   200 Metres Breaststroke
Silver   100 Metres Breaststroke

Britain's most successful swimmer of the modern era, Wilkie became the first man for nearly 70 years to win an Olympic swimming title for Britain when he clinched the gold in Montreal. Of the 13 men's swimming events at the Games, 12 were won by swimmers from the United States, but Wilkie's performance was rated as the best.

In a sport where records are chipped out by hundredths of a second he demolished a world-class field in the 200 metres breaststroke final and hacked more than three seconds off the previous world mark. Wilkie learned to swim in the idyllic setting of Sri Lanka, where he was born to Scottish parents in 1954. He returned to Scotland in 1965 to attend Daniel Stewart's College in Edinburgh, and joined forces with coach Frank Thomas, who put him on the road to future swimming success.

His first major success was a bronze in the 1970 Commonwealth Games 100 metres breaststroke. This was followed two years later by a silver in the

200 at the Munich Olympics, behind America's world record-holder John Hencken. His success had been noticed in the United States and he won a scholarship to the University of Miami, where he studied marine biology, and was given the time, facilities and expert coaching he needed to put him at the very top. The immediate effect was a 200 metres world title and world record in 1973, followed in 1974 by gold at the Commonwealth Games and European Championships, as well as a second world record. The year before Montreal he won both breaststroke events at the World Championships and was awarded the MBE for services to the sport.

Going into the 1976 Games he was among the favourites to win the gold, but his arch rival Hencken, who held the 200 metres world record of 2:18.21, was in fine form. But he had already shown the Americans what they had to beat by winning three collegiate titles in the run-up to Montreal. By then the familiar bobbing cap and goggles were as much a part of British swimming as 'Wilkie first' and hopes were high of landing a British gold in the pool at last. Hencken had to swim a new world record to beat him into second place in the 100 metres, but Wilkie was too strong in the 200, where he swam an astonishing 2:15.11 to take the gold and obliterate the world record.

He retired immediately after the Games and for a while went on the Masters circuit in the US. He is still swimming and made a brief comeback in the run-up to Barcelona but spends more time writing and working in television.

CYRIL WILKINSON

HOCKEY

1920 Antwerp
Gold   Hockey Team

Wilkinson captained Surrey to the County Cricket Championship in 1914, six years before winning his first international hockey cap. A talented cricketer, Wilkinson was born in Durham in 1884, but the family moved to Devon and he played in the famous Blundell's School XI before joining Surrey in 1909. He played his last game for Surrey in 1920, the year in which his hockey career took off.

He had played top-class club hockey with Norwood, Hampstead and Surrey and it was something of a surprise that he should be selected for the Olympics at the age of 35. But he acquitted himself well and played in both England's games en route to the gold – a 5–1 drubbing of Denmark and the more famous 12–1 thrashing of Belgium.

A civil servant by profession, he went on to serve the sport as an administrator and umpire, was elected vice president of the Hockey Association and was awarded the CBE for his services to the sport in 1954. Two years earlier he had played his last game of club cricket for Sidmouth at the age of 67 – scoring 50 runs and taking ten wickets for 27! He died in Honiton, Devon, in 1970, aged 86.

GEORGE WILKINSON

SWIMMING

1900 Paris
Gold   Water Polo Team

1908 London
Gold   Water Polo Team

1912 Stockholm
Gold   Water Polo Team

Wilkinson's goalscoring feats attracted huge crowds wherever he played. But for the fact that Britain failed to send a team to the 1904 Olympics in St Louis and that the First World War stopped the 1916 Games, Wilkinson could have won five straight gold medals. Britain invented the game and dominated in the early part of the century.

Wilkinson, born in Manchester in 1879, swam in many national finals, though he was a far better polo player than race swimmer. His goalscoring average in local leagues earned him selection for the country's top Manchester Osborne Club and in 1900 they signed him up for the trip to Paris, where they represented Britain in the Olympics, without even giving him a trial. He helped the club record two victories over French and Belgian clubs to bring back the gold.

Shortly after the Games he joined the Hyde Seal Club and captained the water polo team for 22 years. During this time they won nine national titles and the unofficial world championship in 1904. In 1908 he scored four goals in the 9–2 final victory over Belgium and made his final Olympic appearance in Sweden, where he scored in the 8–0 drubbing of Austria. He was named as reserve for the 1920 and 1924 Olympic sides (he was 45 at the time of the Paris Games) and retired in the mid-1920s after winning 24 caps for England.

He ran the Wheatsheaf Hotel in Hyde for many years and died in the town in 1946.

HERBERT WILSON

POLO

1908 London
Gold   Polo Team

One of the great curiosities of the 1908 Olympic polo tournament was that Captain Wilson should have been playing for the winning side at all. An influential figure in the sport, he was a member of the Hurlingham Committee and lived a stone's throw from the famous club. But at the 1908 Games he turned out for nearby rivals Roehampton and lined up against his own team.

Born in London in 1875, Wilson attended Eton and New College, Oxford, before joining the Nottinghamshire Imperial Yeomanry, winning a DSO for bravery during the Boer War. A keen horseman, he played top-class polo and rode regularly in the major Quorn, Cottesmore and Belvoir hunts. It appears that he sometimes played at Roehampton and they asked him to take part in the 1908 Olympics. Thinking he would not be required for the Hurlingham first team he accepted. Hurlingham staged the polo tournament and their team was then depleted by injury and the absence of their top player, the Duke of Roxburghe, so Wilson might have appeared for them after all. But instead he played for the Roehampton side which beat Hurlingham 4–1 in the semi-finals and All-Ireland 8–1 in the final, scoring twice in both games.

During the First World War he served with his regiment in France and was killed in action at Ypres in 1917.

JACK WILSON

ROWING

1948 London
Gold   Coxless Pairs

One of the heroes of London's 'Austerity Games', Wilson and partner Ran Laurie came from nowhere to win the gold. The duo had been successful in their Cambridge days and Wilson had rowed in the winning Boat Race crews of 1934, 1935 and 1936. But soon after that last success he left to join the Sudan Government Service and did not row in the Berlin Games, where his presence might have won Britain a medal.

Soon after Berlin, Laurie also came to the Sudan and they got leave to return to Britain in 1938 to make what should have been their farewell appearance at Henley, where they won the Goblets. A few years later Wilson was nearly killed when attacked by a tribeswoman and speared through the abdomen, but he survived and after the war the pair talked about returning for a tilt at the London Olympics.

Most rowing opinion considered them too old, but they persuaded the Sudan Government to grant them extended leave, went into hard training and held off the Swiss Kalt brothers to win a brilliant gold medal.

Wilson was born in the United States, to English parents, and educated at Shrewsbury School and Pembroke College. After the 1948 Games he returned to the Sudan, where he continued his government work until the country's independence in 1956. He then came home and began working in the steel industry, but continued his interest in rowing as a steward at Henley.

He retired in 1974 and today lives in Devon, where he rents holiday flats.

LORD JOHN WODEHOUSE

POLO

1908 London
Silver   Polo Team

1920 Antwerp
Gold   Polo Team

One of the few peers to win Olympic gold, Lord Wodehouse won his first medal while serving as an MP. Born in 1883 on the Norfolk estate of his father, the Earl of Kimberley, Lord Wodehouse went to Eton and Trinity Hall, Cambridge, where he twice captained the polo team to victory over Oxford. In 1906 he was elected Liberal MP for Mid-Norfolk and served the constituency for one term, during which he played polo for Hurlingham in the 1908 Olympics. He was in the side beaten in the semi-finals by great rivals and eventual winners Roehampton.

Lord Wodehouse figured in many Westchester Cup games against the Americans and was a Champions Cup winner on six occasions. During the First World War he served with the 16th Lancers and won three major honours: the Military Cross, the Croix de Guerre and the Italian War Cross. At the end of hostilities he joined Winston Churchill's staff as assistant private secretary in the Colonial Office and in 1925 was awarded the CBE for his work. In 1932 he succeeded to the earldom, but in 1941, on a visit to London from his estate, he was killed in an air raid.

FREDDIE WOLFF

ATHLETICS

1936 Berlin
Gold   4 × 400 Metres Relay

See Godfrey Brown, page 32.

ARTHUR WOOD

YACHTING

1908 London
Gold   8 Metres Class

Wood was a member of the five-man crew aboard the winning boat in the 8 metres class at the Olympic Regatta in Cowes. Blair Cochrane's *Cobweb* won the event after placing first in two races and third in the final race to take the gold ahead of Sweden and a second British boat.

Like the rest of the crew, Wood was a member of the Royal Victoria Yacht Club, which hosted the regatta, and he was invited to take part in the event by *Cobweb*'s owner Cochrane. Born in 1875, in Chester-le-Street, County Durham, Wood succeeded to the family baronetcy on the death of his father in 1920 and, as Sir Arthur Wood Bt., served as Sheriff of County Durham in 1933. He died six years later while on holiday in Scotland.

HARVEY WOOD

HOCKEY

1908 London
Gold   Hockey Team

Not the busiest man at the 1908 Games, Wood was the England goalkeeper in a team that won gold by scoring 24 goals and conceding just three. Wood, born in Beverley, Yorkshire, in 1885, was understudy to England keeper Len Gurney at the West Bromwich club and made his international debut at the start of the 1908 season. Standing at 6 ft 4 in and weighing 14 stone, he was a big man for a hockey goalkeeper, but was also remarkably agile and quick for his size. Despite the England side's success during 1908, particularly their 8–1 Olympic final thrashing of Ireland, Wood did not reappear on the England scene.

VIVIAN WOODWARD

ASSOCIATION FOOTBALL

1908 London
Gold   Soccer Team

1912 Stockholm
Gold   Soccer Team

Vivian Woodward was one of the finest centre-forwards to grace a football field and became a giant of the amateur game in the early part of the century. He was not built like a traditional number nine and he was not even particularly fast, but his science, skill and speed of thought elevated him above the cut and thrust of the games in which he played. He enjoyed a superb career with Spurs and Chelsea, played 23 times for the full England side and scored 29 goals – a record that stood until 1958 when both Tom Finney and Nat Lofthouse pushed their totals to 30. A confirmed amateur throughout his career, he also played 44 amateur internationals and won two Olympic gold medals.

Charles Buchan once wrote of him: 'Rarely have I seen another forward do so much with so little effort. He made the ball do the work, opening up the play with beautifully timed passes. He seemed to stroll through the game. I could not tell, really, if he were fast or not. He seemed to have no concern with speed.'

Born a stone's throw from the Kennington Oval in 1879, Woodward dreamed of emulating his hero, the Old Carthusians and England forward G.O. Smith. He joined his father's architects practice, though he later became a farmer, and played minor league soccer in Essex until he signed for Spurs in 1902. The side was then in the Southern League and he was with them when they were elected to Division Two of the Football League. He scored their first goal in League football. He netted 19 in 27 matches in that first season and the side was promoted to Division One.

He joined Chelsea in 1910, winning his last England cap a year later against Wales, but his club career was interrupted by the war and he was badly wounded in France in 1916 and never played football again. He had won his first Olympic gold helping Britain to a 2–0 win in the final over Denmark, while playing for Spurs and serving on their board. He was in the side that retained the title in 1912, beating the Danes again, this time 4–2.

Woodward continued to farm and did not break contact with football, as he served as a Chelsea director until 1930. He died in Ealing in 1954.

MAX WOOSNAM

LAWN TENNIS

1920 Antwerp
Gold   Men's Doubles
Silver   Mixed Doubles

One of the finest sportsmen ever produced in Britain, Woosnam was a gifted natural athlete who excelled at every sport to which he turned his hand. His Olympic success came in tennis, but he also played soccer for England and golf and cricket for Cambridge.

Born in Liverpool in 1892, Woosnam went to Winchester School, then Trinity College, winning four blues in his freshman year — soccer, golf, real tennis and lawn tennis. He served in the Montgomeryshire Yeomanry and the Royal Welsh Fusiliers during the First World War and at the end of hostilities returned to Cambridge, where he became captain of cricket.

His tennis career really took off at the 1920 Olympics, in which he was also selected for the British soccer team. But the timetable was such that he decided he could not compete in both. He joined forces with Noel Turnbull to win gold in the men's doubles, beating the Japanese pair Ichiya Kumagae and Seiichiro Kashio 6–2, 5–7, 7–5, 7–5, before winning a silver in the mixed doubles with Kitty McKane, beaten by the French pair Max Decugis and Suzanne Lenglen. In the same year he started his Davis Cup career, winning a doubles match against Spain, with Randolph Lycett, and the pair went on to win the Wimbledon title in 1921.

Woosnam was selected for the Paris Olympics in 1924, but was knocked out in the early rounds of both singles and doubles. Throughout this period Woosnam was also playing soccer and building a reputation as a powerful centre-half. He had played for Chelsea before the war and in 1919 joined Manchester City, playing 89 League games and captaining the side to second place in the First Division in 1921.

He played three times for England — twice as an amateur — and captained the full international XI against Wales in 1922. He was poised for a successful soccer career, but he broke his leg shortly after the Welsh game and complications to the injury effectively ended his career.

After the First World War he joined ICI, retiring from the company in 1954. He died in London in 1965, aged 72.

LESLIE WORMALD

ROWING

1912 Stockholm
Gold   Eights

Wormald was a more successful rugby player at school than an oarsman, playing in the first XV for Eton and only rowing in the second eight. Born in Cookham, Berkshire, in 1890, he showed rapid improvement on going up to Magdalen College, Oxford, and in 1910 he was in the college boat that won the Head of the River and the Grand at Henley.

He was in the Magdalen crew that won the Grand in the following year and rowed for Leander in their victory in the 1912 Olympic final — an all-British affair against New College, Oxford. In 1913 he was again in the winning Oxford crew at the Boat Race, this time as secretary of the University Boat Club and captain of Magdalen.

When the First World War broke out he served in France and was awarded the Military Cross in 1918. He died in 1965 at a London hotel on a visit from his retirement home in Spain.

CYRIL WRIGHT

YACHTING

1920 Antwerp
Gold   7 Metres Class

Wright was the helmsman and co-owner of the *Ancora* which won the 7 metres class at Ostend. A naval architect by profession, Wright and his father-in-law Percy Machin bought the boat, but Machin did not take part in the Games. However, the family ties were kept intact with the presence of Wright's wife Dorothy among the crew. The *Ancora* lost its first race to a Norwegian boat, the only other entry, but came back to win the next two to take the gold medal.

Wright, a member of the Royal Burnham Yacht Club, eventually retired to the south coast, where he died in 1960, aged 74.

DOROTHY WRIGHT

YACHTING

1920 Antwerp
Gold   7 Metres Class

A member of the four-man and one-woman crew aboard the gold medal-winning *Ancora* at the Olympic Regatta in Ostend, Dorothy Wright was the wife of helmsman Cyril who co-owned the boat with her father Percy Machin. She married him while he was on Christmas leave from the RNVR during the First World War.

She was also a member of the Royal Burnham Yacht Club and was the only woman to take part in the yachting events at the Games. *Ancora* came from a race behind to defeat the Norwegian boat *Fornebo* 2–1 to take the gold.

Born in east London in 1889, Mrs Wright retired to the south coast when Cyril gave up his post as a naval architect.

GORDON WRIGHT

ASSOCIATION FOOTBALL

1912 Stockholm
Gold   Soccer Team

Wright was selected as a reserve winger for the Olympic team in Stockholm despite being a full international player. A swift, skilful player, he got his chance in the side for the semi-final against Finland and although Britain won the game the selectors made more changes for the final and he was left out. Britain went on to win the match against Denmark 4–2 and retain the Olympic title.

Born in Surrey in 1884, the son of a vicar, Wright began playing competitive football at Queens' College, Cambridge, and played for three years in the university side. It was in the varsity matches that he was spotted by the England selectors and picked for the game against Wales in 1906. The same year he left college and joined Hymer's College in Hull to teach natural history and science. He signed as an amateur for Hull City and became captain, playing more than 150 games for them before

leaving to play at Leyton Orient and Portsmouth.

He won the first of his 20 England amateur caps in 1908 and the last in 1913, when he emigrated to South Africa to work as a mining engineer. He died in Johannesburg in 1947.

JIM ZEALEY

ASSOCIATION FOOTBALL

1900 Paris
Gold   Soccer Team

Born in Mile End in 1868, Zealey was one of Upton Park's star performers in their 4–0 victory over the French representatives in the 1900 Olympic tournament. The Essex team had lost a player to injury in the first half but still established a two-goal advantage by half time. Despite the pace slackening somewhat in the second half, Upton Park scored another two goals. Zealey capped a fine display at inside-left with the decisive fourth goal, assuring Great Britain of the Olympic title.

INDEX OF SPORTS

ARCHERY 65, 146

ASSOCIATION FOOTBALL 15, 18, 26, 32, 35, 41, 45, 53, 64, 88, 94, 95, 102, 105, 109, 113, 121, 134, 146, 164, 165, 175, 179, 181, 182, 193, 196, 203, 205, 206

ATHLETICS 9, 11, 12, 23, 30, 32, 38, 42, 48, 49, 57, 60, 62, 89, 90, 91, 93, 95, 98, 102, 105, 116, 118, 121, 126, 127, 136, 150, 152, 159, 165, 169, 170, 172, 175, 183, 187, 189, 193, 195, 197, 198, 203

BOXING 68, 75, 88, 91, 133, 135, 141, 149, 166, 181, 187

CRICKET 19, 29, 30, 35, 38, 45, 53, 56, 68, 164, 186, 193

CYCLING 19, 107, 108, 112, 114, 138, 158, 174

EQUESTRIAN 11, 36, 86, 100, 109, 121, 137, 156, 162, 172, 183, 196, 198

FENCING 177

HOCKEY 14, 15, 16, 19, 23, 27, 44, 48, 52, 55, 56, 65, 74, 79, 80, 88, 90, 95, 110, 113, 117, 123, 126, 127, 135, 136, 147, 155, 163, 164, 168, 171, 178, 179, 187, 201, 203

LAWN TENNIS 18, 52, 64, 67, 71, 83, 86, 93, 100, 114, 130, 169, 193, 204

MODERN PENTATHLON 79, 147, 155

MOTOR BOATING 75, 168, 192

POLO 18, 26, 57, 109, 123, 128, 140, 147, 166, 202, 203

RACKETS 14, 147, 158

ROWING 15, 21, 24, 27, 29, 36, 38, 41, 42, 48, 55, 56, 71, 73, 74, 78, 80, 81, 103, 104, 108, 110, 112, 113, 114, 116, 129, 130, 144, 146, 168, 174, 179, 184, 192, 196, 197, 202, 204

SHOOTING 12, 30, 44, 53, 70, 77, 104, 118, 129, 137, 141, 143, 145, 155, 159, 162, 163, 184, 200

SWIMMING 23, 36, 51, 53, 62, 78, 79, 84, 90, 100, 102, 107, 109, 110, 121, 123, 143, 144, 145, 158, 164, 165, 171, 178, 181, 182, 186, 192, 200, 201

TUG OF WAR 16, 44, 84, 102, 103, 105, 140, 141, 175, 177, 183, 192

WEIGHTLIFTING 73

WRESTLING 14, 61, 149

YACHTING 12, 21, 27, 29, 30, 35, 38, 42, 48, 52, 55, 56, 57, 64, 70, 74, 83, 89, 94, 117, 127, 128, 130, 134, 136, 144, 149, 156, 169, 170, 184, 186, 195, 198, 203, 204, 205